Life in the Pits

ALOUETTE BOOKS
Madison, Wisconsin

Copyright © 2023 by Nicholas P. T. Maxwell, MD

All rights reserved.

No part of this publication may be reproduced, distributed, or transmitted in any form or by any means, including photocopying, recording, or other electronic or mechanical methods, without the prior written permission of the publisher, except as permitted by U.S. copyright law. For permission requests, contact AlouetteBooks@gmail.com.

For privacy reasons, some names may have been changed.

Book design by Sara DeHaan

Cover: Detroit Receiving Hospital, 2019. Original photo by Erin Kirkland, ErinKirklandPhotography.com.

Publisher's Cataloging-in-Publication data

Names: Maxwell, Nicholas P. T., author.
Title: Life in the pits : a surgeon's awakening / Nicholas P. T. Maxwell, MD.
Description: Madison, WI: Alouette Books, 2023.
Identifiers: LCCN: 2023911551 | ISBN: 9798218228743
Subjects: LCSH Maxwell, Nicholas P. T. | Surgeons—United States—Biography. | Emergency physicians—United States—Biography. | BISAC BIOGRAPHY & AUTOBIOGRAPHY / Medical | BIOGRAPHY & AUTOBIOGRAPHY / Personal Memoirs
Classification: LCC RD27.35.M39 2023 | DDC 617/.092—dc23

Life
in the
Pits

A Surgeon's Awakening

Nicholas P. T. Maxwell, MD

ALOUETTE BOOKS

The surgical resident is like a mushroom:
kept in the dark, fed shit and expected to grow.

CONTENTS

INTRODUCTION

I WAS surprised when I noticed how nonchalant I was about walking into the resuscitation room. Just four short years earlier, the overhead announcement of a life-threatening trauma (a 'code') would have made the few remaining hairs on my head bristle with ignorant trepidation. How things had changed over those intense intervening years! Now, entering the last of five years of surgical training, my nervousness had faded, my naivete had been swept away, my knowledge and experience had soared, and a completely new level of confidence had emerged. I had evolved from being a total novice to feeling comfortable and knowledgeable in the midst of the battlefield that was the Trauma Emergency Room. Every day was indeed a battle, and one in which I had learnt to always expect the unexpected and respect my limitations. So even though I was now prepared, every new arrival was just that: new. Each one had its own peculiarities, its singular challenges, sometimes straightforward but more often than not with unexpected twists, as of course does life itself and perhaps, in part, that's what made it all so very exciting.

It had been four years since I had graduated from medical school and had driven up outside the Detroit Medical Center and the silvery, metallic appearing, modernistic, cubic façade of Detroit Receiving Hospital. I was awestruck, if not stunned, as I realized that this was where I was to spend my next five years. After driving down the concrete ramp into the multistoried subterranean parking structure and carefully locking my car, I anxiously surveyed my surroundings. After all this was Detroit, and I knew its reputation. I was nervous, apprehensive, excited, almost overwhelmed to start my surgical journey, and even though I had absolutely no idea what lay ahead, I sensed that things would never be the same again. I had a feeling that I was entering a one-way portal from which there would be no return. I was right.

As with most trauma centers, ours was located deep within the inner city, where, by design, they were closer to the action. The Detroit Medical Center towered over its surroundings, the sun reflecting brightly off the metallic siding, shining like a beacon, an oasis of care in the midst of an urban desert. The silvery, metallic-appearing, modernistic cubic façade stood out amongst blocks of run-down, burnt out, and boarded up tenements. But deserted? Not even close. They were teeming, and where there were so many in such a poor and dilapidated environment, there was always crime.

Our patients were a combination of inner-city, crime-related injuries intermixed with a sprinkling of multiple-injured trauma victims from high-speed motor vehicle accidents, along with a liberal smattering of injuries from dumb luck.

During my time as a surgical resident, and especially in the stressful environment of the operating room, I was exposed to a diverse assortment of surgical personalities, techniques, and skills. When it came to our educators, there was, surprisingly, a broad variability in knowledge, skill level, and finesse, let alone teaching ability. Some surgeons I trained under were silky smooth, apparently able to tackle problems (it appeared to us) without a significant expenditure of energy, remaining calm, level-headed, and focused, even under the most intense of pressure. They were the gifted. They were the ones who made it look so deceivingly simple.

These were the surgeons from whom I learnt the most, the ones whom I wanted to emulate, and the only ones whom I would wish to have operate on me, should I ever be in need of surgery.

Are we born with surgical talent?

No doubt every prospective surgeon has to have some intrinsic dexterity and ability, but that is wasted unless we have skillful teachers from whom to learn, allowing us to refine our craft. It can be said that surgery is as much art as science, but it is an art that must be learnt, practiced, and carefully honed. It is imperative, therefore, that surgeons have only the best of educators.

I believe I was fortunate to have had exactly that.

I came to Detroit by way of Montreal, where I completed medical school at McGill University. Although I thought my training was outstanding in most areas, I had never experienced any real trauma, and the occasional motor vehicle accident was about the extent of the trauma that we were exposed to. Montreal was, and still is, not renowned for its penetrating trauma, its 'knife and gun club'.

I was, therefore, in for a rude awakening when I started my emergency surgery rotation a few months into my first year of surgical residency in Detroit. It was difficult to comprehend the volume of penetrating trauma and other even stranger injuries to which I was now being routinely exposed. I had erroneously believed that these injuries were solely the domain of Hollywood, yet here I was experiencing the reality: that fact was so much stranger than fiction.

While caring for innumerable gunshot injured patients, what really came as a surprise, a shock even, was how many actually survived. Before my trauma surgery rotation, I had always had the erroneous assumption that a bullet killed, period. As I soon learnt, many were fixed up, just to leave and return, shot again. The majority of survivable injuries were the result of the local 'wars' and disagreements, in sharp distinction to the more professional, often drug related, 'hits' that arrived DOA (Dead on Arrival), usually a bullet through the head or chest.

Yet it was for this precise experience—treating trauma—that I had come to Detroit to train to be a surgeon. It was here that I would follow the immortal words of Hippocrates: "He who wishes to be a surgeon should go to war." I discovered quickly that our institution, like so many big-city trauma hospitals, were indeed on the front lines of an all-out urban war.

Surgical residency was not easy, but then it was never designed to be. It was hard, damn hard, certainly the hardest thing that I had ever done. Frequently it seemed like a nightmare that would not end. We were always busy, as if running on a mouse wheel, day after day, week after week, month after month, not really knowing where the end was or what it even might look like. We just wanted to be surgeons, but then we also had no idea what that really meant. There were so many barriers to be overcome, some subtle and some not. There was the physical pressure of days with minimal sleep, the stress of dealing with the sick and dying, the apparently infinite amount of information to assimilate, as well as the constant psychological battering from our 'seniors' and some staff. As a fourth-year 'chief' at one of the private hospitals, I was constantly reminded by one of the older surgeons that surgery was not 'like it used to be', so why on earth would I want to go into it? A strange thing to be told when your training is almost complete.

Do I feel that way now? Luckily, absolutely not.

I am convinced that ultimately, the harder the training, the better the product. Yes indeed, they were making a product and a very important product: a surgeon. It was a difficult combination of knowledge and experience, skill and dexterity, humbleness and swagger. We went into the 'residency machine' as naive, brash medical school graduates, and after five years, if all went according to plan, the 'machine' would spit out a surgeon. Occasionally someone would fail to make the grade. They were out. Surgery was not for them.

It was this contrast to my relatively sheltered (when it came to trauma) medical school training in Montreal that persuaded me to begin a journal, recording some of what I saw, experienced, felt, and performed. It is those notes that I have used as the basis for what follows.

Life in the Pits is my recollection of a very small fragment (about eight days out of two six-week long rotations) of my emergency trauma experience during the second of my five years of surgical training.

The narrative is interspersed with reflections, *in italics*, based on my subsequent 30 years of surgical practice. During that time, I have witnessed many changes and advances in both medicine and surgery, to the extent that many of our old practices would be barely recognizable to the new generation of surgeons gingerly following in my footsteps.

MY LEGS were heavy, weak, and powerless. I was struggling, as if wading through thick molasses. The effort of lifting each foot was a chore, the sole of each foot held captive to the floor beneath by a strong, tacky, adhesive force. It was dark and sticky, thick and unyielding, with a salty, sickly, yet strangely familiar smell. It was everywhere, and I appeared to be covered in it.

I was so confused. Where was I? More importantly, what was going on? What was this stuff that was all over me? Nothing seemed clear. Everything was just a little out of focus, foggy, as if I had suddenly developed cataracts.

I looked at my right hand, trying in vain to focus. It, too, was covered with the same viscous, sticky, dark, crimson red material. It was not molasses. I looked closer. Suddenly I knew exactly what it was. I had been in medicine for a few years now, so I knew this smell, this texture. This sticky familiar substance that was all over me registered. It was blood. I was covered with blood. But why? My confusion and apprehension increased.

I looked around at the strangely vacant room in which I found myself. My vision gradually returned to focus, and I recognized the cupboards, the door. It clicked. I was in our resuscitation room. But the room appeared strange. It seemed larger than usual, cold, dark, and empty, with the exception of a lone gurney in its center, appearing to be lit, as if by searchlight, by a single vertical beam from some overhead source. My confusion and anxiety were increasing exponentially. My vision was tunneled as if looking through the wrong end of a telescope. Something was not right, but I could not put my finger on it. I couldn't see anyone else anywhere. I was completely alone. Why was I here? Where was everyone else? I made my way very slowly, arduously slowly, towards the light, each leg lifting against an invisible resistance. Yet in an instant, despite ambulating difficulty, I was there. There was still blood everywhere, so much blood, far too much blood. It was all around me. The floor was covered; the walls, the cupboards, the ceiling were all splattered red. Where did it all come from?

There, on the bloodied steel gurney, was a lone, grotesquely pale, lifeless body, its motionless sunken eyes unfocused, looking up aimlessly into nothingness. My own eyes shifted slightly to the right. and I looked just below the neck, where I could see that the chest had been longitudinally split wide open. Getting closer, much closer, I reluctantly peered in, like a child frightened of looking into a dark recess. I saw nothing, at least nothing that I expected. In front of me was a large empty shell. Nonetheless, a human shell. A dark, blood stained, crimson cavern, its walls comprised of widely separated arching ribs, covered here and there with pieces of bloodied tissue. It was a chest cavity completely devoid of all its internal organs.

I felt something now. In my left hand, I felt something. It was wet and sticky, yet firm. Looking down, I gasped. I was stupefied, stunned, shocked. What on earth was I holding? How did it get there? I lifted my hand up to look at it more closely. I stared in disbelief at the double-fist-sized bloody object as I turned it around in my hand. As I looked at it more closely, the muscular anatomical structure was unmistakable, even though I had not had one in my hands since my first year of medical school. I knew it was a heart. A human heart? This man's heart? How could that be? I rapidly looked back and stared at the empty carcass that lay before me and then again at the bloody contents of my hand. I tried to drop it, shake it off, but yet it stayed fixed, somehow firmly adherent.

What had I done? But then, how could 1 have done anything? What on earth was I going to do now? How do I put it back in? A myriad of questions rapidly came in and out of my consciousness like waves. For a few moments I had the futile thought of trying to put it back. How would I sew it in? But then, sew it to what? Where were the lungs? For that matter, where was everything, everyone?

I was now perspiring profusely, anxious and agitated. I could not think straight. What was going on? All I could focus on was that my future surgical career was now over. All those years of hard work, all the ceaseless hours, the days, the months spent in the library studying, all down the drain. And for what? For nothing, it now seemed. How could I have let this happen? What would I tell my friends, my family? I had let them all down. I had let myself down.

I was drenched in a cold dampness, but this was different now. There was no blood, no stickiness. Yet still I could feel that I was being held captive. My legs flailed in an increasingly frightened attempt to free themselves. Slowly I came to the realization that my adversary was the tight, constriction of my entangled, sweat-soaked bedsheets. Still confused I looked around, still attempting to get my bearings and even in the darkness I began to see some recognizable shapes. I could make out my bed, my alarm clock. Indeed, it was my room. After a few more anxious seconds, I was relieved to finally comprehend that I had woken from a dream, or more accurately, a nightmare, and one that had been a recurring companion ever since I had begun my residency the previous year.

This was not a particularly auspicious start. It was my first shift of six weeks on 'days', my second-year daytime emergency trauma rotation, in the 'Pits', as the trauma module had been affectionately named.

DAYS

The Resuscitation Room

I FELT a gentle, almost polite, tap on my shoulder as I was hunched over, evaluating a man's finger injured during a football scrimmage.

"Nick, you'd better get to the resuscitation room. We've got a code coming in."

I looked up, to locate the source of the subdued yet authoritative request.

It was Dr. Peter DeMuth, the senior physician in charge of the emergency room that day. He was calm. He was always calm, never a strand of his neatly cropped salt and pepper hair, which topped his rugged Florida tan, ever out of place. His clean, bright, sage green scrubs were freshly pressed. He was clearly proud of his chosen profession, and over his left chest pocket, his name was boldly embroidered in dark blue cursive above a caduceus flanked by the letters E and R. Our emergency room was physically divided into separate 'modules' for surgical and non-surgical (medical) patients. Module one specifically was designated for surgical patients. Dr. DeMuth would rarely, if ever, be found in our surgical module. More frequently he would be teaching the medical and emergency room residents in the two non-surgical modules. It was, therefore, a bit of a surprise to see him, and for a few moments I guiltily and rapidly reflected on all my recent activities to be sure that I had not done anything which now warranted this personal visit. But that would have been impossible, I rapidly surmised, for this was my first day. As I turned to greet his gaze, I likely had an apprehensive, inquisitive, and probably guilty look. My first thought was, "Why are you telling me this? Go tell my senior resident."

I had been a resident long enough (just over a year) to know how the medical chain of command functioned. The attending physician (who was the physician ultimately responsible for the specific patient) spoke to the senior resident, who in turn spoke to us more junior residents, the peons at the bottom of the surgical food chain. However, that thought was short lived, as it soon dawned on me that in fact, I was it. I was now the second-year in the Pits. I was the one in charge of the trauma module. So, although still very much a newbie, it was my job, my responsibility, to run the surgical/trauma codes.

This was definitely a daunting prospect for me, just as it was for my six general surgery co-residents, who had all begun their surgical journeys with me. We rarely saw each other, catching up at the weekly conferences where we rapidly exchanged our stories and fears. We were all starting our second year. I had been an MD now for just a year.

All I could really think of was, "Shit! Here we go." It's time to jump in the deep end. It was sink or swim time.

It was now time for second-year residents to shoulder more responsibility, and one of the ways in which responsibility was given to us was by placing us in charge of the ER surgical/trauma module. Each of the four modules could hold about twelve patients. This seemed like a huge step but was still minor in comparison to being in charge of the trauma 'codes'. Sure, it was a matter of going through the basic trauma algorithm, which had been drilled into us repeatedly during our busy and intense first-year nighttime trauma rotation. The real question was: did I remember all that stuff from eight months ago? The answer was very simple. No.

Hopefully it would come back and quickly.

While these thoughts were busy taking a whirlwind tour of my consciousness, an overhead page resonated through the module and the entire emergency room. This announcement became all too familiar.

"Surgical code one to resuscitation. ETA five minutes."

No matter how many times I heard it, it always got my heart racing, my adrenaline pumping, and my sweat glands flowing. It caused my senses to become heightened as well as my clothes to be drenched. It was accompanied by a distinct queasy feeling in the pit of my stomach. With time and experience, this 'sympathetic' response was tempered somewhat, allowing me to function better under stress. You never knew what to expect at any code, so we were trained to expect nothing, or actually expect everything, taking nothing for granted, always preparing for the unexpected.

With time, and with the seemingly slow acquisition of knowledge and experience, I gained small aliquots of confidence. But too much introspection resulted in an unwelcome rise in anxiety, as I realized how little I really knew and how much I still had to learn.

In medicine the more we know, the more we come to realize how much we don't (know).

But as for now, on this day, it was up to me. I was the one in charge, and this code was my responsibility. It was my problem to deal with.

It started to sink in. "Oh, shit! Now what the hell do I do," I thought briefly to myself. People were counting on me, and no one more so than the arriving victim. I was in charge, and truthfully, I was terrified. While my mind was racing on the inside, outside I tried to stay calm. *Never let them see you sweat,* was the mantra. Keep your poker face. The team must at all times have confidence in their leader. Now I certainly did not have much confidence at that stage of my training, but I knew that no one else could know that. I needed to keep my little secret under wraps. How about my fellow residents? Did they know what they were doing, or were they all just faking it, too? I soon discovered the feeling of general insecurity and inability was endemic amongst us. We were like runaway trains barreling along, hoping to stay on the (residency) track but very easily derailed at any time.

Every resident (and every physician), who is honest with himself or herself, must always be aware of his or her deficiencies. Confidence comes from knowledge gained from experience, and this only comes from hard lessons learnt, which means making mistakes. I made a lot of mistakes as a resident, hopefully not too many serious ones (although there were some), but still, lots of little ones. Mistakes will always be made as such is life, and mistakes are one of the frailties of being human, yet the trick is to have checks and balances in place to minimize the frequency and impact of our all-too-often uneducated errors. This is true in all parts of hospital life, but the potential for harm is magnified when decisions have to be made quickly and under pressure as, for example, in the operating room or during a trauma resuscitation (code).

I was young, nervous, inexperienced, and let's face it, I knew next to nothing—or at least that's what I thought, and certainly that was how I felt. Perhaps it was not exactly nothing, for by this point I had completed my first year of residency in addition to four years of medical school, so I had five years of medical education under my belt. I knew a lot of book knowledge but felt as if I knew very little that was truly of practical use. My every action was being watched, second guessed by everyone (which in a strange reassuring way, I hoped it was), including the nurses, who had seen far more than I ever would. It was experience that I lacked, but that was precisely why I had come here and had chosen to train at a major metropolitan trauma center. I had come to learn, to learn medicine, to learn surgery, to learn how to become a surgeon. I wanted to get the most valuable of all medical commodities: experience. Experience in dealing with all types of surgical patients and their injuries or diseases.

Being placed in charge of the trauma module on days was our 'reward' for surviving our intern year, which itself was never a given. It came with the expectation (fanciful perhaps) that we had gained enough experience from our busy night trauma rotation the year before. However, once on my own, I certainly felt somewhat, if not completely and woefully, inadequate. It was on the job training at its best, a true apprenticeship.

"Surgical code one to resuscitation. ETA one minute," the increasingly familiar overhead page announced with a great deal of static.

It was time for me to get my act in gear. Mobilizing my inner troops, a million thoughts pummeled the distant recesses of my brain. What was this one going to be? A shooting, a stabbing, perhaps a car accident? The possibilities were always endless. I needed to clear my head and mentally prepare.

I had to leave my young charge with his football hand injury, so I could get over to resuscitation.

The resuscitation room was an area specifically designed for the acute, life-threatening medical and trauma emergencies (codes), which sadly here were all too common. Strategically located a straight shot down a long bare-walled hallway, it could easily be seen by ambulance crews as they pulled up onto the expansive, metal canopy-covered, concrete emergency-room driveway. The walls were covered with layers of peeling and faded old beige paint, the surrounding counters full of even older and more obsolete equipment. On the wall, adjacent to the double-doored entrance, hanging like trophies, were well-worn wooden backboards with faded, and now barely legible, black and red stenciling.

My team on 'days' was spartan: just a medical student (stud), the nurse, and me. We sat on edge of the gurney, in our usual 'ready' position, while waiting for codes, looking expectantly along the vacant hallway towards the entrance. I mentally began preparing myself while at the same time trying to appear confident (poker face!), ready for anything, making small talk and cracking jokes, all in a desperate attempt to lighten the atmosphere.

We began receiving assorted and conflicting reports of the code that was coming in. First we were informed that nothing was known. Then barely a minute later another message trickled back saying that we were receiving someone found with no vital signs at the scene. This information was likewise short lived, as we were soon informed that he was responding. So as was typical, we had no idea of what to expect. Although it was great to receive a heads-up from EMS (Emergency Medical Services) as to what they were bringing us, it was often a far cry from what we actually received. It taught us to be skeptical of any and all information not directly obtained.

Maybe we would need to 'crack' the chest (open the chest to access the heart), perform open cardiac massage or release a cardiac tamponade (a life-threatening condition where the heart is squeezed by surrounding blood). One could only hope. This was what we, surgical residents, lived for: the chance to do something very dramatic, very machismo, fun even, though it may not actually make any difference to the outcome. But, as in all training, we learnt techniques and tricks that, even if they were of minimal or no help at the time learnt, enabled us to become proficient so that in the event where it might make a difference, we would have the knowledge and skills to be successful. But on that particular day, my first day as the lone soldier, the lone surgical resident in the module, I was hoping for something a little more straightforward.

Finally, the distant wailing of the doppler-shifted sirens became louder. This crescendo-decrescendo sound was soon replaced by static as the overhead paging system again crackled to life. announcing:

"Surgical code one now arriving."

The blue EMS-emblazoned, white, boxy, ambulance screeched to an exaggeratedly abrupt, noisy halt outside the entrance, its red and white flashing lights dancing seductively towards us on the bare walls of the hallway like the dance floor of a suddenly evacuated seventies discotheque. We watched intently as two paramedics dressed in matching navy blue jumpsuits leapt from the cab and hurried to the rear of their rig. They rapidly extracted a stretcher with a patient on it and, assisted by two nurses, hurried down the empty corridor and into our receiving hands. It was immediately apparent that nobody was doing CPR. This was either a good sign or the exact opposite. No sooner was his cart alongside, then with a well-orchestrated brisk and efficient motion, he was transferred onto our gurney.

He had barely landed, his blood-soaked clothes having only just struck our crisp white sheets, when we started our barrage of questions. He was completely surrounded by wildly gesticulating arms, questions and orders flying every which way. With the rapidity of bacteria multiplying in a warm petri dish, we had suddenly expanded from just three to a heaving mass of medical professionals who now engulfed him. We got on with our business. The EMS team was also there, standing relaxed, off towards the door, watching, chatting, loudly critiquing our every move, as if they were standing behind a one-way barrier. But there wasn't one.

Soon more nurses, respiratory techs, and many who I had not the faintest idea who they were but later was informed they were residents from the medical modules, had come to join in or at least to watch. I soon discovered that watching the drama, gore, and intensity of a 'surgical code' was deemed high entertainment by our nonsurgical colleagues. We always seem to draw a crowd. But still for now, I was in charge. It was my job to take control. I needed to block out all the distractions so I could concentrate. But there was a part of me that was happy I was not alone. Were they really helping? Not really. But at least there was help, I thought, if I needed it.

"What happened? When? What kind of weapon was used? Where do you have pain? How is your breathing? Does your belly hurt? Can you move your arms, your legs? Stick your tongue out. How did this happen? Don't move, we are trying to put an IV in. Do you take any medication? Does your neck hurt? Who did this to you? Follow my finger. How many can you see? Do you have any medical problems?"

The commands and questions were flying in, so hard and fast that I doubt if anyone, let alone the sick, blood-streaked patient, had a chance to process one before the next was hurled at him. Could he tell the difference between the questions we were asking him and those that we were posing to each other? It was a nonstop verbal assault. Truthfully, in all the commotion, it made it close to impossible to hear his answers.

In all 'codes', much of our information was gleaned from the delivering paramedics. Here, they explained, our patient had been found shot in the chest, lying face down in a pool of blood outside of what was probably his local bar. When the paramedics arrived on the scene, they found him somnolent, not really even rousable, and were unable to obtain a decent blood pressure reading. This, at the best of times, was near to impossible due to the intrinsic low blood pressure, ambient noise, and ongoing resuscitation.

Following a 'load and go' philosophy, they brought the patient in as quickly as possible. In trauma, time was always critical, and the clock started at the moment of injury. Each valuable second counted.

This skin of this young man was a pale, silvery grey, looking for all the world like a department store mannequin. Except this one could move and talk. He was agitated, belligerent, and clearly very weakened. Where meaningful words failed him, profanity did not.

One of the nurses called out with a blood pressure. "Fifty-five over palp," she almost screamed. He needed fluid and fast. We needed IV access. I searched in vain for a usable vein. They were all collapsed. I needed to do something. He needed fluid ASAP. The only solution was to immediately place a central line.

This central line was a long plastic catheter that was threaded into one of the main, or central, veins that returned the blood from the upper extremities back to the heart. 'Placing a line' was one of the first procedures that I had learnt as an intern and, because of our high volume, I quickly became proficient at it. Actually, as surgical residents we took great pride in being able to rapidly 'slam' them in, even in the most difficult of situations, the bloodiest of 'codes'. The needle we used was huge, more of a size used to draw blood from a horse. Once accessed, a catheter was threaded into the vein through the needle's central bore. This was not so bad when the patient was 'out of it' but was definitely no fun if awake. His skin was cold and clammy. Clearly, he was in shock; he was losing a large amount of blood. He did not complain of any difficulty breathing, but I still needed to listen. I grabbed my stethoscope—at least I had not lost that yet—and placed its diaphragm over his chest. He appeared to have normal breath sounds on both sides. However, due to the ever-present commotion, any attempt to listen to breath sounds during a code was almost always futile. This was a difficult environment in which to apply the subtle skill of auscultation (listening to the lungs). However, we were not looking for subtle findings; we just wanted to know if we could hear air exchange.

After rapidly placing the central line, we immediately started pouring in fluids.

On his left chest, just beneath his left clavicle (collar bone), was a dark, well-punched-out hole, slightly larger than the size of a nickel: the gunshot entrance site. Pink froth was welling up at the edges of it. We log-rolled him to one side and checked his back. No exit wound. His blood pressure slowly began to rise as he responded to the fluids.

We immediately requested a chest X-ray (CXR), hoping that this might shed some light on the nature and extent of his injury. Now even this seemingly straightforward task could be quite an undertaking for the critically injured.

Almost immediately, the radiology techs arrived with their X-ray machine. They were already aware of the code from the overhead page and had been patiently waiting outside the door, ready to be called into action. The cumbersome 'portable' X-ray unit (which looked somewhat akin to a sawn-off forklift) rolled into the resuscitation room with all the finesse, maneuverability, and stealth of a World War One tank. Just the apparently simple task of shooting of a chest X-ray could lead to all sorts of trouble, including the patient often being neglected for a few moments. More than once, a severely injured patient had taken their last breath while having their chest X-ray 'shot'. With our patient sitting half-upright on the gurney, the machine's red crosshairs were carefully targeted upon his chest. The X-ray 'tech' spoke authoritatively, while adjusting the various mysterious knobs (she was not going to miss her chance to tell the doctors what to do):

"Step-back six [feet]. Shooting an X-ray," she would say calmly.

Responding, the now radiation-panicked occupants of the room instantly evacuated. The bustling throng that had been busily fussing over the patient was now scurrying, like rats from a sinking ship, for the exits. There was an audible, high-pitched beep signaling that the invisible X-rays had begun and almost instantaneously completed their light-speed dash through the patient's chest before imbedding themselves in the silver emulsion of the photographic plate behind him.

Only after hearing the single beep did people slowly filter back into the room, and the organized chaos resumed.

As the X-ray was being developed, we continued with our methodical examination.

Now portable X-ray machines have also entered the digital age. Today, smaller, sleeker units with high-resolution digital screens roam the halls. There is no longer any waiting for the photographic plates to be lugged into a darkroom and developed, as we are now able to see the pictures almost instantaneously. We truly get to have our cake and eat it without having to wait.

When I placed my stethoscope on his chest and listened again, I now could not hear anything on his left side. I looked at the bell of the stethoscope as if it was defective and checked to see if I had put the earpieces in correctly. This was a rookie error, no doubt, but one that I find I am still occasionally prone to. Had his lung sounds really become more distant and muffled, or was it just because the room was so noisy? I was not sure. I asked for some quiet.

Indeed, now with the room quieter, I could hear (or rather, not hear) a huge difference between the breath sounds rushing in on the right compared to their complete absence on the left. His lung must be collapsed on that side due to air leaking out into the chest cavity from a lung injury, which had caused it to collapse (a pneumothorax), but there could also be bleeding (a hemo-pneumothorax). It seemed to me that the latter was the most likely, but in any event the treatment was the same; stick a chest tube in—the bigger the tube the better—and suck out the air and blood, allowing the lung to re-expand.

Now, I had placed a whole bunch of chest tubes during my intern year, and unquestionably I knew how to do it. But still it was different when there was no senior resident right next to me. There was no one to look up to for moral support. There was no little nod of agreement, encouraging me to proceed and reassuring me that I had indeed made the right decision and even the right diagnosis. On this day it was all up to me, and just as every pilot takes his first solo flight, today I was 'flying' solo.

A chest tube is a three-foot long stiff, clear plastic tube with multiple side holes set towards the farthest end. They come in a wide range of circumferential sizes, from tiny and pediatric to huge. Placing this tube in his chest would not only confirm if there was blood or air present in his chest, but more importantly it would remove it and hopefully allow our patient to breathe better.

I started unwrapping a tube, a big sucker, about the same diameter as my thumb. With the chest film snapped up onto the view box, I could see the normal lung, which appeared darker, on the right side, whereas on the left side there was a large, light grey area filling the chest halfway up, representing fluid, or more likely here, blood. I felt strangely better, not really for my patient, but that chest film reinforced my decision to place a tube.

I generously painted his entire left chest with brown antiseptic 'paint'. Sometimes there was not time for careful skin preparation, and we had to just dump the solution over the chest. I was nervous. I did not want to screw up. This was my first real one under the gun, and I knew everyone was watching. (We were all a little paranoid that way.) I made a very conscious effort to externally remain calm.

I unwrapped layers of the sterile blue paper wrapper that covered the stainless steel chest tube tray. I stared. There were so many instruments glinting in the tray, and I wondered what many of them were for. I hoped I would not need the majority of them. Rapidly donning a pair of brown sterile gloves, I took four sterile blue cloth towels and draped the area around my planned entrance site. Again, a thousand images rushed through my head, mainly recalling the disaster stories that we had been told. I did not want to end up being someone else's "you won't believe what happened" story.

After choosing the site, I made a small incision. Using a hemostate, I spread the fat until I could feel the underlying rib. I advanced the clamp over the rib and with some significant force, penetrated into the chest cavity. This was the most painful part of the procedure but after some practice, it became quite rapid. I was always impressed by the force it took to push the clamp through the intercostal muscles and into the chest cavity. It was a shove—definitely a two handed, full force, don't go easy, shove.

Once in and opening the clamp, a prolonged hiss of escaping air followed, reminiscent of a tire being punctured, along with a gush of bright red blood as the chest cavity decompressed.

We had learnt how the left ventricle of the heart was one of many organs that could be inadvertently injured. Although it did not happen in my time (really!), we all had heard the story of a former resident who had the misadventure of placing a chest tube directly into the left ventricle with the resultant rapid and fatal exsanguination. Of course, this story had the desired effect of making us exponentially more apprehensive but also safer.

To be aware of the potential disastrous consequences of our actions is essential in all aspects of surgery, and the more we learnt, the more procedures we performed, the more complications we saw, the more we understood. Experience was never gained easily.

With the tube in, it was then connected by a long rubber hose to a

Pleur-evac (a device that enabled us to control the amount of suction and collect and measure the fluid removed). When it was all done, I felt a huge sigh of relief. First code down and no major screw up, so far. So far . . . so far. The words resonated within me. I knew that my time would come. I was only at the start of my second year after all. I still had such a long time to go. Or as we were all reminded, so much time in which to screw up!

As soon as I had placed the tube, over a liter of dark blood gushed with almost explosive force. Now that amount warranted a thoracotomy to locate and repair the injury. I called my senior. He needed to know.

The patient continued to put out lots of blood from his chest until we had removed over two liters. We were pumping in saline and blood, and he became more alert and much more coherent. His blood pressure improved and his breathing had become much easier.

Reviewing his CXR again, I saw a bullet fragment in the right upper chest. If this was the culprit, then it must have passed all the way across to the other side, also penetrating his right lung on its voyage of destruction. He needed a tube on the right side, too. Taking a deep breath and knowing I could step off the accelerator slightly, I placed a second chest tube on his right where immediately 200cc (cubic centimeter, each equivalent to one milliliter) of blood came out.

The bleeding on the left side had not let up one bit. I knew that he needed to have his chest explored, and while the staff surgeon for the day was on his way, I went around the business of getting him ready. I explained to him that he needed an operation, to find and fix the damage caused by the bullet. I then went searching for his family and repeated my discussion.

Since both of his lungs had been damaged, both sides of his chest would need to be explored. But even more important would be to check the possibility of damage to the 'middle area', the mediastinum, the area occupied by critically important structures, not the least of which were the major blood vessels that entered and exited the heart.

I was, by his time, getting a little excited. I knew that this was going to be a great case . . . except . . . except that I would not be there. Yes, I knew that. I knew that I needed to remain in the module and take care of all the other patients that had piled up while we were busy with this man's resuscitation. Still, it was going to be a great case.

With his IV fluids and blood hanging (from an attached IV pole), his chest tubes draining, and all his laboratory results taped to his chart, we wheeled him out the side door at the rear of the resuscitation room, heading down behind the modules, around a few bends, and into the hands of the operating room staff. This trip took all of a minute, a huge advantage having the OR so close to the emergency room. Now, that was a good bit of design.

Meanwhile, back in the resuscitation room, work continued in our absence as the carnage was cleaned up. If there was one thing that was never a priority during codes, it was tidiness. Clothes were ripped, torn, and cut from the helpless individuals, allowing us access to them and their injuries (Exposure: a vital surgical axiom. You cannot fix it if you don't know it's there). Blood-soaked bandages and syringes were every-where. The clean room of half an hour earlier now appeared more like a battlefield.

Back in the surgical module, with my heart rate having slowly returned to normal, I contemplated the mountain of work that awaited. Now this was not the mess of the resuscitation room but the steady unrelenting influx of patients and their associated paperwork that had accumulated during my absence.

The young football player who had lacerated his hand during a game earlier that day was still waiting patiently to be attended to, his hand soaking in a brown antiseptic concoction of Betadine and saline. This had been given to him by one of our experienced module nurses. I immediately went over and attended to him.

The laceration had torn through the skin at the base of his thumb and had nicely exposed the layer beneath; globular, pink-tinged, yellow fat in the depths of the wound. My examination appeared to be causing him significant consternation, his look of fear seemingly a little out of place for a man of his overwhelming physical presence. His forehead beaded up with glistening droplets of sweat that rapidly combined themselves, forming small rivulets that made their way down the side of his face. He was in pain, yet he remained silent. His hand was not yet anesthetized, and he was certainly not enjoying my examination. Visually I could not see any evidence of deep tissue, muscle, or tendon involvement.

He was lucky, as this could very easily have been an 'ugly' injury had the cut been a little deeper and could also have necessitated a trip to our already backed up operating room. I checked the motor and sensory function of his hand. He stayed still, but not without grimacing, as he tolerated my probing. I could not find any evidence of a deficit, and he appeared to have full function. This confirmed my visual findings. I located the 'stud' who was with us that day and delegated him the task of irrigating the wound and sewing him up.

The ER trauma rotations were part of our pre-surgical training, teaching us how to handle critically ill patients and improving our meagre decision-making skills. It taught us to function under stress, for there was no higher stress than caring for a full-blown trauma 'code'.

I rapidly learnt that it was the minority of trauma victims that ended up in the operating room, yet these were the exciting ones, the challenging ones, and usually the bloody ones. This was precisely why I was here. I wanted to learn how to operate and fix people. What could be better, I thought, than to use one's own hands to save someone's life? Not only was it a privilege, it was also a massive adrenaline rush. *(These feelings have not changed 30 years on).*

On 'nights' we occasionally made it to the operating room. If we were lucky, or more likely deemed worthy, we might be 'thrown a bone' by our 'chief' and be allowed to drain some 'butt pus' (a peri-rectal abscess). Going to the operating room was an opportunity that had to be earned, a reward for hard work, especially if we were able to keep the pressure off our chief and keep our end running smoothly. We needed to make him look good (which was not always easy).

Going to the OR, even on 'nights', presumed that the module was not too busy and there was enough help to tackle the load. During 'days' however, it was different story as there was never the manpower available as on 'nights'—typically we were there alone. Occasionally we would be lucky enough to have a 'stud' or an ER resident to help out. An extra set of hands prevented me from becoming bogged down, enabling me to keep track of the big picture, get the critical patients attended to, and see consults. These were requests that we received for help, for an opinion with respect to a specific patient problem, usually in one of the medical modules.

It was a constant flow of interesting characters interspersed with the occasional serious injuries, which were sometimes triaged, in error, to the module instead of the resuscitation room. The easiest patients to evaluate were the gunshot or stab victims, and although these may have involved life threatening injuries, their more easily understood mechanisms allowed for a better estimation of their potential injuries. Blunt trauma, on the other hand, which we most commonly saw as a result of high-speed motor vehicle accidents on one of the many nearby freeways, was much more difficult to assess and required a great deal more time for its proper evaluation.

Residency is an apprenticeship, and with that in mind, everything I saw and did, no matter whether it was good or bad, easy or hard, was still essential experience. Knowledge was what I needed, and I needed to absorb every morsel that I could. Before starting to learn how to operate, I needed to learn how to decide when to operate, who should be operated on, how to prepare my patients beforehand to maximize their outcome, as well as how to take care of them afterward. It is not good enough to just be technically adept at operating without the other two pieces (pre- and post-operative care) of the surgical care triad. During my residency we were constantly reminded that a surgeon needed to know as much as an internist (internal medicine physician), and in addition must also know how to operate. These were very lofty goals indeed.

Each of my multiple ER rotations added a further layer of knowledge and was associated with an incremental increase in responsibility. In our first year, as interns, we were junior members of the extensive night trauma team, where we learnt trauma basics and the seemingly impossibly complex task of its evaluation and treatment. It was both mental and sensory overload! As a second-year we 'enjoyed' both a 'solo' day rotation as well as another as a member of the 'night' trauma team. Two years on, as a fourth year, we graduated to being 'IT', the night trauma service 'chief'. Then we had Saturday night off, which was covered by a fifth-year resident (see The Visiting Professor, p. 279).

Being tired was an occupational hazard as a resident, as we never had the opportunity to get enough rest. During our second-year daytime trauma rotation, the one to which I was currently assigned, we did twelve hours on and twelve hours off for six days straight, but the days always ended up being a whole lot longer than just twelve hours. Sign out to the oncoming team every evening could easily add half an hour. In addition, if I was in the midst of a code or laceration repair, then that would have to be completed and the appropriate documentation written up before I could even contemplate leaving. In the end our shifts always ended up closer to thirteen hours. Now that was only if there wasn't a good case in the OR that I wanted to watch or scrub in on, for once my shift was over, I was free to go to the OR if I chose. Being in the OR is always where we would rather be.

Keep Me Alive

ONE MORE down. Who knows how many to go?

Back in the module, I kept working my way slowly but systematically through the backlog of patients that had accumulated during my time away at the code. I was always amazed how much stuff would pile up while I was tied up. A young child with a dog bite, a girl with a sprained ankle, a laceration caused by a lapse of concentration while opening a can of pork and beans.

Dog bites were exceptionally common, especially in kids, but for the most part they were an easy fix: wash them out, close them up. The face was especially prone, perhaps due to a combination of its relatively large surface area, and that kids, innocently, love to get up close to play with their family (or someone else's) pooch. Where they might have been just expecting a sloppy lick on the cheek, they might receive a little more for their attentions. Although keeping the child still during repair could be trying, it was not as difficult as keeping their parents under control. These lacerations almost always healed up well. There is no substitute for young healthy tissue.

Now human bites, well, that's another story altogether. Some of the worst infections I have ever dealt with have had their origin from the bacterial soup residing in the human mouth. The most frequent culprit, the roundhouse punch, a favorite of Westerns, usually results in the knuckle of the aggressors' clenched fist striking the teeth of the recipient. In the movies you don't see the guy who threw the punch holding his fist in pain because he just lacerated it on the foul teeth of his opponent. Instead, they return to the bar to down their double whiskey. But then that is Hollywood. It is far from reality, and too many people only find this out the hard way, often being surprised when experiencing the unpleasant truth.

The skin overlying the knuckle is very thin, and the smoothly gliding tendons that extend the fingers reside barely a millimeter or so beneath. It is because of this anatomical proximity that a laceration caused by contact with sharp, bacteria-laden, teeth (the combatants in such altercations are not renowned for their superior oral hygiene) may lead to a severe infection of the immediate area if not of the underlying tendon itself. This can rapidly develop into a devastating infection, which without timely and aggressive intervention can result in permanent scarring. We are not talking about superficial cosmetic scarring here, but a more serious functional one whereby the ensuing chronic scar can lead to impaired mobility of the tendons, sometimes permanently. This type of infection is treated by opening the tendon sheath and draining any pus that is hiding there. This hospitalization may be inconvenient but certainly is far better than the alternative of a life-long stiff finger, or worse, losing it.

Finally, as I continued my tour of the module, I got around to seeing a man who had arrived on 'nights'. He was a smartly dressed, pleasant but anxious middle-aged gentleman with a jet black closely trimmed beard that unlike his hair had not yet begun to grey. He had been driving home from his work as a second shift supervisor at the nearby Chrysler plant. It was well after 1:00 when he had finally gotten behind the wheel of his car, exhausted, his mind singularly focused only on getting home to his bed, when he stopped at a red light.

As the story unfolded, I found myself surprised. I shouldn't have been. But I was still very naive and new to inner-city ways. This incident seemed personal and yet at the same time very random. He explained that while he was stopped at a light, which he further explained was not in one of the better areas of the city, he noticed two men, materializing out of the shadow of a nearby building, rushing towards him. He immediately tried to drive away, stalling his car in his hurried attempt. Try as he could, he was unable to restart it quickly enough to make an escape.

It was a typical hot, humid, summer night in Detroit, a thunderstorm having passed through, and without the benefit of a functioning air conditioner, he had been driving with his windows down. This fact he had completely overlooked during the ensuing 'stressful' confusion. While one man ran in front of his car, the other went to the driver's side door, opened it, and dragged him out onto the deserted street. Pressing his face against the uneven, rain-drenched asphalt, they immediately set upon him, kicking him relentlessly with multiple blows to his head, chest, and abdomen. They not only proceeded to rob him of his wallet, keys, and of course his car, but they also stripped him and took his pants. As strange as it might seem (and with time I learnt that some of the seemingly strangest things were in fact routine), it was a common tactic in an attempt to impede him from rapidly obtaining help. He was able to reach help and was soon brought to us, pant-less. He was lucky to have escaped with his life.

My immediate thought, rather selfishly, was what would I have done in a similar situation? I had no idea. I need to make sure my doors are locked and windows closed, I told myself.

On arrival, he was found to have been beaten with such ferocity that his face was bruised and cut up all over. A deep laceration above his left eye had already swelled and burst. There was more bruised than normal skin. He would be hurting for many days to come. Luckily he had passed a full eye exam performed the by the night crew, who fortunately for me had found time to do some of his evaluation.

He had been sent to the X-ray line to await specialized views of his spine. Here he joined the long parade of patients, lined up in their carts, winding down the hallway like cars lining up outside a service station during a gasoline shortage. With his spine finally cleared and neck brace removed, the grime that had collected under it was cleaned and that area of his neck examined.

He had two large lacerations, each about five inches long across the back of his skull, which we sutured, and we dressed a number of abrasions. He was very anxious and eager to get home, but mainly he was just scared. He was frightened not so much for himself but for his family. His assailants not only had his car and keys, but having taken his wallet, they now had his home address as well!

As my weeks of working in the emergency room went by, I found myself listening to many unfortunate tales almost identical to his. It was becoming clear to me that these types of incidents were surprisingly common, so I took notes, at least mental ones, trying to make my own map of these locations. I hoped that this knowledge of potential trouble spots would perhaps allow me to avoid them, even in broad daylight. If nothing else, it certainly changed the route that I drove home, as I had to drive through some very questionable areas. I began regarding deserted stoplights as more of a suggestion to slow down and look carefully than to come to a complete halt. I rapidly became more 'street wise' with the information obtained from our many less fortunate 'citizens'. I soon discovered that there was a bigger problem and one which I could not so easily overlook. I was currently living in just such an area to be avoided!

It was not so much the apartment complex itself, which was relatively safe with its gated security, but more the location, which, although ten years previously was very desirable, had now become rundown and downright dangerous. It was not uncommon to hear, more typically on muggy summer nights, the rat-tat-tat of automatic weapons being discharged. Even though I was probably safe, it was still a little unnerving. Hell, it was downright frightening. I appeared to be living in a war zone.

I made my way over to the nursing carrel to write up charts, sitting down to 'enjoy' a little breather while documenting the morning's events. I could feel my pulse slowly returning towards normal. The carrel almost eliminated the noise and bustle of the outside world and enabled me to block everything else out from my immediate surroundings and concentrate on getting my notes written.. I scribbled rapidly on a blue progress note sheet that I had pulled from the file tray on the shelf above me. I never knew how much time I had to get it all done, so I wrote fast, as fast as I possibly could. It was no wonder our handwriting was always such illegible scrawl. It was born out of necessity. There was no time to ever go slow, go neatly. If I did not get it done right away, I would either forget to do it or begin to get patients mixed up with each other. Either way it wasn't good. It was never long before I became inundated with even more work, more patients, more details, more paperwork. It was imperative to stay ahead.

Now that we have entered the age of the Electronic Medical Record (EMR), physicians no longer have to write undecipherable notes or prescriptions. Although I doubt our illegible scribble will improve, at least now it matters less. EMR should increase efficiency (we are not there yet), which should translate to more time with the patient (definitely not there). Hopefully, we can find a way to spend more time taking care of patients—not charts.

Another tap on the shoulder brought me rapidly back to reality. I backed out and swiveled around on my stool, glancing up to see one of the nurses who was working with me that day standing directly over me, her short black hair framing a round, overly tanned, smiling face.

"Well, hopefully it'll be pretty quiet from now on," she said with a glint in her eye and a slightly forced smile. She knew better. "Looks like we've had our quota for the day," she continued.

She was right: it had already been busy enough for two days.

"If not for the day, then maybe at least for a few minutes," I said. But I also knew better and immediately regretted my words. Emergency room personnel specifically, and nurses in general, were a superstitious lot. They really disliked it if you said if as you left, "I hope it stays slow for you." This was sacrilege and tantamount to asking for the floodgates of hell to be opened. I was pretty sure that we would receive at least one more code that day but was still hoping that it might not come for a while.

But as was typical, it was not to be.

"Surgical code one to resuscitation, ETA two minutes." The familiar voice echoed its staticky notification around the entire emergency room.

The sound reverberated in the recesses of my cranium.

But then what was I thinking? Clearly, I wasn't. I knew that the little bit of quiet I was expecting was just too good to be true. I had been warned that it was always hard, if not impossible, to ever really get caught up on 'days'. Just when you were close to being all caught up another patient or code would roll in.

It only took only a split second for the adrenaline surge to kick in and whisk me away from my temporary pleasantly relaxed state. I dashed back to the resuscitation room, my heartrate once again rising exponentially, my mind being jolted to an almost hyper-aware level. Perhaps this feeling was similar to how athletes felt prior to competition, the adrenaline surging through their bodies, permeating every distant cell.

In the resuscitation room, we (all two of us) once again assumed our positions. Even though it seemed like we had all only just left, the room was already 'spick and span'. I made sure that I had everything ready and at hand. From the top drawer of the crash cart, I removed an endotracheal tube and then grabbed the Laryngoscope. I flicked it open to check that the light was working. But of course it was. I had checked it less than a half hour earlier. But it kept me busy, kept my fingers occupied and threw a little oil on my mounting anxiety. Perhaps it also made me look as if I knew what I was doing (that always helped!).

Going over to one of the side cupboards, I removed a cutdown tray placing it nearby and armed myself with a couple of 'red-devils'. These were 14-gauge IV catheters that were so named because of their scarlet packaging and their huge size, the diameter of a ballpoint pen refill. They allowed us to infuse fluids much more rapidly than through the more usual smaller catheters. These 'red devils' were always our preferred IV access during a trauma resuscitation, when speed and volume of fluid infusion were paramount. Truthfully, we never really got much of a chance to put them in. They were, naturally, very difficult to insert, especially as the patients who really needed them often had the worst veins. But really the main reason for having them was that we looked (so we thought) 'cool' with a couple of these monsters sticking out the top of our scrub pockets. Surgical machismo!

While we were preparing, the ambulance came flying into the ER, accompanied by its usual noisy, rapid, and overly dramatic screeching halt outside the entrance. Some loved to put on a show, as if competing for the longest tire skid tracks. I walked briskly over to the side of the room, stopped, and for a couple of seconds stared pensively at the telephone that hung expectantly on the wall. I knew that it was my responsibility to inform my chief, so lifting the receiver I pressed zero. I wondered if this was how Commissioner Gordon felt when he picked up the Bat phone. But then again, I was not being put through to 'Wayne Manor', just the hospital switchboard. I asked the operator to page my senior resident to the resuscitation room 'stat' (an overly used medical term for 'rush' or 'immediate'), knowing full well that he was likely tied up in a case. Nevertheless, it was still my duty to inform him that a code was coming in. Once in a while (quite rarely in my experience) my page would be answered by my chief's timely arrival, usually with one of his or her juniors in tow, their long white coats trailing behind them as they swept into the room, dynamic duo style.

Moments later, the expected page reverberated noisily overhead.

"Surgical code one now arriving."

From our vantage point, we could see pretty much everything, or at least everything that we needed to.

We were ready or so we thought. Once again, everything around us appeared to be taking place in slow motion. Just watching the patient being wheeled towards us seemed to take forever. Was this already starting to become routine? Was that what this was? I really doubted it. In my head everything was still crazy, a hundred possibilities rapidly coming into focus and just as quickly vanishing. A jumbled mosaic of potential life-threatening scenarios played out in my mind. All I could think about was who and what was coming in. What should I do? Was I really ready?

Let's go. Let's get the patient in here. It was always the waiting that was the hardest.

We did not move, our eyes were still fixated on the cart being whisked (a very slow whisk, it felt to us) down the hallway towards us. Once again, I repeated my mental sifting of diagnostic possibilities, trying to make sure that I had a logical plan ready. I had no real idea what this code would be. He was still 25 yards off but closing fast. What would it be? Another gunshot wound? A stabbing? It could be anything.

A year ago or so, I never would have thought that the consideration of all these potential life-threatening injuries would have become so routine. Not just daily, mind you, but numerous times a day. I thought my list was complete, exhaustive, but that was my inexperience talking as, in truth, I did not yet realize how much I didn't know!

The patient came closer. The waiting always made me anxious. This was the time when I would second guess myself. Could I really take care of this guy? Would he have something that was beyond my abilities?

An instant later, they were here, alongside our gurney. It was clear that this patient was not dead, but nevertheless was clearly a great fan of 'the Dead', as was attested to by his black t-shirt with the faded but still recognizable silvery grey likeness of Jerry Garcia and his band's logo emblazoned in green and white. The collar of his shirt was partly covered by long strands of thin grey hair that were, in all likelihood, darker and much thicker when the shirt was purchased.

With his transfer over to our gurney completed, the order of apparent disorder rapidly returned in full force. It was controlled chaos, a barrage of interrogation and information, orders and actions flying in from all angles. His face was pale, grimacing, deeply contorted, a combination of pain, fear, and panic.

"You are at Receiving Hospital. We are all here to help you." I weakly attempted reassurance and then continued. "Can you tell us what happened?" I caught myself speaking too quickly, so I purposefully slowed my speech. I needed to remain calm, to act calm and in control.

I tried to put myself in his place, scared, in pain, as he stared blankly at me. What did he see? A kid? A doctor? Hopefully he would continue to remain blissfully unaware of my ignorance and inexperience.

"This guy robbed me. Then this." His eyes slowly tilted downward, almost as if ashamed, his gaze settling on the blood-stained shirt covering his abdomen.

After a slight pause, he added in a tone of disbelief. "He had my money. So why? Why this? Why? I just don't understand."

Instantaneously it appeared, our nurses had him stripped bare, cutting away his Grateful Dead t-shirt, its tattered pieces of black cloth receiving their final coup de grace. His newly bared abdomen revealed a six by a half inch gaping gash, its edges surrounded by partly congealed black clot. However, from under this meandered a slow yet continuous stream of bright red blood, following the irregular contour of his skin, running over the side and dripping onto, and forming an enlarging stain on, the starched, white sheets.

It was all too easy to be fooled by the obvious, as Sherlock Holmes might assert, so we were taught to take note of the obvious but keep on guard for problems that might be easily missed, camouflaged even. The most visible and most painful injuries were frequently not the most serious.

"Do you hurt anywhere else?" I asked. Then as he replied, we log-rolled him, first to one side and then the other, checking for other injuries.

"No, I don't think…" His voice trailed off as he grimaced, then grunted, clearly with increased pain from the movement.

Holding him over on his side, we quickly checked his back. Finding nothing, we gently rolled him back.

"Oooh, my belly. It really . . . really hurts, Doc."

He moved his hand rapidly down towards his injured side, almost pulling out his IV.

I watched him staring, slightly catatonically perhaps. For a few moments I felt disassociated, an outsider floating above him, looking down on the surreal scene unfolding. There we were, all huddled around this poor guy. I could hardly see him through the almost impenetrable jungle of hair (this was 80s big hair time) as we arched over, intently caring for him. But there on his left side was the dark bloody slash.

"I know, I know. We are going to help you and get you fixed up." I repeated reassurances, but my words seemed so meaningless, so impotent. My mind wandered again as I tried to imagine what had gone on in the mind of his assailant. Why on earth did he do it? Why would he want to? Why would anyone? These were questions I would ask myself again and again as we cared for patients with life-threatening injuries caused by the hand of a fellow human. But I also knew I would never discover the answer.

Laying the young man flat again, I returned my focus. I turned to the nurse taking the vitals.

"Blood pressure?" I asked.

"120 over 60. No change"

Almost right away we had two good sized IVs in place, and the 'Ringers', was running in, full bore. 'Ringers', which is short for Lactated Ringers (abbreviated LR) is a particular formulation of IV fluid favored by many surgeons, especially in trauma.

I stood on his right side, my hand on his bloodied, hairy belly, as I systematically began a visual tour of his abdomen while simultaneously beginning my examination, starting away from the site of obvious injury. As I pushed in (not as gently as I should have) with the tips of my fingers, they were met with a sudden resistance, his abdominal muscles instantaneously contracting up against my fingertips. He flinched, grimaced, and cried out with excruciating pain. I was a little surprised. There was serious trouble going on in there. This was guarding, a sign of serious inflamma-tion within the abdomen cavity that caused his muscles to involuntarily contract, reflexively attempting to prevent me from pushing in deeper.

Peritonitis, or irritation/inflammation of the peritoneum, the nerve-rich inner lining of the abdominal cavity, is the technical term for the cause of this (physical) finding, and it was immediately clear to me that he needed to go to surgery. Most likely the knife had penetrated a por-tion of bowel, spilling its, foul, highly corrosive, bacteria-laden contents inside the abdomen, causing the irritation and consequently the severe pain elicited by my examining fingers

I now started to consider all the possible internal injuries that he could have sustained. The knife could have struck anything—the stomach, the small bowel, and what about the colon? Could the colon be injured? That, naturally, was also a possibility and a potentially much more serious one—one we would not know about until his belly was opened. If the knife had caused a significant colon injury, he might need a colostomy, a 'shit bag' as it was so often described by our patients. Some things you just could not sugar coat.

Here, after removing the injured portion of colon, the two ends are not reconnected. Instead, the upstream, cut end, is brought out through a surgically made defect in the side of the abdomen. This newly fashioned 'ostomy' allows the colonic contents—fecal material (shit)—to exit the colon directly into a bag secured to the skin. As awful as this sounds (the right decision for the patient is not necessarily the one they will always like), it is far superior to the alternative of attempting to primarily repair the injury and subsequently having it break down, its contents oozing into the abdominal cavity, leading to severe infectious complications, further surgery (the colostomy that they should have received in the first place), and possibly death.

Right now, we needed to get him ready.

Having just caused him exquisite pain from my exam, I could barely imagine how frightened he must have been. I leaned over him and made sure I was making good eye contact. Maybe he thought I was going to tell him that there was nothing more that we could do. Well, at least if that's what he thought, then I had some good news for him.

"The knife has gone into your belly." I began with the obvious. "It has done some damage, but exactly what we don't know. At least not yet. We need to get in there, find out what's wrong, then fix it. You need an operation as soon as possible."

He seemed almost relieved with the news, appearing overcome with an almost Zen-like calmness, perhaps born from the knowledge that the injury was potentially fixable and survivable. With almost childlike naivety and complete trust, he replied,

"OK, Doc. Do whatever you have to do. Just stop the pain. Please."

I then went on and explained to him about the possibility of colon damage and that he might have to temporarily wear a bag.

"Just keep me alive for my boys." He looked up as he spoke, staring at me with dark, pleading eyes. His eyes were tearing up. These were not tears of pain but rather the tears of rekindled hope.

Here I was, an inexperienced second-year resident, a surgeon in training. I was the one that he was looking to for help, to save his life. This is real, I thought. This man might die. He needs a real doctor, a real surgeon.

I tried not to think about the incredible responsibility that had been thrust on us, let alone the expectations of our patients. It was almost too overwhelming. Right now, I needed to get this man off to the operating room and return to seeing my other patients. There would be time for reflection later, at least that's what I always told myself. In reality there never was, as when later arrived, sleeping always took precedent over dwelling on the day just passed. The next day would be the same and so the day after. There was only ever time to reflect on the moment, which we vigorously avoided. We needed to keep moving—fix one problem, deal with the next, and attempt to keep our heads above water.

All seemed to be good, in control, at least for now. My patient was stable and ready for the OR. Well, almost ready. I turned and spoke to the pharmacist standing over by the door. They were always present during 'codes', trying impossibly to look inconspicuous as they stood out in their never wrinkled, starched lab coats.

"Let's enter him into the penetrating abdominal trauma protocol."

He answered with a simple nod.

I hoped that there would not be a long delay, and that as soon as the current OR case was completed, they could start on my stab victim. As I was finishing scribbling down the particulars of his physical examination, happy that I had managed to get everything done, another overhead announcement interrupted my thoughts. I stopped while quickly attempting to listen through the background barrage of noise and static.

"Surgical code one, times two. ETA three minutes."

"Oh shit, here we go again," I thought to myself as I completed my illegible rushed note on the blue progress sheet, describing both the presentation and the findings of my exam. We had not even managed to get him out of the room, and now there were two more coming.

I have to admit that a part of me felt excited, exhilarated even. I was on a trauma high. Bring them on. I don't care if it's one or five. We can handle it. I can handle it. The adrenaline was re-surging through me, tingling every pore of my young, tired but hopefully resilient, body.

We were all adrenaline junkies (that summarizes most surgeons), and even now, that has not changed much. When I talk to other surgeons about why they do what they do and continue to do so after so many years, it is rarely for financial gain but usually for the rush. The rush you receive when you tackle a difficult problem and overcome it; the deep satisfaction of using your hands to make a sick person better. What bigger rush is there than saving a life?

It was precisely this craziness that made our ER rotation such an invaluable experience and was, after all, why I chose to do my surgical training here, at an urban trauma center. So here I was, in the fast lane, the insane high octane, stressful terrain of trauma. I wanted to see, experience, and learn all I could about trauma and how to care for the severely injured. Everybody had told me it was the best way, if not the only way, to properly train to become a surgeon. It was here, in the heat of battle, that I would hopefully learn the skills to save lives.

When the adrenaline surge receded, my mind returned to hounding me with its repetitive nagging questions. Will I be able to handle this one? What about the next? When will I start to feel comfortable? Was I the only one to have such thoughts? Although fleeting, such thoughts remained a frequent visitor to my psyche. It was a constant yin and yang and one that I tried to relegate to my subconscious (hence perhaps, the nightmares).

As I constantly learnt and relearnt, at least half of the battle in dealing with acute life-threatening trauma was making sure that we are adequately prepared mentally as well as clinically. This ability came painfully slowly as we gained hard earned experience. As many have noted, inexperience leads to complications, but complications lead to experience. Decisions needed to be rapid, almost reflexive. We could not waste precious time. Every patient needed to be evaluated in a specific and logical sequence, such that decisions could be efficiently made, most of which would become second nature but were still essential to ensure the best possible outcome. In the end it was always time that was our enemy, and it was always the one commodity that was in short supply.

We were taught to keep emotions under wraps as we evaluated each new patient, absorbing the information—what our ears heard, our eyes saw, and our fingers felt, along with the results of any tests performed. All these varying sources of information were inputted into the 'CPU', our brains. Just as with computers, the output obtained is only as good as the input and the software programming, which in this case was our experience and education. With incremental adjustments in programming, our output became more refined. It was a little detached, inhuman almost, but it was (and is) the best way to ensure that we obtained the best outcomes. It was paramount that we, the physicians in charge, keep clear heads and follow a systematic and organized sequence. Although there are many times in medicine where it is appropriate to show emotion, this was not one.

Working smoothly and efficiently, our module one nurses rapidly set up the two remaining gurneys in the room. We put a call through to our surgical module to see if they could take our 'stab' patient, but everyone there was busy, too. He would have to remain in the resuscitation room for the time being. The three minutes were almost up, and the atmosphere in the room was a thick with anticipation. We were like a herd of sharks circling before a feeding frenzy.

Just then Dr. Bouwman, our staff surgeon for the day, poked his head around the corner, unannounced and at first unnoticed. He was a physically imposing man, tall, husky, with broad shoulders, looking more like a professional football player rather than a knowledgeable surgeon and outstanding surgical educator. His face was framed by tightly cropped black hair and a salt and pepper beard, and his abdomen bellowed out under his scrubs like a yacht's spinnaker pulling with air. He was our residency program director, at least for that year, and was universally well liked by all the surgical residents, having a reputation, above all else, for giving it straight. He was friendly and always helpful but was never somebody that you wanted to cross.

He had been in the operating room dealing with the bilateral chest-injured patient (our first code that day) and had decided to come by and see if there was anything waiting in the wings. Clearly he was not in earshot when the most recent 'code page' had been broadcast.

I had no idea how long he had been observing before he announced his presence.

"What have you got?" he asked.

"Oh, hi!" I replied, trying hard to tone down my surprise as I turned to see him. My first thought was, I wonder how long has he been standing there, and had he seen me screw up at all? I gathered my wits about me, and pointing to the man on the first stretcher in front me, I continued.

"This guy sustained a stab wound to his lower abdomen, and on my exam is very tender with guarding and rebound."

"Sounds like he needs an operation," Dr. Bouwman replied

"Yup, I think so. He's all set up and ready to go. Consent signed," I responded.

"Antibiotics?"

"He's on the protocol."

After some further brief exchange of information, he seemed satisfied.

"Great, looks like you have everything under control." With those words of encouragement, he started to leave the room. But what about the two more we had coming in? Without making it look like a plea for help, I thought I had better tell him about our imminent new arrivals.

"Oh yeah, and we have a double code on the way in," I said, pretending all was under control.

Did I say too much? Was I asking for help? A sure sign of weakness.

He stopped in his tracks, turned, and suddenly appeared a little more attentive.

"What are they?" he asked.

"Don't know yet," I replied.

Once again, we were all set, poised, and ready. But now Dr. Bouwman decided to hang around for a few minutes to see if we, or rather I, needed help.

Within seconds the next two victims' arrival was announced. As it turned out, they, too, had been at the same bar as our stab victim, and they also had managed to get in the way when knives and bullets began to fly.

With our new arrivals, the resuscitation room was full; there was no room for any further codes. Dr. Bouwman went over to examine the man in the far gurney while I began on the man who occupied the middle one. He was in a great deal of pain, but his vitals were rock steady, and while I got on with my examination, the nurses commenced their routine, starting IVs and drawing blood.

As it turned out, his injuries did not seem at first all that bad, but then that all depends on your perspective. At least they did not appear to be life-threatening. He had been shot at an oblique angle to his left leg, the bullet tearing through the base of his penis, through the right testicle, and then out through the right flank. Ouch. It appeared to have missed the major blood vessels that supply and drain the legs. However, he still had been left with a severe soft tissue injury to his genitals, which would require extensive reconstructive work from our Plastics team.

After completing my examination and finding no other injuries (but then surely, he had enough), I knew he was one patient that I would not have to worry too much about, at least not for the short term.

Dr. Bouwman meanwhile, had just finished his examination of our third code patient. He had ordered a chest X-ray, and the nurses had the IV in even before he had a chance to ask for it. With this patient stable, he walked across the room and spoke to the senior ER doc on that day. The resuscitation room was full, and it looked to stay that way for a while.

"We're going to close down as a 'code one' destination until we are cleared up," I overheard him saying to the ER attending.

There was a strict hierarchy for trauma patients, and it was the attending surgeon on call who had the last word. It was his or her decision whether or not to temporarily suspend the ability to receive trauma code patients. We had some attendings who never closed, even if the resuscitation room was bursting at the seams. I think they looked at it as a sign of weakness and that we were just not being efficient enough. It would be expected for us to raise our tempo, to take care of all the patients we had, even if perhaps some of the care might have suffered. Certainly, we suffered, and if nothing else our stress level shot through the roof when we though it impossible to raise it any further. But then this was all part of the training, and some Attendings certainly had adopted a more 'trial by fire' methodology. If we had a pressure relief valve, it would have blown long before.

Dr. Bouwman explained to me what he had in the last gurney.

"Nick, this guy got stabbed in the left chest, up high. Chances are he has a 'pneumo'. Wait for the chest X-ray. He's stable."

"Okay," I replied. "I'll get a tube set up. Sounds like he's going to need one."

"I'm going back to the OR now. Okay? You can handle it?" I was not quite sure if it was a statement or a question.

"No problem," I said, confidently as he walked out of the room. It was not as if I was going to say anything else, I just needed to get going and get the room cleared out.

As he left the room, I wondered to myself, "Did I do OK? I think I did. I don't thing I made any blunders or at least no major ones." Again, my insecurity topped with a large dose of paranoia was trying to get the better of me.

Looking up at the clock, I could hardly believe it was already 6:30 p.m. The four codes and the many module patients had kept me very busy, and the day had flown by. I had not even had time to see all the patients that had accumulated in the module. I would have to donate them to the oncoming night crew. They would not be happy, but at least they would have enough help, and it would take their larger team little time to get it all sorted.

I was glad to get out of there. I was physically and mentally exhausted, and more than anything glad to have my first day on 'days' under my belt.

Another Chest Tube Save

HOPEFULLY EARLY in our training, there is a day, a time, a moment when everything clicks, things go right, we have a great experience, maybe even save a life, and so despite the long hours, the days without a break, the never-ending studying, the sleepless nights and nonexistent social life, it reminds us of why we are here. This was my day to realize that perhaps it was all worth it, and like a high handicap golfer who makes a really great shot, it keeps us going with the belief that it will, or at least might, occur again.

So many times in medicine, we know our actions will make little difference to the overall outcome. Our actions are temporary, a Band-Aid at best. We frequently treat only the symptoms of a problem, and while certainly that has merit and even benefit, it leaves us wanting for more.

For many of us, we want to really fix the problem This is why we endured the laboriously long years of medical school and residency. This was, for me, one of my main drivers to pursue surgery.

I have always been a fixer. I see something broken, and I want to fix it. Maybe I need to, and perhaps it is about the challenge (then and now) to see if I can. It might be the need for immediate gratification, whereas in so many areas of medicine, results are gained slowly, sometimes painfully so. It is hard, frequently impossible, to change most of our patients' unhealthy habits or to try to effect meaningful change in a difficult and complex social situation. But surgery is much more Pavlovian, much more stimulus-driven with a well-defined reward. A person comes in with appendicitis, a rotten gallbladder, and you take it out, fix them. You cure them. Now that feels good. No, actually it feels great! Maybe surgeons just need their gratification immediately. We typically were not the ones writing poetry or painting pretty pictures as kids, but rather, I like to believe, we were the ones with the erector sets, taking things apart and putting them back together and hoping that when we did, they still worked.

> *We would like to believe that when we put people back together, they always work, but sadly, that is just not true. Although we know a great deal, the human body remains incompletely understood. We do not know why many of us get certain diseases or how to prevent or fix them. Unlike the futuristic 'docs' on Star Trek, we don't yet have a 'tricorder' with the ability to diagnose and fix everything with just the push of a button (not yet anyway!).*
>
> *In the end I don't really know the exact reason I went into surgery (does there have to be one?). I'll leave that one to the psychiatrists to figure out. Of course, many of them think all surgeons are ego-centric, maniacal, prima donnas.*
>
> *Hmmmmm. Perhaps there is some truth to that?*

This morning, after I had finished sign-out rounds with the impatient-to-leave outgoing night crew, I started heading around the module again. I attempted to familiarize myself in more detail, at my own pace, with each patient I had been left. I needed to get organized, to know exactly what I had in 'my' module, so that I could formulate a strategy of care. This involved triaging, prioritizing everyone in my mind. I knew that I was being a little overly compulsive, but for me it was the most efficient way to get everyone properly cared for, out of the module, freeing up space for the next influx of patients, all the while trying to keep my sanity. It was a never-ending revolving door; the only thing that ever really changed was the speed at which the door rotated.

Every day, although early on it was far more frequent, I would second-guess myself as to what was I doing here. Did I know enough to take care of these super sick people? Sure, I knew I was here to learn, but I was alone, so who was teaching me? In the end the answer was and will always be the same: It is the patients who are our teachers. It was through their illnesses, their misfortunes and resilience, along with some (not always a lot) guidance from our Attendings and senior residents (and the nurses!) that we learnt the practical side of medicine, surgery, and patient care.

There was little time for formal education. We learnt from textbooks, from careful observation, and from listening to anecdotes on rounds. We learnt by watching and then doing. This accounts for why there is such variability in surgeons depending on where and under whom they had the fortune (or misfortune) to train. The old adage "see one, do one, teach one" was an accurate way to describe the residency process. You can't expect to see every surgery or to experience every scenario we might expect to encounter in practice. So we mastered the basics and learnt more complex techniques that, when necessary, could be extrapolated to almost all situations. In surgery, just as in the building of a house, the key is to have a broad, sturdy foundation, and just as every builder is taught slightly differently, so it is with surgeons.

Clearly the system had some degree of confidence in me, and so now it was up to me to have confidence in myself. This was something that was not very rapid in coming. Just to make me feel even more self-conscious, I noticed that some of my colleagues appeared to ooze confidence. Later I discovered that it was not real but just well-faked. As for myself, I was wearing my familiar cologne, 'Eau de scared shitless'. Could everyone smell it?

During our training, we were constantly reminded of our ignorance—most frequently by our more senior residents but also by our Attendings, the individuals who were charged with our education (no touchy-feely here). Of course, this was all in an attempt to encourage us (while staring down the barrel of a gun—the threat of being tossed out of the program) to constantly better ourselves and increase our knowledge. However, the constant berating and demeaning assaults certainly didn't do our 'delicate' psyches any good. To make us feel better, we would then take it out on our juniors (medical students when we were interns and junior residents when we were more senior), and so the problem was perpetuated, as it likely still is to some degree today. It was the classic 'shit flows downhill' phenomenon, and we just needed to hurry and get off the bottom, which took at least one year. It was teaching by intimidation, definitely not the most efficient or constructive of educational methods.

After five years, on the day of my residency graduation, I remember discussing with one of my fellow classmates whether or not we really knew enough to be entering into practice. We started naming the cases we thought we were capable of doing. It was a short list, very short, surprisingly short.

As it turned out, we all knew much more than we thought, and surgical practice came much more easily than any of us could have anticipated. So many times since, I have been thankful for having had the very thorough, diverse, intense, and (let's face it) bloody difficult training that I went through. This became especially evident in practice when I had the opportunity to work with and observe surgeons who did not have such a rigorous training, leaving them with a tremendously misplaced and dangerous overconfidence.

I had barely started seeing my patients when I heard the familiar overhead refrain: "Surgical code one to resuscitation. Now!"

Well, actually most of it was familiar except for the last word: "NOW!" It took me a number of seconds for this to register, so much so that I waited for the announcement to be repeated. I did indeed hear it right; they did say "NOW!"

The paramedics were not on their way; they were already here. Typically, we had a few minutes of warning as they called ahead to let us know what and when to expect. No such luck here. There was no warning. This patient had been brought in directly by our Detroit Police Department colleagues.

I dashed to the resuscitation room, and, as if landing at home base, I slid into position at the head of the gurney. I barely had a few seconds to arrange my thoughts as the nurses wheeled in the code.

"Male, stab to the left chest," one of the nurses announced to us, catching her breath.

In a single, synchronized movement, we lifted him from the stretcher and onto the empty waiting gurney.

I started out with our usual questions. It did not take very long, however, to figure out that those questions were getting us nowhere. He was not really responsive, at least not in any meaningful or useful way, but just moaned. We began our frenzy of random-appearing, yet highly organized, activity. In moments his clothes were off with the speed and agility of a professional car stripper.

"Let's get an IV in and send off bloods!" I said somewhat redundantly, as the nurses had already seen to it. But then it was my job to take charge or at least to sound and appear like I was.

Examining him, my eyes and hands keenly surveyed every inch of his young muscular body, scanning him like a searchlight combing a lake at night. I sequentially organized and prioritized tasks as I rattled off orders. Bloods. Already done. I needed a type and cross and a chest X-ray. What about his abdomen, was that injured? I made a mental note to make sure to get a nasogastric (NG) and bladder catheter (Foley) in and perform a rectal exam. But hold on, let's not forget the ABCs: Airway, Breathing, Circulation, the basic tenets of any resuscitation. There were so many things to sort through, get in the correct order, and not forget. His airway was fine, I could tell that from his complaining, but I needed to check his lungs anyway, and what about his blood pressure, was that OK? What about other injuries? I needed to slow down. Prioritize. Prioritize, I kept telling myself.

Another resident who had come in to help me with the code was about to start a central line under the patient's right collar bone. Right then, that was not what he needed. His veins were fine.

"Mark, he's got great veins. Just put a regular IV in," I suggested firmly. He backed off immediately, clearly receiving the gist of my tone. The last thing the patient needed was a central line and the concomitant risk of collapsing his good lung. However, I still appreciated the help.

At first the patient would not stay still, but with a lot of help holding him down, we were finally able to get two large caliber IVs in and running. He appeared no older than his early 20s and a little on the skinny side, emaciated by Midwestern standards. His skin appeared stretched over his ribs, and he had a tattoo of a large bald eagle superimposed on the stars and stripes. He had a two-inch long stab wound to his left upper chest going right through two of the stars. Although his color was good, he soon began having difficulty breathing.

My mind absentmindedly wandered as I thought he was lucky that the knife had missed the eagle and just hit a small part of the flag. The cut must hurt like hell. What kind of knife was it? What was the fight about? Did it take place in a kitchen or in a bar? Was the fight really worth dying for? So many random thoughts flitted through my brain.

The entrance wound must be open to the chest cavity, as with every breath, small, bloody, pink bubbles came spewing out of the wound, followed by a slight but still disturbing sucking sound when he took in a breath. I needed to listen to his chest, but unlike the stereotypical TV doctors, most surgical residents didn't have a stethoscope draped around their necks (the emergency medicine residents did! They still wanted to look the part). But if we did, we would lose them. I borrowed one from the nurse next to me. Adjusting the earpieces in my own ears (I hoped her ears were clean), I placed the diaphragm on the chest wall, which was covered in dried blood, and attempted to listen. I could not hear breath sounds on the left side, but I could feel crepitus all over. I knew he needed a chest tube.

Crepitus is a crackling, popping sensation that can be felt under the skin resulting from gas, usually air, forced into the subcutaneous (fat) tissue. It felt a bit like pushing on a bunch of Rice Krispies or crushing tiny bubble wrap. The feeling is so unique that even feeling it for the first time, you knew immediately what it is. Classically, it's a sign of a collapsed lung (pneumothorax) and air being forced from the chest cavity into the subcutaneous tissue.

"IV's in. The first liter of Ringers is running. and the labs are off," I heard someone blurt out. It sounded like they were so far away. My mind was still focused on completing a thorough evaluation.

"Do you want to have blood set-up?" I heard another nurse's voice rise above the background babble as she also announced the blood pressure.

"What was his blood pressure again?" I asked, acting as if I could not hear her properly. I had heard her just fine, but I wanted (needed?) a few extra seconds to sort out my options and come up with a plan.

"130 over 80 on arrival," came the immediate reply.

"And now?"

"The same."

"Just type and screen for now then," I replied, still trying to concentrate on my examination while I partitioned a little part of my brain to deal with the continuous stream of incoming data and questions.

Blood and blood products are vital and indispensable for surgical patients but never more so than in the bleeding, severely multiple-injury trauma patient. For them, blood was truly a gift of life.

As an undergraduate, donating blood was always fun and really more of a social event. We really had no idea how important it was. Sure, we had all heard the term 'gift of life', but I didn't really understand it until years later, when I had a chance to witness first-hand its life saving properties. Along with food and a movie ticket,

*we were given a pint of beer for every pint of blood donated. Food,
booze, and a movie—just what every college kid wanted—sorry, no
altruism there. The beer seemed to act like two, giving us a good,
and more importantly free, buzz after we had just donated.*

While still juggling priorities, I completed my exam. The nurses, meanwhile, had stuck gel-backed electrode pads on his chest and hooked him
up to the monitor. It appeared pretty clear that the knife had penetrated
his left chest and had collapsed his lung on that side. Had it hit any of the
great vessels? This was always a possibility, especially given the location,
but he looked too stable for that, so I thought that was unlikely. I hoped
I was right.

"Let's get a chest tube tray set up with a number 40 tube, please, and
call for a stat portable chest X-ray," I said, again trying to stay calm and
act with authority now that I had made a decision. I found it difficult
telling nurses with a decade or more of experience what to do. After all,
they seemed like experts compared to me. However, lest I forget, I was
still the doctor, the one who had gone to medical school and the one
responsible for this patient's care. Learning to delegate with confidence
without being disparaging or condescending was an important skill I
would acquire. Sadly, many surgeons never learnt it.

He appeared to be holding his own, breathing comfortably, and so I
planned to get a chest X-ray first and then place the chest tube, if indeed
my clinical suspicion was correct. I wanted to be one hundred percent
sure that I had the correct diagnosis before I proceeded to shove a huge
tube in his chest. I turned to collect some necessary gear: a pair of sterile
surgical gloves and a large wad of gauze from the supply cart. My back
was turned for barely a few moments.

Turning back, gloves in hand, it was immediately evident that something had changed and dramatically so. It was if I was looking at a completely different patient; his skin had taken on a purplish-blue color
(cyanotic), he had become a lot more agitated, and his breathing was

now rapid and labored. We rapidly log-rolled him, something that I had failed to do initially, to look at his back. There was no sign of any injury there, so returning him onto his back, I once again asked the nurses for his blood pressure.

"120 over 70," came the reply.

"Well, at least his blood pressure was good," I thought, as I again borrowed a stethoscope again from where it hung around the neck of the nearest nurse and, wiggling the soft rubber earpieces into my ears, I leaned over him and pressed the diaphragm hard against his bloody chest. I listened intently for what seemed like an age, although it was likely only just a few seconds. I could not hear a thing. Was I deaf? I asked for some quiet. Then I listened again, first on his right side where immediately I could hear the somewhat faint, but still clearly present, sounds of air rushing down in and inflating his lungs microscopic air sacs (alveoli). Switching back to his left side again, I could not hear a thing. Nada, not a sound. This was a very dramatic change from earlier, when I was sure I had heard at least some sounds. I rechecked him, my mind now racing a mile a minute. I placed my index finger in the gap where the clavicles met in the middle, the sternal notch, and felt for his trachea (windpipe). It was not there—at least not in the middle where it should have been. It had shifted to his right. Suddenly a light went off in my head, and everything started to make sense. Despite his pulse and blood pressure still being fine, he was getting bluer by the second. He was in trouble. He had a textbook tension pneumothorax.

This is a potentially lethal situation in which air builds up under pressure in the chest cavity and compresses the lung. It can rapidly progress and put the lung under so much pressure (tension) that not only can oxygen not be exchanged, but as it continues, it pushes the heart, kinking the great vessels leading to cardiac decompensation and arrest if not immediately treated.

This air under pressure must be relieved, and rapidly. This can be achieved simply by sticking a needle into the upper portion of the chest, allowing the pressurized air to escape, or by the expeditious placement of a chest tube. The needle has one main advantage of being quick and can buy us precious time until a chest tube can be inserted.

Just as words were about to exit my mouth saying that we needed to put in a chest tube, a nurse called out,

"X-ray is here. Do you want to get a chest X-ray now?"

"No!" I responded tersely. I was becoming even more nervous now. I needed to get cracking; seconds counted. This guy was in trouble. It was so different being on my own. Doing the procedure was one thing but taking the responsibility for the decision was still new. Now I had to do both. I could feel my own blood pressure rising, but I needed to stay calm, focused, and get a move on.

"They'll have to wait till I get a tube in," I abruptly replied. This was no time for explanations.

The X-ray techs appeared a little miffed that we did not stop everything to accommodate them as soon as they entered the room. A swift glance and glare over my shoulder (a maneuver that I have since masterfully perfected) put to rest any brewing comments. I knew they were not happy waiting, but this guy needed help, and he needed it now.

I rapidly opened up the chest tube tray, organizing the instruments I needed. Without even asking for it, antiseptic solution was poured over his chest, and his arm was moved out of the way. After freezing the skin, I grasped a scalpel and made a quick one-inch incision on the side of his chest. Just this incision allowed some air to be quickly released from the subcutaneous tissue. With one quick jab, I pushed a large hemostat through the recently made wound and into the chest cavity. Opening the jaws of the hemostat slightly, there was a much more impressive gush of air, its forcefulness, reminiscent of a submarine blowing its ballast tanks. I shoved a number 40 chest tube through it and into the chest cavity, looking at the numbers printed on the side of it to make sure it was in far enough. Now he began to complain of pain, yet glancing at him, I could see his color was already improving. He was out of the woods—for now at least.

It was a complete turnaround. His breathing was easier, his skin pinker, and his previous agitation had disappeared. Sure, he now had pain, but that was easily taken care of with some IV morphine. Using a heavy silk suture, I stitched the tube in place.

While reaching for the end of the chest tube to hook it up to suction, I was unaware that the nurse helping me had the end of the tube inadvertently aimed in my direction. Accidental? But then perhaps not. At that same moment the patient decided to cough, and I was immediately caught in a broadside of blood and clot shooting out from the end of the tube. Luckily I was only wearing surgical scrubs, which were now drenched with polka-dot bloody splotches, much to the amusement of all present (except me).

In retrospect we were very nonchalant in our approach to individual protection. Being splattered with blood was commonplace; leaving the operating room with blood-soaked underclothes, bloody socks and shoes, was the norm. Perhaps we even regarded it with some pride.

Today, this type of practice is appropriately condemned, and such reckless disregard for safety not tolerated. Everybody wears gloves when examining patients, and when there is a chance of gross contamination, such as in a trauma code, then gloves, face masks, eye protection, and frequently a protective plastic face shield are donned. The modern trauma caregiver is fully encompassed in protective gear which, although makes it more difficult to examine the patient, certainly represents a dramatic advance in personal protection.

In the operating room there has always been a culture of protecting the patient from the team (external contamination), despite the fact that the majority of surgical infections occur from the patients' own bacteria (usually skin) as opposed to that arising from the team ('break in technique'). This philosophy is slowly changing as we have come to understand that risk goes both ways. Now in some specialties, orthopedics for example, they often wear more of a full-face protective gear, as much to protect the surgical team from blood and aerosolized fluids (from power tools) as it is to protect the patient from them. The pendulum is swinging and as always will slowly come to rest somewhere in the middle such that both patient and caregiver will be equally protected. The time is not too far away when every surgical team will be suited up with space-suit-like protection.

All in all, it had taken only about ten minutes from the time the code was called to the time that we obtained the final chest X-ray, but it seemed much longer. When the adrenaline was flowing, time seemed to slow down. (I wonder what Einstein would have to say about that.) Now that the patient was stable, we wheeled him off to the X-ray department for more definitive films and once again turned our backs on the bloody-clothing and supply-littered battleground that was our resuscitation room floor.

I stopped and reflected for a few moments on what had just happened. This is what I thought it should feel like to be a doctor. I felt like I had actually accomplished something. I had examined a patient, made the correct diagnosis, and fixed it. It felt great—like I had really made a difference. This man could have died had I not intervened. Well, probably someone else would have done the same thing. But they didn't, and I did.

That is what surgery is all about. Timely intervention. That is why risks are taken. Sometimes the risks are high, but then the alternative of doing nothing can be fatal.

I was still in my dirty, blood-splattered scrubs. Looking in the mirror in the locker room, I was quite surprised to find that I had blood splattered everywhere: on my scrubs, my face, my glasses, my hair. I was a mess. I took a quick basin bath and threw on fresh scrubs before heading back.

Love Hurts

I HAD been the 'lone soldier' for a couple of weeks now and even began feeling comfortable with the routine of working 'days' solo. But then that right there was the real danger. The danger of complacency, of thinking that I actually had the hang of it, that I might know what I was doing. It was a great feeling to think that I could be comfortable running the surgery and trauma module. But still I had little idea of just how much I didn't know.

Most days followed a routine. The majority of the morning was spent cleaning up from 'nights'. I needed to triage: sort out who could go home, who needed to be admitted, who need more testing done, and find those who had eluded the night team altogether. It was not always too bad to be a little busy right before sign-out, as we did not want the incoming team to think (which I did, when I was on 'nights') that we had it easy all day.

Fortunately, I had two nurses with me that day and we could always use an extra nurse rather than more docs. The evaluation of the patient usually did not take that long. What did take time was drawing blood, starting IVs, cleaning wounds, bandaging, and the hundreds of other jobs that our nurses performed while we, blissfully unaware of their unwavering industry, were off complaining to anyone who would listen to our puerile rants. Much of this care we tried, often poorly, to do ourselves. I was happy to have nurses who were both experienced, knowledgeable, and willing to help us greenhorns.

When I was on 'days', no matter if I had help or not, it was my responsibility to examine every patient in the module at least once and quite often, many times more. When it became busy, I would rapidly go over a patient, examining them to make sure they had nothing life threatening, make a quick mental plan, order blood work, X-rays, and decide if they needed an IV.

With the initial decisions made, they would either be wheeled off to the X-ray line, have blood drawn, or get in line to be stitched up. The X-ray department was a bit of a black hole, sucking our patients in, sometimes not spitting them out until hours later. We always needed to make sure that they were stable before they were warped to that part of our universe. It was frequently a couple of hours before I had the chance to see them again, during which time I would have examined many other patients, many with similar injuries, some identical. By the time they returned, I could almost guarantee that I would have completely forgotten their history and what I had found on my initial exam. It was during this time that I learnt and honed the skill of multitasking and compartmentalizing my memory between patients. This ability was essential to keep the module running smoothly.

Most surgeons take the ability to multitask for granted. We do it all day every day, whether on the patient floors or while in the operating room. We might be in the middle of surgery, trying to always think two or three steps ahead, while fielding calls from the floor nurses, from the clinic, the ER, or about our last or next patient. We can't be five places at once, but we still need to train our brains to be. Is this a naturally occurring gift? No, I believe it is a skill learnt out of necessity then developed and refined.

It was only 8:00 a.m. when the first code of the day came in. In the hour and a half since I arrived, I almost had the module sorted and the backlog of patients dealt with. Well. Almost.

There was minimal fanfare accompanying the announcement, and we were given scant information from triage. Multiple stab wounds. That was it . . . . Great. That's helpful. No, not really. Were these stabs in his chest or his big toe? The knowledge would help us prepare both mentally and physically. We could get the appropriate tools ready, if any. But we knew nothing until he (we knew it was a man!) arrived.

When he was finally being wheeled down the hallway, it became immediately clear that he was not in any way critical. He was very much awake, talking so loudly that any respiratory compromise was certainly not in question. But then, really, he was not even talking so much as just shouting, and the first exchanges that we, as his caregivers to be, were privileged to hear were pure profanity. But all interactions, no matter what emotions they might conjure, always contained reams of hidden information.

"Shit, what you doin'? Fuck this! I need to get out of here, man," was the first complete sentence to reach our ears, while he, squirming on his cart, was brought through the double wide resuscitation room doors. As his arrival was announced overhead, he increased his flailing. The EMS crew tried their best to calm him down while trying even harder not to get themselves injured in the process.

"Where the hell am I?" he asked repeatedly.

"Sir, you are at Detroit Receiving Hospital. Can you tell us where it hurts?"

"I'm going to get that motherfucker." It was clear that his own injuries appeared for the moment to take a backseat to other goals.

"Yes, sir. I understand. But do you hurt anywhere?" the nurse immediately chimed in, not missing a beat.

"I got cut. That motherfucker cut me." He was staring at no one in particular as he continued his rant. "I need to get outta here, dammit."

"We need to make sure you are okay first," I quickly added.

"Fuck that, man. I just need outta here!" he rapidly retorted. "I'm going to get that fucker. I'm going to cut him up, kill him. You'll see."

I turned towards the nurse who was in the process of trying to take his blood pressure.

"Let's get a couple of IVs in." Then feeling a little sorry for her, I added, "and good luck."

"Where are you hurt?" I tried once again to try to tease some information from him.

"Fuck, man, you're the doctor, ain't you? It fucking hurts everywhere."

Now I felt a little uneasy. This guy wasn't our usual code patient. He was wide awake, and I was a little worried that he might do something crazy, maybe even lash out at one of our nurses. Our nurses did not give his attitude a second thought, having appeared to have developed a very strong AI (Asshole Immunity) over the years.

Beginning my exam, I rapidly focused on his abdomen, the obvious site of injury if the blood all over his shirt was anything to go by. He remained completely uncooperative. There were multiple cuts—stab wounds—the largest of them was a slash over his left upper abdomen, deep enough to expose muscle. This was not just an accidental stab; he had been in a full-blown knife fight.

I was pretty sure that his chest was fine, but I still needed to listen to it. His breath sounds were excellent (but then I already knew that from his forceful comments on arrival). But when he spoke or exhaled, his breath stunk. In fact, his whole body stunk like some long dead half-decomposed animal. His abdominal examination, on the other hand, appeared to be completely benign.

After a slightly more lengthy evaluation and still with rock solid vitals, it was clear that he did not need the resources of the resuscitation room, so we shipped him off to the module, where our nurses continued their valiant, but in-vain, attempts to calm him while making arrangements to get his labs and X-rays done.

In his calmer surroundings, I was able to obtain a version of what had occurred, although it seemed to change every time any of us asked.

He had been out drinking with his wife and his 'best friend' that night, and they had still been going strong in the early hours of this morning, when his friend, who was a whole lot more intoxicated (at least that was the inference), had decided to drive himself home. So, as a good friend should do, our patient attempted to prevent him from doing so.

The exact sequence of events that followed is unclear except that his friend, now influenced by the combination of booze and stupidity, took exception to the suggestion, grabbed a deer knife, and proceeded during the ensuing 'discussion' to swing randomly and slash him up in the many places that we now needed to deal with. Our patient made it crystal clear that he wanted to leave so that he could go and take care of his 'friend' (not his exact words).

A little later they brought in his wife, her clothes also blood soaked, who attested that she had been more than just a witness to the altercation. Also highly intoxicated, she was both agitated and unreasonable, demanding to know why her husband's wounds had not already been cared for.

His largest laceration was, in my opinion, too large to be adequately cared for here, especially as I had neither the time nor personnel available. Far better, I thought, to fix it in the operating room with the better lights, instrumentation, and help. However, I had already spent far too much time trying to arrange this. I contacted my fourth-year chief, who said he would be right down, yet it was about four hours before anyone actually showed up. Although this was not uncommon, it just added unnecessary fuel to an already out of control fire.

Not long after the belligerent 'knifing code' came in, his 'best friend' wandered in. Not surprisingly he was also extremely intoxicated, his entire face covered with dried blood. Our nurse was appropriately reluctant to put this man in the module, worried that there might be an unplanned reunion. However, he was in no condition to go anywhere, and I for one, certainly wasn't going to tell him about his 'buddy's' previous arrival. I must admit to not being too excited about having husband, wife, and 'best friend'/assailant in the same room and only a few feet from each other.

Soon, when things eased up a fraction, I took the opportunity to dash off and see a couple of the consults that awaited me. Despite this, I still needed to keep check on the module, to make sure nothing new had been brought in that needed my immediate attention. Seeing consults was a great lesson in multitasking and time management. We tried to see them as soon as we could. We knew it was just a matter of time before the next rush or code arrived.

During the day we always had an assortment of 'head bonks'. This was our euphemism for patients who came in with a non-serious head wound. This was in contrast to a 'head injury', which denoted a much more serious condition. This usually involved an underlying, even life-threatening, brain injury, for which we would need the services of our neurosurgical colleagues.

One such arrival had been found face down downtown in the road outside of a rundown, uninviting (EMS's description) corner bar. He was short, almost squat, with cropped yet disgustingly filthy dark hair. His face had an "I bet you don't know what I've just done", intoxicated, imbecilic expression plastered across it, as well as being adorned by a long, jagged laceration just above his right eye.

Approaching him I was almost flattened as I hit a wall of perverse odor, reminiscent perhaps of the olfactory challenge experienced by brewery employees cleaning out the debris at the bottom of huge fermentation vats. I struggled to overcome my initial wave of nausea as I tried hard to keep my gastric contents in their rightful place. I still needed to sort out what was going on. Never twice did he answer the same question with a similar reply. Although flatly denying any recent alcohol intake, his exhaled breath was causing me to become intoxicated.

"Do you know where you are?" I asked him in an effort to determine his level of orientation.

"Yooou . . . yoou . . . know," came his prolonged, slurred, and stuttered reply.

"Are you at the hospital?" I tried continuing with a simplistic line of questioning, thinking this should be an easy yes or no.

"Yup, a horsepital, that's it," came his reply.

Ah ha, maybe that was the trick. Keep it simple. I had renewed hope that I was making progress and maybe, if I was not pressing my luck, I could get the history completed before the night crew returned in another four hours!

"Which hospital?" I continued my overly simplistic interrogation, still attempting to figure out his level of orientation.

"Yoooure horsepital," he responded correctly but yet without really helping. He was not making this easy, and I needed to get a move on as he was not my only patient. I really did not have time for this. I could see that I was going to have to make my questions much easier from now on. Maybe I would get better results if I switched to multiple choice.

"Are you in a hospital, a church, or a bar?" I tried my luck here, but still no progress was forthcoming.

"Yup, that's it," came his reply, followed by the slow return across his face of his sheepish, asinine grin.

"I need to piss," he then volunteered without prompting. "I need to piss, now," he repeated.

"I need to piss. Bad!" he continued, now with obvious irritation, the nostrils on his reddened face flaring as he noisily took a breath and gritted his teeth.

Well, some of his neurons were still functioning, at least the ones that originated in his bladder. One of our nurses immediately returned with a plastic urinal, then, closing the side curtain and blocking his view of the patient next to him, politely gave him the container.

When examining him, I was forced to intermittently turn my head to inhale much-needed fresh air. Finally, I concluded that besides the laceration, the only thing really wrong was that he had drunk far too much. While the nurses started an IV, I began to evaluate the next patient. I'm sure that somewhere there is a warning sign to never turn your back on an intoxicated man with a urinal. If there isn't, there should be.

Although the curtains gave some privacy on the sides, we could still see him from the bed opposite. He took a hold of the empty urinal and gently and slowly turned it around in his hands, lifting it up, letting the light filter through the opaque plastic, inspecting it as though it was a priceless antique. Suddenly he spoke very clearly, the words somewhat incongruent given his recent pleadings.

"I can't piss in here. It's not big enough."

His comment went mainly unheeded.

Next to him, was a man who had been just brought in after losing a fingertip with a new circular saw. There was nothing to sew back on. A good inch was gone, the cut end of bone clearly visible in the bloody stump. Before I went off to see another consult, I cleaned and blocked his finger, always the key to any procedure on fingers or toes. I knew I could fix this at his bedside. But I at least needed to have some tissue to close over the exposed bone. I cut away the macerated skin, trimmed back the bone, and smoothed its rough edges. Using a few carefully placed sutures, I brought the deep layer over the bone and then finished the job with simple nylon sutures for the skin. It looked pretty good, I thought. It was swollen and would stay this way for a few days. I wrote out a prescription for some antibiotics and pain medication, and soon he was on his way. We advised him to stay away from power tools for a while, but we doubted the advice would be heeded.

In the bed opposite our urinal connoisseur, the occupant explained how, while mowing his lawn, he had slipped, and his left heel was caught and sliced by its blade. I was always at a bit of a loss to figure out how these patients actually managed such a feat. He expressed the classical incredulity common to people with such injuries and could not fathom why the mower had done such a thing. The blade had cut right through the thick, but soft, rubber heel of his sneakers, flaying it open and leaving a two-inch gash in the soft tissue of his heel pad. Carefully removing his shoe, I separated the sharply cut edges with my thumbs. It had gone in pretty deep, but miraculously the bone appeared not involved. To save time I would sew him up first and then send him off to get the requisite X-rays.

While sewing his heel back together and listening to a litany of excuses as to how the mower had gotten the better of him, I recognized the unmistakable splattering sound of water striking plastic. I turned my head slightly, looking for the source and expecting to see one of our nurses pouring water into a plastic basin. To my surprise, I saw that my intoxicated urinal fondler was now standing next to his cart, his stained tan pants around his knees. He stood calm, oblivious, self-focused, a steady four-foot parabolic arc of urine cascading directly against the clear plastic liner of a small circular trash can. He did not seem in the least bit fazed by this. His bladder was full, and he had no intention of allowing the overpowering call of nature to wait any longer. He certainly did not appear lucid enough to comprehend the complexities of using the plastic urinal given to him. I suppose it was better that he hit the trash can rather than releasing the entire contents of his bladder in the bed or on the floor, although he still managed to leave a good sized puddle nearby.

We could not let this intoxicated man leave, especially once we received his blood alcohol level: 424. Yet another who would join the illustrious ranks of the '400 club'. During my short time, I had already come across at least a dozen or so new inductees. We set him up with an IV and 'banana bag' and shipped him off to the OCU (Observation Care Unit) to sleep it off. With luck we would get his forehead laceration taken care of when he was more agreeable and especially more sober.

A banana bag was a specially blended concoction of vitamins and minerals mixed into a saline IV that we gave to the severely intoxicated. This nutritional supplement usually contained, amongst other things, thiamine, folic acid, and magnesium sulphate, the first two giving the solution its characteristic yellow color. Although its use was controversial, it was thought by most to be an inexpensive therapy for our many malnourished alcoholic patients. It also gave us an instantaneous flag to recognize patients who had 'overindulged' it as they spent quality time sobering up under the yellow banana bag insignia.

The observation care unit, which we derogatorily called the 'occasional care unit,' was about as far away from the trauma module as you could get and still be officially within the emergency room. It had the capability of holding about 20 patients in an arrangement where the majority of beds were arranged along the wall opposite the nursing desk and entrance. It was perennially understaffed, and as such, the nurses had little hope of completing many of the tasks asked of them. It tended to be a dumping ground for patients awaiting 'dispo(sition)' and for those waiting for consultants. It was most often used by us as a drunk tank where we would send our intoxicated patients for the night, with their accompanying yellow IV bag insignia, to sober up. It would help us clear out of the module, giving us room for new arrivals, and enabled us to focus on those that really needed our help.

One of the drawbacks was that patients sent there were easily overlooked. It was truly out of sight, out of mind. It was as if they had been sucked into a black hole at the other end of our ER universe, perhaps never to be seen again. It was common that patients sent there were not reevaluated or even remembered until rediscovered at the next sign-out rounds. Because of this, sick patients or those that needed frequent checks were always kept in the module where we could keep a closer eye on them.

Later that afternoon, after hearing sirens, we waited for the inevitable code to be called. It never materialized, but instead we were introduced to a 'stretcher sandwich'. Our new arrival, clad in an orange jumpsuit, was sandwiched between two securely bound blue stretchers and an entourage of officers. There was no way out (hopefully). As usual, the writhing was not silent. It never was. And along with the visible contortions, there was the unending barrage of occasionally obscene, but for the most part unintelligible, verbal diarrhea.

Following an overhead request for help, we were soon inundated by extra nurses and orderlies, always accommodating but mainly just inquisitive. Once placed on a regular gurney, all four extremities were secured with thick leather restraints both to protect them as well as all of us. One indisputable fact was that crazy people tended to do crazy things, and no doubt he fit the bill. The officers looked on indifferently, quietly backing off and observing from a safe distance. They never liked to get too involved once they had completed their delivery duties. They certainly did not want any further paperwork. However, if something did go awry, they would always jump in to give us a hand.

Once safely secured, the patient explained in no uncertain terms that he had had enough of this world. The word was that he had loaded himself up with vodka before slashing his wrists with a kitchen knife. The police had been kept at bay outside for more than three hours while he threatened to harm someone with a knife. They waited until he gave up, as they had no idea what he might have hidden in his arsenal. Once all went quiet, they dragged him out, and with the help of EMS, brought him here.

It appeared that all attempts to rationalize with him were in vain. He fought all our efforts of help and just kept screaming. Earplugs would have come in handy.

"No needles. I don't want no damn needles." He stared directly at me with an unpleasantly vacant stare as we tried to hold his arm still. "Don't give me needles. You hear?" He kept on as we tried in vain to locate a vein with which to start an IV.

Should we even put an IV in if he didn't want one?

"Let the cops have me," he said, semi-coherently. Was he really fine and just playing with us? It wouldn't be the first time. We were rapidly becoming tired of his antics and were tempted to give him to anyone who would take him. But then that was the problem. No one really wanted him. The police certainly didn't. That's why they brought him in here. They wanted us to deal with him. The last thing they wanted was another 'crazy' in their custody.

Once he settled down a little, we could evaluate his injuries. He was now sitting up, if somewhat awkwardly, still strapped in four-point leather restraints. Once his forearms had been cleaned, the only real injuries he had were multiple lacerations to his wrists—mostly just scratches, yet a couple were quite deep and likely capable of causing significant blood loss. Patients who slashed their wrists tended to extend the wrist before cutting, causing the artery to hide deeper behind tendons. In general, it was a poor method to reach their apparent goal. On the other hand, if the real goal was seeking attention, it worked brilliantly.

Many of our less belligerent visitors were placed only in two-point restraints. It took only one bad experience to learn how to approach the visitor correctly when they are restrainted this way. Those who were new and naive, the internus ignoramus maximus, thought it best to approach the patient from his or her restrained side. We found out rapidly how incorrect our assumptions were. Sure, they may not be able to hit you with the restrained side, but the unrestrained arm is free to swing across, gaining momentum, before striking its now surprised target. This was quite a frequent occurrence with our belligerent alcoholics, and after being nailed once, I learnt to approach the patient only from the unrestrained side.

Luckily for us, he had both his hands and feet restrained, so at least that was not a worry. Nonetheless, he could still spit, bite, and even head butt, so we were, by no means, out of harm's way. Here some professional wrestling training would have been at least as useful as medical knowledge. I was just completing my exam when he started up again taking a different tack this time.

"I can't see. I can't see. Help me," he went on.

That certainly did not sound like someone who was trying to commit suicide only a few hours earlier.

"Oh, man, I'm getting dizzy," he said again in a much weaker voice. Now all profanity was gone.

He was pale and now acting as if he might have lost a substantial amount of blood, despite his blood pressure remaining essentially unchanged. He soon became unresponsive, and we seized our opportunity.

"Let's get the IV in now. Quick, while he is out." I reiterated the obvious to the nurses helping me. We quickly had one in and bloods drawn. He did not even let out a whimper, but as soon as we lay his head down, he began to vomit violently, a bucket load of clear watery stuff. We slipped an NG (nasogastric tube) in and sucked out the remaining contents of his stomach. Still there was minimal response. His vomit smelt like pure alcohol in addition to the usual 'puke' smell. We kept the tube in, at least for the time it took me to stitch up his lacerated forearm. I turned his head away from me so as not to be incapacitated when he exhaled. I didn't have as much time as I had hoped, as soon he began to wake, moving, making it difficult if not almost impossible to administer the local anesthetic. I needed to speed up. I scrubbed his wound and proceeded to quickly stitch him up. Slowly it appeared that he was coming around, returning to some semblance of normalcy or at least partial sobriety, no doubt aided by the sucking out of booze remaining in his stomach. We kept his IV in to help, hopefully, with the detoxification process. Once done, we donated him over to the psychiatric (psych) unit, where not only did he need to be, but where he would be out of our hair.

Across the room, I could hear my next patient, a gentleman who had been injured as he disjointedly explained.

"I was hurt because . . ."

He appeared well dressed, wearing a crumpled, dark grey business suit with a bloodied white shirt and blood-stained light blue tie. He spoke slowly, softly, enunciating clearly between sobs, his shoulders drooping and his eyes watering slightly. His chin trembled just a little as he stuttered, swallowing hard, almost choking on his words in mid-sentence. At first, no more words were forthcoming. Then shaking his head ever so slowly in disbelief, he continued.

". . . Because I love. . . ." There was another long hard swallow. ". . . loved someone."

As he spoke, his already puffy eyes were welling up. Was he truly one of the good guys? He was propped up in the gurney and recounted his sad story.

He had been living with his girlfriend for five years in an apartment in a newly renovated portion of the city, just off downtown, and he (of course) thought that everything was just fine with their relationship. (Don't we always?) He was returning from a business trip to Chicago and had arrived home a little earlier than (she had) expected. On entering his bedroom, where he was hoping to surprise his girlfriend (and he did!), he was stunned to find another man, naked under the sheets with her. According to him the 'intruder', who appeared just as surprised, spurted out:

"Please don't shoot. Please! Please! I didn't know."

This was either, truly a complete shock (I very much doubt it) or more likely not his first rodeo with a surprised boyfriend.

After seeing many people come in on both sides of similar situations, such a plea for clemency was not so crazy. More often than not, if a gun was available, it was used; and perhaps if one had been more accessible, then things might have turned out very differently, as the old shoot-first, ask-questions-later philosophy was one that was frequently adhered to.

He explained that he was more stunned and upset than physically hurt. He kept repeating that he just could not understand why it had happened. Despite his shocked state, he gathered his wits and forced himself to continue recounting to us the afternoon's events.

Without saying anything further, his girlfriend's startled bedfellow quickly ran out of the house, barely half dressed, not even stopping to pick up his pants. Meanwhile she grabbed a nearby glass vase (a birthday present that he had recently bought her) and whacked him on the head with it. Now, not only did he have a large gash in his heart, but he also had one on his head to match.

Every day brought with it new surprises, and even though patients might present with the same type of injury, each was unique, whether it was the way in which they were sustained or frequently outlandish stories that accompanied them. This was one of the reasons that I began a journal. What I witnessed on a daily basis was just too crazy, too outrageous, and sometimes too morbidly depressing to ever be made up. The expression "It's so crazy, it has to be true" seemed to have been written about our patients. It was certainly something I was neither used to nor had ever experienced during medical school where, you might say, I had a somewhat sheltered experience.

There was one fact that remained constant, it was that nobody who said they were just minding their own business ever was. They were often trying to make somebody else's business theirs, and in doing so would end up making it ours.

As is typical in all metropolitan trauma centers, we saw countless injuries related to celebrations gone wrong. One of the busiest times for all of us was the night when the Detroit Tigers won the World Series in the summer of '84. (I was a few weeks into my first year—an intern on 'nights' at the time.) Even though you would think everybody would be happy and celebrating the victory, alcohol took control, and after the bars had closed, the merriment and mayhem erupted out onto the streets. We ended up having one of our busiest nights, continuing into the early hours of the following day.

Another evening that will forever be etched in my memory was an evening in August 1987. It was at around 9:00 p.m., during my first month as a fourth-year chief on 'nights', when we received notification that there had been a serious plane crash at Detroit Metro Airport. This immediately initiated our mass-casualty plan. The entire hospital mobilized its resources in preparation. We waited and waited. As it turned out, there was nothing to wait for as this was the infamous crash of NW flight 255. This terrible tragedy took the lives of 156 passengers and crew with the only survivor being a four-year-old girl who was rushed to the children's hospital, next door. That evening was a roller coaster of emotional extremes. From pumped up, almost excited to be able to help out with treating the victims of such a high-profile disaster, to tremendous anxiety and apprehension as we knew we were soon to be swamped with a deluge of critically ill patients, to despondency after an unusually long wait to hear the devastating news. At first it did not seem real, and we felt almost a little relieved at not having to deal with a large influx of patients, but this short-lived euphoria was rapidly replaced when the shattering, sad reality that so many had perished began to sink in.

Showtime

DAY 4 —For a Friday it had been uncharacteristically quiet.

Around noon I caught myself gazing out over the module, from the nursing desk where I was sitting. Doing what? Absolutely nothing. Really nothing for a change. What a wonderful sight—an almost empty module lay before me.

Empty except for a young man, who had been mugged and had his wallet stolen. He had failed spectacularly trying to defend himself, his skin now covered with bumps of blue, purple, and red interspersed with abrasions and a few bloody, jagged cuts that had already been sutured. There was even an area on his forehead that looked very much like a large footprint.

It is a common occurrence for us to care for patients who almost, and some that do, lose their life over a little cash and a few sentimental photographs. Certainly a wallet or its contents are not worth dying for. Yes, I know, it's the principle, right? Pride, principle, or whatever you want to call it. Suck it up, swallow the pride, ignore the principle, give them your damn wallet, and run. Sure, you might be a chicken. But you'd be a smart chicken and more importantly a live one.

Dangerous yet delicious visions of leaving on time began creeping into my consciousness as I reveled in the rare, relaxed feeling of a few moments slack. But I knew better. It was only 3:00 p.m., so it was still far too early to have hopes of getting out on time. But that hardly stopped me, and with every passing minute that the module remained empty, my fantasy strengthened.

When we were busy there was never any complaining, but when it was slow even the slightest interruption seemed an inordinately aggravating inconvenience.

Maybe I could actually get a few things done that evening, I continued musing. My to-do list was increasing exponentially. But then if I really had spare time, there was always reading to catch up on.

Reading was a never-ending battle that went on for the entire five years of training. No matter how much reading I did, there was always more, a lot more. There were more books to read, more journals to muddle through, photocopied papers that I always had the intention of reading but just never got around to. They made their way lower in the ever-growing pile on my desk. Finally, with guilty relief, they were ditched, unread. It was a constantly moving target that always seemed unreachable. As it was, I was never much good at reading, as the more I concentrated, the more rapidly I fell asleep, my head collapsed, plastered to the glossy pages of a surgical textbook. Now there was at least one thing that I could claim to be an expert at. Later I would awake confused, not knowing if I was at home or in my call room, or what day was it? I was exhausted, but I felt pressure as I thought that my fellow residents always seemed to find the energy. I guess we all had our skill sets, and reading was not one of mine. If I was not physically moving, I would crash (surgical residents also had a terrible habit of getting into car accidents while driving home exhausted).

Around 5:00 that afternoon everything changed. We knew it would. It always did. And to think that we had been doing so well! The triage desk notified that a number of EMS trucks were on their way with a bunch of young kids who had been 'shot up' at their school. We should have been surprised, but we weren't. I soon realized that in Detroit anything and everything could happen and frequently did.

That's all we knew until the kids began to arrive. Until then, it was left to our overly fertile imaginations to guess what we could expect. My mind easily ran rampant, picturing ravaged children with all sorts of terribly painful, disfiguring, and mutilating wounds. Luckily I was far off the mark. The majority had received only minor injuries, mostly scrapes and bruises sustained during the ensuing panic. As the ambulances unloaded their young cargo, we spoke to the adults accompanying them and attempted to piece together what had happened.

After school the children were walking over to watch a school baseball game when a lone car drove slowly into the parking lot. It remained unnoticed until someone unleashed a hell-storm of buckshot from one of the rear windows towards the kids.

In what appeared to have been a totally random event (although truly they rarely are), which ended as rapidly as it began, when the car drove away. Fortuitously, most of the injuries were sustained as the children ran from the blasts, their backs to the shooter. By the time the pellets struck, the shot had spread out, and their velocity had decreased substantially. Had this insane outburst been carried out with an automatic weapon, the damage would likely have been catastrophic.

The first child that I saw was a calm, almost overly subdued, 13-year-old boy, the left side of his back and shoulder peppered with pellets. His bright yellow shirt, still tucked in his blue jeans, was torn and stained with his own blood. He was in a great deal of pain, the pellets having torn through the skin and muscle of his upper back. I imagined in slow motion each pellet striking his skin, and the kid squirming as if trying to avoid the pelting of hot ash from an erupting volcano.

With his eyes welling up with tears, he stayed stoically still, which helped us immensely in completing his assessment. X-rays showed that none of the pellets had entered any of his body cavities; instead, they were all lying in the soft tissue of his back, and that's where the majority of them would remain.

Going after bullets may look and sound great in the movies, where an unsterile clamp is used to magically locate and remove the life-threatening projectile. But I was quickly educated that bullets do not need to be retrieved for the well-being of the patient. Sure, it might sever bowel or blood vessels, but once the bullet has come to rest, removing it does nothing to fix the damage already inflicted. If the bullet penetrates the bowel, then the risk of infection is much higher, and along with fixing the bowel, we might try to locate and remove the offending lead fragment. However, frequently it is not in a location where it will cause harm and therefore not worth retrieving.

Almost all the kids were evaluated and discharged, including an 11-year-old girl who had the top of her left ear clipped. At first it appeared as though her ear been partly shot off. But once cleaned, we could see just how lucky she had been. If she had turned her head it could have blinded her, and a larger caliber weapon would have instantly killed her. After sewing her up, we returned her into the waiting, shaking arms of her petrified parents. Although for the kids the physical damage would likely be short-lived, it would not be so easy for their parents who would have lasting emotional scars.

It did not take very long for the local media to get wind of things, and they soon found their way down to our ER. They were always on the lookout for a good story, and young kids being shot surely filled that bill. The local TV channels sent their crews with accompanying bright lights and cameras. They swarmed the waiting room and commandeered it into a media control center.

Enough was enough. This was still an emergency room. It was a place for the care of the sick and injured, not an arena for a media circus. It was time for one of our more senior ER physicians to take control. It was their responsibility to keep the cameras away so that we could continue our work unimpeded.

This unenviable task fell to Dr. John Enders. He was diminutive but nevertheless very arrogant with a bit of a (actually, pretty much a full blown) Napoleon complex. However, here it appeared that he might have finally found his calling, for he quickly corralled all the media personnel and herded them back into the triage area. Bonanza's Big Hoss would have been proud of his marshaling abilities. The media, with their over-zealous, entitled, and let's face it, just plain rude crews reluctantly acquiesced.

Dr. Enders remained front and center in the triage area, giving the media his own somewhat embellished narrative which they consumed ravenously. He pontificated to the press, carrying on with the camera crews, clearly having found a new home in front of their bright lights. The way he was prancing around in front of them, it appeared as if he was auditioning for a new ER sitcom.

The biggest hurdle we faced was trying to convince the distraught families that their kids were well enough to go home. We spent far more time talking, explaining, calming, and reassuring families that their children were okay than we did actually caring for them. Anyway, in a half an hour or so, the night crew would be coming in, and it would be their problem.

Out of all the kids that we saw, there were only two who had serious enough injuries to require admission, both young girls. One, with a tiny skull fracture directly where one of the pellets had impacted, was admitted to neurosurgery. The other, struck by pellets to the side of her left knee and despite no obvious bone damage, was admitted by orthopedics. This appeared to be mainly for PR (public relations), or rather parental relations.

While we were dealing with the kids and their concerned families, a code was brought in. This one essentially arrived unannounced, as it was almost impossible to hear anything on top of the very noisy and distracting commotion.

Our code was a very tall, thin, black gentleman, brought in face down, covered only with a white sheet. Removing it revealed a large, black, plastic knife handle protruding from the left side of his shirtless back. Luckily, the EMS, following protocol, did not attempt to remove the knife, and he was transported here lying on his stomach. As we were preparing to 'start in' on him, he lifted his head slightly and gave us a huge smile. Gaunt, almost emaciated and with a head topped by a mop of curly grey hair, he appeared like an elderly Abe Lincoln. He was wide awake, chatting as if he were relaxing over a cup of coffee, with an added 'Oh, by the way do you know I have this thing sticking out of my back'. Maybe this was not his first time.

Cocking his head awkwardly, he answered our questions with ease and an unexpected politeness. It was impossible to lay him on his back, and we were not ready to pull the knife out, at least not yet. Immediately a couple of large IVs were placed and fluids begun. The X-ray techs materialized, 'shot' a chest film, and then just as rapidly evaporated. While we were waiting for the films to be developed he shared with us his version of what had occurred. The story, like so many, was not really much of a surprise, and it was one we probably could have surmised just by looking at the knife and its location.

After coming home from the bar (well before 6:00 p.m.), his wife met him in the kitchen and accused him of having an affair with her best friend. (We never did find out if the accusation was valid.) While his back was turned, she plunged the knife deep into where it now appeared stuck firm.

I soon learnt the truth of domestic assaults. Men were stabbed by their partners in the kitchen, while the women more usually were shot in the bedroom, often still in their beds (although rarely alone).

His X-ray did nothing to alleviate my concerns. Although there was neither a pneumothorax nor even evidence of any blood in his chest, the blade was huge. It was much longer than any of us (especially me) had expected. The frightening image now scared the hell out of me, and I knew that at any time we could have a huge problem on our hands. There were many potentially life-altering (ending) large vascular structures that lay directly in the path taken by this pointed hunk of kitchen hardware. It might easily have struck the aorta or vena cava on its perilous journey before finally imbedding itself into the bone of his spine. None of the scenarios I could envision were good.

So now what should I do? If it had struck the aorta, its continued presence was more than likely preventing any bleeding, but if removed, then all hell could break loose. He might bleed with such force that we might not be able to get in and stop it in time. No, it was better that I not make any rush (or rash) decisions. At least not yet. He was stable, so I had time.

Talking to the radiologist did not make me feel any better. Actually the opposite. It made me far more concerned. He was convinced that the blade had likely penetrated one of the 'great' vessels. If he was worried, then I was doubly so. I knew I needed help with this one. This was not a time to do and then think. Again, I had time, so I decided to defer to someone more experienced, which meant pretty much anyone but me. I thought that it would be best to have the knife removed under direct vision, meaning with the chest open, but certainly that was not a decision I was qualified to make. I put another call in to my senior (I had already notified him of the code), who quickly returned my call, or rather the circulating nurse in the operating room, where he was still tied up, did. He was satisfied for now that the patient was stable and did not need to be rushed over immediately. Somewhat dismissively, he told me to discuss it with the incoming 'night chief'.

My patient remained frozen, lying on his belly, the knife sticking out of his back tenting up a plain white sheet. I explained to him my proposed yet still tentative plan. Sure, it was so tempting to just yank the knife out, and chances are he might be fine. But then again, maybe not. He was all ready to go to surgery, if needed, when the night shift began streaming in, so I began my sign out with him remaining in the resuscitation room.

I presented the case to Randy, the night chief, explaining as best I could my thought process (except for the part that I really wanted to pull the knife out!!!). He agreed with my assessment, and that it would be safest to remove the knife in the operating room under direct vision. There we would be able to see and repair any damage that we might encounter.

Sign-out was quick, mainly the two kids from the school shooting. Randy briefly took me aside.

"Nick. I know you're already done for the day, but this is your case if you want it."

It took me a couple of seconds for me to realize that he was offering this case to me. "You bet," was my quick, slightly stuttered, but excited reply.

I could not believe my luck. There is no way I was going to go home and let a thoracotomy fall through my fingers. They were hard enough to come by on a good day, and rarely did a second year (and only just a second year at that) get a chance to do one. Anyway, I was not really tired, especially not now, as I felt a new wave of adrenaline surge through me. This would be a very cool case.

In the operating room, we positioned him with his right side down, for a true left lateral thoracotomy.

Wow, here I go.

Now although the chief made it sound like it was my case, he was there every step of the way. If I was just slightly off, he would rapidly steer me back on course. I began and made a long, curved incision through the skin of the patient's left chest, beginning between the shoulder blade and the spine and extending down and around, following the curve of the ribs and towards, but falling a good four inches short of, his left nipple. Using the electrocautery, I slowly cut my way through the thick muscles of the lateral chest wall. I could not believe how much muscle there was to cut through, yet he appeared so skinny. I then cut between the ribs and entered into the chest cavity. There was a small amount of blood that we sucked out, maybe a cup full, certainly not enough to ever show up on his chest X-ray. I slipped the rib spreader in place between the ribs and cranked it open. With the chest open, I tentatively retracted the soft pink spongy lung out of the way then followed the knife blade towards the back. Expecting to see that the knife had cut directly into the aorta, we were all surprised to see that it had slid along the side of it, impaling itself into a vertebral body. He appeared to have missed everything. How was that possible? There was no evidence of any injury to the aorta, barely a millimeter away. If the blade had been turned only a few degrees, it would surely have been a different story. Could he have been any luckier? I doubt it.

"OK then," Randy said. "Go ahead and pull the knife out."

I grabbed the handle and pulled. Nothing. I pulled harder, much harder. Still nothing. It didn't even budge. I felt like a medieval knight failing in his attempt to pull Excalibur from the stone. This sucker was stuck hard. Finally, bracing my right foot on the edge on the operating table and using two hands, I pulled like hell. With an added wiggle, I managed to finally release it from where it seemed inexorably imbedded. The sudden release caused me to lose balance, and I fell back slightly but luckily remained upright and held on to my prize. Whoever stabbed him had done so with tremendous force. Now I really wondered what he had done.

The knife was huge. A 14-inch sharp skinny blade attached to a six-inch scratched-up black plastic handle. We looked back in the chest, surprised at the minimal damage. I could hardly believe how lucky he was. It had missed everything vital. It was as if it had been surgically placed between the two huge blood vessels. You could not get luckier (OK, well, maybe not being stabbed!). Still, he would have a pretty big slice in his chest as a souvenir of his afternoon's encounter with his pissed-off (and very strong!) wife. After placing a couple of chest tubes in, I cranked his ribs together and closed him up. I stopped by to see him after my shift a few days later, and he appeared no worse off for his experience as he was being readied for discharge.

It was great to be able to do a thoracotomy in the operating room without all the added stress of someone trying to die right in front of me, as they were apt to do when such procedures were performed in the resuscitation room. But still, we didn't really know what we were going to find when we opened him up. It was always a crap shoot.

I made it home much later than expected based on my earlier afternoon's assessment (fantasy). Slumping on my couch, I turned on my small TV and channel surfed until I found the local news. Within seconds I was looking at our emergency room and apparently the latest star of the screen, Dr. Enders, who was describing in 'Hollywood style' the details of the injuries that had befallen the unfortunate young school kids that we had cared for earlier that day. I had a good chuckle when I heard our new celebrity explain how one young girl was admitted in critical condition. Although a complete exaggeration, it certainly made for great television.

All over the viewing area, I'm sure there were families glued to their TV screens gesticulating with a lot of 'oohs' and 'aahs' as the story unfolded.

Stupidity and Brain Farts

DAY 5 —It was a miserable, fall, Midwest morning, and the penetratingly moist cold made the darkness of the early hour seem even darker and the hour itself even earlier. I shivered under the minimal protection afforded by my scrubs covered with an old, poorly insulated, faux army jacket, driving along Jefferson Avenue waiting for my car's unreliable heater to finally kick in. It was the kind of morning that made me wonder why I had chosen a city so far north to be my home for five years.

When I arrived at the hospital at just after 6:00, even before stepping foot inside the module, I knew it had been a busy night. A bloody busy night. I went to the locker room to switch into a clean pair of scrubs. I had learnt to save time and laundry by wearing scrubs to and from the hospital. Entering, I was immediately confronted by a pair of discarded, blood-soaked scrubs, on the floor under the sink. From what I could tell, the only portion that remained unadulterated was a small green strip running around the waist. Clearly these scrubs and their occupant had witnessed an eventful night.

I still had a few minutes, so I popped by the front desk of the OR to find out what had transpired overnight. I knew there was a good chance that one of the night crew might still be there.

Sure enough, Randy, our night chief, who had so generously helped me with the thoracotomy the previous evening, was there, sitting half slumped over a paper littered desk. This was not an unusual place to find him, as he tried extra hard to stay awake and chat with the nurses sitting behind the thick glass of the control desk.

It was from this glass-enclosed area (the fishbowl) that during the day, the OR secretary orchestrated the flow of patients on their journey to and from the various surgical suites. She was not only the traffic controller, but it was through her that all elective cases were scheduled. We quickly learnt to make her an ally, as she was the one who could help us get a case on when necessary.

This 'fishbowl' was also a popular gathering spot where the more senior residents would hang out after a case. It was their safe haven, a place where they could sit and chat, yet if an Attending were to happen by (and here they might have adequate warning), they could instantaneously appear busy. It is a funny thing about surgical residents: We never wanted to let the attending see us acting tired or resting; for that, we thought, would be an admission of weakness. Of course, we were surgical residents, surgeons to be, so we were never weak, never tired, we just wanted to operate all the time. At least that's what we wanted everyone to think. And isn't that how we were supposed to be?

The Attendings knew, all too well, that we were tired, hungry, and exhausted. They had all been through it before. They had also experienced the pain of long nights that seemed to never end, the chronic fatigue, but also the exhilaration of a life saved. For some of our younger staff, it had not even been that long. Perhaps this was all a rite of passage? A Darwinian filter to weed out the weak? Who knows, but it seemed to work. Some of them liked to really grill us hard, never relenting, no matter how tired we were. They kept at it until you stumbled or admitted defeat (a bad option!). Kill or be killed; knowledge was survival. They would push us as far as they could, trying to find a weak chink in our armor. But then why should we expect less? Disease did not take it easy on anyone. Life threatening trauma did not take a day off. It didn't give us a reprieve because we were tired. Therefore, if we were to learn, how could we expect anything less? We needed to learn to function well, to excel even, under the harshest of conditions, when we were exhausted, and a life was on the line. Was it any different than a marine going through basic training? The goal was the same: to always perform at the highest level, even under the most stressful of conditions. We were told, and more than once: If you can't hack it, there is no place for you in surgery.

Although perhaps now controversial, I believe this stressful educational environment actually was incredibly beneficial—teaching us to think ahead, to problem solve issues, especially when we were the most stressed, such that we were able to make logical and, more importantly, correct decisions. One of the biggest challenges I faced when I came out into practice was that there was no break, no one to pass on the responsibility and care of patients, even after a grueling day and sometimes night of operating. No matter when, day or night, I was responsible for my patients, and I had to always be prepared for every eventuality, every phone call, whether it was 2:00 p.m. or 2:00 a.m. It was where the harsh, stressful environment in which I trained paid huge dividends.

Randy was half asleep, slumped forward, his head on his folded arms. He gazed up briefly as I entered. He looked awful. His bloodshot eyes were barely open under their dark, drooping lids. Waking slightly, he began re-hashing the details of his night. The bloody scrubs in the bathroom were his and were just one of the casualties of his last case. He had just finished operating on one of two victims of a horrific motorcycle accident.

A couple were riding their bike, pre-dawn, on what they likely thought was a deserted road. They had just left their local watering hole and were well 'fueled' for their voyage home. While taking a sharp corner, they veered into the oncoming lane, where they were met head on by a jeep with two off-duty police officers. The result was carnage.

The man, who was on the front of the bike, was thrown off and instantly decapitated after striking a fence wire. The rear passenger, a woman in her twenties, sustained an extensive avulsion injury to her right hip—essentially her right leg had been almost completely ripped off her pelvis. Randy deliberately slowed as he continued to describe the subsequent devastating and depressing events.

As soon as she had arrived at the hospital, she was rushed straight to the operating room due to the severity of intra-abdominal bleeding and her almost-completely-severed right thigh, which was barely hanging on by a few inches of devitalized muscle and tendon.

Her surgery lasted for a few hours, while Randy, along with the Attending, struggled trying every trick they knew in an attempt to stop her from exsanguination. No matter what they tried, they could not stem the torrential bleeding. Soon she succumbed to the overwhelming blood loss, and died on the operating table.

An operating-room death is devastating. It is demoralizing, even though perhaps not always entirely unexpected. No matter how hard we try, sometimes we are doomed to failure by the nature of the injury, damage so extensive that it is not survivable. It doesn't make a difference how many times a death occurs in the operating room, you never get used to it, and it is always painful for those involved. Our self-imposed expectation of 'no failure' did not help, but just made the feelings of helplessness and inadequacy even more pronounced. Here was a woman who came into the operating room alive (granted in critical condition), yet left lifeless. It made me wonder how the medical personnel who cared for the critically injured, maimed, mutilated, dismembered troops on battle fronts dealt with it. Did they ever get used to it? Of course not.

Strangely, EMS had brought in both victims of the motorcycle accident together, including the man who had been decapitated. I could only wonder, what were they hoping we could do? Sew it back on, Frankenstein-style? Even more bizarre was that when they wheeled him in, his helmet was lying between his legs, his head inside. Word of our headless motorcyclist spread quickly, and he became an instant in-house celebrity, a macabre tourist attraction. Almost all the ER staff found time to swing by and take a look. I tried to picture the scene. Everyone standing around the gurney of the headless man, helmet between his legs, eyes wide open, lifeless, fixed, dilated, yet nevertheless somehow still piercing. He along with his head were soon transferred to the decontamination room, waiting to be taken down to the morgue.

'Down to the morgue'. Now, that was a seemingly ubiquitous expression in hospitals. Morgues always appeared to be 'down'. Did anyone ever go up, 'to the morgue'? I don't think so. They are typically located in an obscure area of the hospital, frequently in a basement (just to make it that much creepier), purposely away from accidental, prying eyes, and often close to the mechanicals, in a world of oversized pipes and noisy valves, peeling paint and bare concrete walls, hidden passageways and long forgotten storage rooms. This was a world inhabited by the numerous ancillary staff who helped keep a hospital running smoothly. Here lay the hospital laundry, the boiler room, and maintenance areas. Here, down another obscure unmarked passage, lay the morgue, its entrance a single steel door dented by the many carts that carried patients on their last journey. Why the rush? On the wall, a small, difficult-to-read sign with the word 'morgue' and its Braille equivalent beneath. Inside, almost an entire wall was covered with stainless steel refrigerated drawers, whose current inhabitants might well have been talking just hours before. The middle was occupied by a single autopsy table: a large, cold, stainless steel shallow pan with a somewhat uncomfortable appearing, heavy plastic headrest at one end and a drain in the center to aid in the removal of body fluids during the 'postmortem'. Above each hung an old, large-dial scale (the morgue was never first on the list for updated equipment) used to weigh the removed organs. Off to one side was a large, stainless sink, with an industrial appearing spring covered hose. The morgue always felt cold, grim. and uninviting (a good thing, I guess), and its poor lighting gave it that extra feeling of foreboding. I must admit that personally I always felt apprehensive, fearful, and even a little panicky when I was down there alone. Scared of what, I wonder? Who knows? One too many horror movies, I suspect.

The morgue served not only as the holding area for the dead but was also where autopsies were performed. As residents, it was mandatory that we attended the autopsies of anyone who died under our care. Occasionally, and luckily only occasionally, we would witness the ravages that occurred when surgery did not go as planned.

Today, autopsies are rare and are usually only performed for deaths that occur under unusual circumstances, mainly because of lack of reimbursement, insurance companies being reluctant to pay for a procedure when the insured party is already deceased. Although I understand their fiscal responsibility, we also have a responsibility to learn as much as we can and use the information to benefit future patients. What was once a common adjunct to our arsenal of educational tools, is sadly, now a rarity, and one that cannot be replaced by books or computers.

It did not take very long that morning for things to heat up, and soon they wheeled in our first accident of the day. This man, who was, luckily, dressed in full leather motorcycle regalia, including a pair of long, steel-capped leather boots, had been involved in a near head-on collision with a wayward car. Causing him to lose control of his bike, he 'laid his bike down' and slid along the road for some distance with it before coming to a halt. He tore up the entire left side of his leathers down to their lining. They were history but had successfully done their job of protecting him from what would otherwise have been a limb-threatening soft-tissue injury. In the end he suffered only a few abrasions and a left elbow fracture besides the loss of his expensive, but replaceable, red and black leather biking outfit.

Soon after caring for him, we received a couple brought in by the police, one of whom was far beyond any earthly resuscitation. They had decided to leave this world together in a suicide pact. The plan was that they were supposed to stab themselves, or each other, then in turn hang themselves. Why this plan? We had no idea, but it certainly turned out in her favor. The first part of the plan went off as scripted, but after he hung himself, and she saw the grotesque way in which his eyes bulged out, she could not complete her part of the pact and instead called for help. The police brought them both in to see us. He was rapidly determined to be brain dead, while she, in the end, merely suffered a bunch of relatively minor lacerations. The lesson? Never go first in a dual suicide pact.

Our only code that day came in at almost exactly at 6:20, just a little sooner than would have been ideal (at least for me). EMS brought in a heavy-set man, who had the left side of his forehead blown away by a close-range shotgun blast. It was a gruesome sight. A large, fist-sized, chunk of his head was missing, and visible at the base of the crater was a mass of bloody, grey, gelatinous tissue. This was the remnant of his frontal lobe. I stared and wondered about all the memories that had been instantaneously erased by the blast and were lost forever.

Despite his injury, he had a pretty good blood pressure and an almost normal EKG. While working on him and trying to get any kind of history from the crew who had delivered him, his face continued to swell. Now this was not just a little swelling, the kind that you would expect if you had been hit on the arm or leg. It was massive. In the short time since his arrival, his left eye, which had been only a little swollen when we first looked, now had swelled to the point that it appeared ready to pop out of its socket. I realized that we were rapidly going to have an airway problem, and my concerns were confirmed when blood-tinged fluid began trickling out from between his now massively enlarged purplish, and hard to separate, lips.

I thought about our options. Trying to intubate him orally or nasally would not be a smart option, as I would most likely fail and at the least make things significantly worse. The only choice remaining, I thought, was to perform a cricothyrotomy (crike).

A 'crike' is an emergency procedure to get access to someone's trachea in order to secure an airway when all other routine methods of access were not possible. Most often it was performed in cases of severe head and facial trauma. Textbooks make it appear straightforward, especially with experience (but then, of course, everything is straightforward with experience). But I had no experience. This was my first time.

I hurriedly arranged the instruments on a tray next to me—at least what I thought I needed. But did I know? I was nervous. The last, and in fact, the first and only time that I had ever done one before was on a pig during my ATLS (Advanced Trauma Life Support) course the week before residency began. That was way over a year ago. I knew the steps. I just had never done one, at least not on a human. I know I needed to stay cool, recall the steps, and do it. It sounded so easy.

The ATLS course was essential practical training, learning skills that we would all use, sooner than any of us would have guessed. No matter what our medical school experience, it placed us all on an equal footing when we began. It also gave us a chance to meet our fellow interns.

As I prepared, a small wave of relief broke over me when my nurse said that she had never actually seen one done before. Great—if she had never seen one then she couldn't critique me. This latter thought propelled a resurgent rush of confidence through me. I looked down at my patient, lying there with a chunk of his brain missing. What on earth was I worried about? No matter what I did, his outcome was sealed. He was never going to make it no matter what. But still, I needed to do the best I could.

I poured antiseptic over his neck and felt for the soft spot below his Adam's apple, the cricothyroid membrane. I carefully injected the area with a local anesthetic, more for the epinephrine's vasoconstrictive effect than for any attempt to really numb the area. He would not feel any pain. A few moments later, I made a longitudinal cut and kept going, luckily not too far, until I reached his windpipe.

I was getting ready to pop a hemostat through the tough membrane when a much more relaxed and rested Randy returned, wondering what

I was up to now. He looked a hell of a lot better than when I last saw him about 11½ hours previously. I rapidly gave him a 'CliffsNotes' summary, and he immediately gloved up and gave me a hand. Just moments later we had a small endotracheal tube in his trachea, and then we were able to ventilate him easily through it.

Standing back, we all stared at the unreal picture before us. A man, his face so massively swollen with half his head blown off, was almost unrecognizable. Yet his heart rhythm and blood pressure were both pretty normal. What to do now? We all knew the answer.

Call neurosurgery.

But we also knew that there was not much they could do except possibly discuss organ donation if and when any family showed up. But we did not even know who he was. He was just another 'John Doe'. The nurses put the call through to 'neuro', and I began sign out rounds. The rest of the night crew had arrived, congregating as usual around the nurses' desk.

Occasionally we experienced a lighter and more human side to our training. Every couple of months or so a quick hand-scribbled note would appear, loosely taped to the department notice board, and word would rapidly disseminate among the residents of 'Fluid and Electrolyte' rounds. The first time I first heard of this, I thought, "Oh, great, here we go again, more quizzing." But, surprisingly, it was actually quite the opposite. It was purely a social gathering, a time when the off-duty surgical residents would meet in a bar across the street from Harper Hospital, and one or more of our staff members, usually led by Dr. Bouwman, our residency director, would come over and buy drinks. I guess it was their way of saying thank you for all of our hard work, the long hours, and that the 'abuse' was not personal. Perhaps it wasn't, but even so it took quite a few drinks before we started to believe it. Then we got on a roll and just kept going, usually (pretty much always) overdoing it. It was fun to laugh and joke with our 'Attendings, and for a short time, anyway, we were on par—fellow physicians, fellow humans, enjoying a drink and exchanging stories. The next day was never so good, as we usually returned to work with a stinking hangover. Still, we enjoyed it and looked forward to the next one.

Not uncommonly we were up for 36 hours straight which is not to say that we thought this was something to be proud of. It just was the way it was. It was expected. So we learnt to function and to make important decisions while, tired. Hell, we were probably half asleep some of the time. We would try to nap wherever and whenever we could. It was no surprise that we could sleep anywhere and at any time.

When we were not on call, we slept. Going out on a date was pretty much impossible. But that did not stop us trying. After all, we were young and wanted to have some fun. But our amorous fantasies were rapidly replaced by fatigue, and we would frequently fall asleep at the dinner table, often mid-meal, perhaps even mid-conversation. A movie was generally a far better option, not because I would actually watch it, but because I could hide my exhaustion, sliding down in the seat as the lights dimmed, the music serenading me as I got a couple of hours of uninter-rupted shut-eye.

We often saw injuries that were simply the result of plain stupidity. We called them accidents, a brain fart, perhaps, as most were totally prevent-able if only the victim had bothered to think. But then it was the activity of 'thinking' that for some appeared to be so alien. Then, sure enough, there were those who just happened to be around when fate was dishing out an extra helping of misfortune.

Later that afternoon, I saw just such an 'accident', one of the infamous yet all too common lawn mower injuries.

A young man (they are always young, for those with such minimal common sense rarely become older) brought himself in with his right hand wrapped in a bloody wash cloth. 'I thought I could get my hand out of the way in time,' he told me when I questioned him. He was wearing a filthy t-shirt, and a pair of equally nasty jeans. An apparent tan made it appear that he spent a lot of time outdoors, although much of it came off with an alcohol swab, perhaps revealing an apparent dislike for soap.

I unwrapped the makeshift bandage to assess the injury. He had neatly severed the three middle digits of his right hand, leaving one-inch-long bloody stubs. He explained that he had been mowing his wet lawn when the lawnmower stopped cutting. Looking under the mower deck, he noticed a thick wad of wet grass jamming the blade. The engine was still running, attempting to rotate the blade at its normal speed of 60 revolutions a second. He thought (or in truth perhaps, did not) that he could quickly remove the offending blockage before the blade would continue spinning. Granted, this might not have been an issue if he had a lightning-fast bionic arm, but he soon discovered that humans are not that quick. Wrapping his hand in a moist sterile gauze, I contacted my surgical chief on call that day and prepared him to go to surgery to have his stumps cleaned and closed over.

Then sometimes the lack of thought hurt someone else. It was about 2:00 in the morning, during 'nights' in the ER, when a mother brought her 13-year-old son into the emergency department after he had been shot in the leg. He hardly even let out a whimper as we went through our evaluation. His mother, now that was another story. You would think that she was the one who had been shot. She was in the hallway wailing as loud as her lungs permitted. We just could not get her to shut up, so we ushered her to a room as far away from the patients as possible, and not surprisingly, without an audience she rapidly acquiesced.

The bullet had penetrated through the thigh muscle of the boy's left leg, shattering his femur. While he was being admitted to the hospital, I took the chance to chat with his mother and found out more of what had really happened.

She explained that it had been just after midnight, and having finished cleaning up her kitchen, she wanted to take the garbage out. Now, why was it so important to take out the garbage at midnight? Who knows? But on top of that, she decided that she did not want to do it alone, explaining she was scared that there might be someone out there. She was smart enough to figure that much out yet not smart enough to wait until the morning. But no, she had an even better idea. So she woke up her sleeping teenage son so that he could go out with her. Now did she really think that her 13-year-old son could protect her? He certainly appeared brave enough, but on the other hand his slight frame did not really present an imposing threat to any intruder or would-be mugger. As they ventured out into the unlit alleyway between her house and her neighbors', with her son out in front, they were jumped, and he got the bullet. It all seemed a little strange, almost as if she had expected it.

Blown Away

DAY 6 —Wow, another Saturday already.

It had already been over a week since I had jotted anything down in my journal. The week had passed in a flash. But then, that's the way it always was when it was busy. There was no break. You arrived, you worked, you left. There was no downtime, no break, no time for lunch, and definitely no time to scribble down even some of the more memorable highlights. Consequently, the busiest days often failed to make it into my journal. Work, eat, sleep, read (not much), repeat. Sleep was paramount, certainly more important than jotting notes in a journal or even reading for that matter. I always planned to write things down when I had a break or when I got home. But when I did finally make it home, it was always to stumble then crash exhausted on my mattress, and despite good intentions, nothing would stop me, not even my clothes. When I awoke, it was a new day, and the jumbled faded memories of the day before became just that: faded memories.

The wonderful thing about all Saturdays (at least, when I was on the ER 'day' rotation) was that I was only 12 hours or so from having 36 hours off. Sunday. Oh, glorious Sunday. This was my one day off every week, only during the ER days rotation, and I was planning to enjoy it, even if all it meant was more sleep. Lord knows I could always use that.

Except for vacations and our six-month research rotation, these

Sundays were the only time during my five years of residency that I had the chance to enjoy a whole day to myself. It was a wonderful day—one where I could act like real person, hang out with friends and family without patient responsibility, without wondering if my beeper (pager) would go off at any moment and interrupt a rare family gathering or perhaps an even rarer, intimate moment.

Beepers (pagers) have now been replaced by the incessant, and frequently unnecessarily intrusive, interruptions of cell phones. We are now all constantly tethered to each other by these invisible cellular umbilicals. How did we ever survive before? We did, and so did our patients.

My first serious injury that day was Tyrone. Ty was a head-shaved-smooth, muscular black gentleman in his late thirties who was well dressed and articulate, or at least as much as anyone could be who just had a chunk of the back of their forearm blown away by a shotgun. He spoke quietly with a softness that belied his strength and the severity of his injury. His right forearm, wrapped up in a blood-stained white towel, was limp, its weight being wholly supported by its healthy counterpart.

He had been heading to his local grocery store in a car driven by an elderly neighbor. Trying deliberately to accurately recall the sequence of events, he explained that as they sped down the street, he had asked his friend to slow down a bit. His friend overreacted a little, and the rapid deceleration was a little too much for the car directly behind them. Unable to slow down fast enough, they were slightly rear-ended. It was the kind of minor fender bender that would usually be resolved with an apology and perhaps the mutual exchange of insurance information. But then this was not just any place. This was Detroit, and this was just not the way that such issues were resolved.

The little tap did not go over well with the occupants of the trailing vehicle, who drove up alongside. As they pulled up, the man in the rear seat rolled down his window, and after pumping a sawn-off double-barreled shotgun, took aim. Ty, realizing the danger, reacted in a flash and brought his right arm up in front of his face. In a split second it was over, and Ty had caught the brunt of the blast directly in the back of his right forearm and wrist.

Removing Ty's bandage, I was met with an unrecognizable bloody mess. There was no flesh remaining anywhere on the back of what had been his hand and wrist. It was all just a bloody pulpy mess, littered with a lot of shotgun pellets and debris imbedded amongst fat, muscle, skin, tendon, and even some bone fragments. More notable was that there was not even very much bleeding. Not only had he lost a great deal of the soft tissue of his wrist in the blast, but it had also disintegrated the majority of the underlying forearm and wrist bones. Reviewing his X-rays plainly revealed the lack of any anatomical skeletal definition; his wrist now could be best described as a 'hazy mush' with lots of lead.

We pounced on him as soon as he hit the mattress, immediately giving him a good slug of morphine and antibiotics. As for the wound, we covered it. There was not much that we could do until we could get him to surgery. Would we even be able to save any of his hand? Would he ever have any functional use? These were all tremendously important questions, but certainly none that we could even begin to tackle right then. Somewhat surprisingly, and fortuitously, there was little other collateral damage. His cheek had been hit by just a couple of pellets as well as one to his forehead. The rapidity with which he had reacted and blocked the blast had likely saved his face, his sight, and in all probability, his life.

He was still in a state of shock, as was only to be expected from someone who had just had half of forearm blown away for no apparent reason. Part of him, I'm sure, was just trying to comprehend what had happened, let alone why.

As with so many of these severe, unexpected, and apparently random attacks, it did us little good to dwell on the why. But still, we wanted to know, I wanted to know. I wanted to understand why this kind of senseless random violence occurred. Was it really random? Perhaps it would make me feel better if it wasn't just chance, for it was precisely the randomness, the unpredictability, that made it so frightening.

Once we had him stabilized with his pain under control, he was transferred to 'plastics' (plastic surgery service). There he would spend many weeks and had numerous trips to the operating room, at first for debridement, which involved cutting out pieces of flesh, bone, clothing, glass, and lead pellets. Later, after the amount of viable tissue could be more properly determined, the surgeries became more reconstructive in nature. Finally, he was returned to the operating room where the massive defect on the back of the wrist was covered by a large thigh 'pedical' flap.

This 'pedical flap' is a technique used by reconstructive surgeons to cover areas of significant soft tissue loss, where simple closure or even the use of a skin graft would not be optimal. Here, it was used as a way to replace the missing soft tissue of the back of his forearm, wrist, and hand. In this tricky operation, three sides of a large rectangular flap of skin and its underlying soft tissue were dissected free from the lower abdomen and elevated, while the fourth side remained attached, supplying blood to it. This large flap of skin and its underlying subcutaneous tissue were then sutured down onto the defect, in this case his forearm and wrist, all the while still remaining connected to his abdomen. If successful the flap will, with time, begin to receive its blood supply from the underlying wound as it adheres, hopefully without infection. The attachment point to the lower abdomen is separated in stages months later, by which time there should be enough circulation coming from the underlying tissue, to keep it alive. For a few months, Ty, with his hand stuck to his lower abdomen, would look a little like a gunslinger getting ready to draw his weapon, but can't.

As with almost all major trauma centers, our hospital was situated deep in the bowels of Detroit's inner city, where a large proportion of the patients that we treated sustained their injuries as a result of the incessant urban warfare. After working there for a number of weeks, I started to learn a little of the 'epidemiology' of such injuries, and it soon became clear that rarely was a truly innocent person the victim. Despite this knowledge, during my first year, I continued to be inappropriately reluctant (scared shitless) to go anywhere, as I did not want to end up a statistic. It took a while before it finally dawned on me that most of the 'accidents' involving guns and knives were not random at all. Now, that is not to say that these things never happened to innocent people, because they did, but it just wasn't common.

Sure, once in a while someone's car breaks down in the wrong neighborhood, and the occupant falls victim to a mugging, a carjacking, or even homicide. However, most of the time (and again, this was very much a revelation), the injured (if they survived) knew exactly who was responsible. Many a patient, who had come in shot, had, by the time of discharge, confided in us their plan of revenge, telling us that we could shortly expect the one they held responsible. On a couple of occasions, we indeed received a patient an hour or so later, who came in exactly as predicted, frequently dead, often with a large hole in the center of their chest. We could not be one hundred percent sure (we did not have the glove to see if it fit!), but we had a pretty good idea who was responsible. It was street 'justice'.

With Ty all squared away, it was off to see Tony, a much more typical module-one patient. Sitting up in a bed tucked away in a corner of our module, he would not lie down, despite frequent requests. He had decided that sitting up on the edge of his bed was all that he was going to do right now, besides ignoring instructions. His head was covered with a bloody rag, his poor attempt at a bandage, and as he repeatedly informed us, in a very slurred and profoundly intoxicated drawl, that there was nothing wrong with him, and he just wanted to go home. He looked at least ten years older than his documented age. His rugged, bronzed, wind-burnt face was unwashed, crisscrossed with irregular, ragged crevasses packed with enough dirt that if seeded would sprout a garden quicker and thicker than any beard. Removing the 'bandage' exposed a large flap of scalp hanging from the side of his forehead, covered on the one side by a knotted clump of bloody grey hair, beneath which his pale, pink-white skull was visible.

Unable to get a story from him, I caught up with one of the EMS drivers who relished the opportunity to give details of his recent delivery. Speaking loudly to be sure he had an attentive audience, he explained how they had found him on the floor of his kitchen, his neighbor having called 911 after hearing him fall, the sound apparently having travelled easily through the thin apartment walls. The flat, according to him, was a veritable 'pig stye', with garbage and empty beer and liquor bottles everywhere. On the kitchen table was a nearly empty bottle of Mad Dog 20/20 (an inexpensive fortified wine that along with Wild Irish Rose were perennial local favorites). They deduced after chatting with the concerned (? nosy) neighbor that our patient had probably gotten drunk, slipped, and struck his head on the side of the kitchen table, a fresh blood trail still marking the spot where the metal table edge had neatly sliced a large hunk of scalp away from his underlying skull.

In some hospitals he would have been taken directly to the operating room, but not here, not today, and not with the operating room occupied and a long list of cases waiting to go. Only a life-threatening emergency would be allowed to 'bump' these. My 'scalp guy' certainly did not make that category. I would just have to figure it out and deal with it here.

At first he would not let us do a thing, and it was a major coup just to examine the wound. But slowly with time and a banana bag pouring in, he let us at least start cleaning it. With an IV bag hung high and with his head tilted back over the edge of the cart, I irrigated his scalp with a continuous jet of fluid from the end of cut IV tubing. I flushed what appeared to be months of accumulated debris into a large, round, metal basin under his head. Then while attempting to evade his highly toxic breath, I began the laborious job of sewing it all back together. I lifted up the bloody, silvery-grey-hair-covered hunk of scalp, but as large as it was, it did not seem anywhere near large enough to cover the defect. How the hell was I going to get this all back together? I was becoming increasingly apprehensive as there just seemed to be nowhere near enough skin. Then I remembered what I had been told by one of my seniors: that these types of injuries always looked worse (he was right there—it looked awful) than they really were, and that there was usually never any tissue loss. The intrinsic elasticity of the skin caused it to shrink as soon as it was cut, making it appear that it would never fit. I just needed to make sure I could get it all together. Slowly I worked on matching the edges where I thought they fit and began stitching the tough deep layer of fascial tissue together. Even after all the irrigation, I was still pulling out pieces of stuff that did not belong. Soon his head was adorned with a crown of thick, bristly, black sutures, but at least it was closed. He alternated between sleeping and snoring or awake and antagonistic, each just as foul smelling, although with the former he was much easier to work on. I still found that I needed to frequently look away and allow the waves of nausea to pass.

Scalp lacerations rarely become infected due to their great blood supply. The only souvenir was a scar, which in most cases, would be covered by hair.

This 100-proof breath, a rotten, rancid combination of old, stale alcohol liberally mixed with vomit and frequently other bodily fluids, we nicknamed 'Module One Breath'.

Even to this day, when I have the misfortune of smelling such a putrid concoction, it instantaneously transports me back to my time working in the 'Pits'. It is another testament to our powerful olfactory-cortical connections.

Suits, Accents, and Accidents

DAY 7 —Later that same afternoon, I experienced yet another wake-up call. This was an invaluable lesson that really did little else except highlight my own naivete.

At the far end of my now crowded module was a middle-aged gentleman, sharply dressed in a tailored two-piece, navy-blue suit, crisp white shirt, light-blue silk tie, and matching pocket square. He appeared ready for a business meeting but completely out of place in our bloody urban emergency room. What was he doing here? We had not received a report of a car accident, and anyway, he did not appear injured, at least not significantly. As I went to see him, things progressed from slightly odd to strange indeed, as not only was he here, but he could not leave. He was handcuffed.

I found absolutely nothing wrong with him with the exception of a few minor scrapes and bruises. So, why was he here, and why the handcuffs? The nurses (who usually knew all the gossip) were unable to shed any light, telling me that he had been brought in by a couple of officers for us to 'clear'.

While I was finishing up my examination, without my even inquiring he launched into a discourse (his version) of everything that had occurred leading up to his being brought here. It was a simple case of mistaken identity, he assured me. It was all a big mistake, and that as he felt fine, could I please let him go. He sounded so genuine, so sincere, and with an added rare politeness that we were not accustomed to. Had he not been handcuffed, I would undoubtably have succumbed to his wishes. Even though there appeared to be nothing medically wrong with him, I could not let him go. I did not have the keys to his Smith and Wesson Detroit PD 'bracelet'(cuffs).

Our emergency room always had a couple of police officers assigned to us. Moreover, in one corner of the complex, a little away from the patient care modules, was a 'lock-up' or police holding area. Here there were two cells (or bull pens as they were known) used to hold detainees until they were sent on to the local precinct. It was another revelation to work in a hospital where there was so much police presence, which was both reassuring and at the same time worryisome. These armed officers were there to protect us, the staff, but also to help process and detain the many 'undesirables' that made their way through our doors on a daily basis. I wondered why I was working in an emergency room that appeared to be so 'unsafe' that it was necessary to have police on site. But then I also knew the answer. This was where I needed to be if I was to become a surgeon. It was the price that I needed to pay.

My curiosity over our smartly suited handcuffed gentleman soon had the better of me, and I decided to go over to the lockup to find one of the officers.

The officer on duty that night listened patiently as I asked him if he had any information on my patient. While I tried not to look as obviously ignorant and naive as I was, he proceeded to tell me the story behind my 'polite' patient. It appeared that he had an outstanding federal felony warrant for the trafficking of automatic weapons across state lines. When finally apprehended, the trunk of his car was a veritable mobile arsenal, stuffed full of illegal weapons. He was, perhaps, not really the nice guy he had us all believe.

I learnt another very valuable lesson and felt much safer knowing that he was in custody.

We all want to trust what people tell us, for that is our nature, and it is especially true in medicine where trusting what we are told is so important in figuring out what is wrong. However, it is exactly this type of experience that made me wary and often distrustful of the stories I heard. What patients told us was frequently light years away from the truth.

We learnt to be detectives, not only sorting through the clues to help diagnose disease but also to figure out if they were themselves being truthful.

'Tito', a man of Eastern European descent, who spoke with a strong but still understandable accent, had sustained two gunshots to his left buttock. He also complained of pain in his left ankle, which prevented him from being able to walk or bear weight. His story, which he was reluctant to share, was a familiar one, as he first explained that he had been caught in a crossfire and had accidentally received two in the 'butt'.

Rock stable, he was whisked directly into the module and soon sent off to the X-ray line to get zapped. He looked unusually comfortable for someone who had just been shot, probably relieved that now he was where he thought his assailant would not try to follow (which was not always a valid assumption).

As I made him aware of the severity of his injuries, his story changed until he settled on one that at least sounded plausible. In his final version, while 'visiting' with his girlfriend, her husband returned home unexpectedly (same old story) and surprised them both.

Realizing that three was a crowd, he hastily retreated, half dressed, via an open window at the end of a long hallway. He undoubtedly did not look before hurriedly leaping from the first story window. His luck was short-lived, as the irate husband quickly managed to get a number of shots off, two of which found their target in his butt as he fled. Things were not improved by an uncoordinated hard landing on his left ankle.

Out at the nurses' desk, we snapped Tito's films up on the view box, which clearly showed a non-displaced tibial fracture involving his left ankle. A cast would take care of that. His belly films, however, told a different story. One or both of the bullets had shattered his sacrum on their destructive journey. It was not so much the bone of the sacrum that concerned us, as much as the anatomical proximity of his rectum which lay just in front. The bullets had likely injured a great deal more than just his pride.

We needed to find out if the integrity of the rectum had been violated by one or both bullets or by the sharp shards of bony shrapnel. The only sure way to know was to look. After explaining the plan to him, I wheeled him over to the endoscopy room, which fortunately was empty, and used a rigid sigmoidoscope to look into his lower bowel. This 'sigmoidoscope' is nowhere near as fancy as it sounds. Unlike its newer high-tech flexible brethren, this was just a stainless-steel tube with a hand/eye piece at one end and a light at the other (the business end). It is carefully inserted into the rectum, while hand-pumping in air to distend the bowel walls. Now, on a good day this is not that much fun, especially when the patient was not 'cleaned out'. This truly was a 'dirty job'. We only managed to get about four inches in when we were met by blood and clot mixed with a generous quantity of stool obscuring our view. This was not a subtle finding but a sure sign that the bowel had been penetrated.

Despite telling us he was feeling a little better, this new finding would not be welcome news. It meant that he now needed major surgery. If the rectal tears were left untreated, stool would find its way out through these defects, leading to a severe infection with potentially fatal consequences. I explained to him that he now needed to have a colostomy to divert the stool away from the site of injury such that it could have a chance to heal, the site being far too low to be repaired primarily. This surgery would involve a relatively large incision, a week of hospitalization, and the necessity to have a colostomy for at least six months before any consideration was given to reverse it. This was certainly not what he expected when he arrived just 'shot in the butt'.

While informing my chief, my ears perked up like a jack rabbit emerging from its burrow as I heard another overhead page but it wasn't the usual code announcement.

"Assistance needed in module three. Bring leathers," came the raspy, staticky, overhead call. Although sounding a little kinky, they meant leather restraints, our heavily padded, light brown ones, which had likely seen a previous life on the psychiatric ward.

My curiosity again was peaked, this announcement sounding promisingly different. Deciding it warranted further investigation, I wandered over to module three to see what was going on. Who knows, perhaps I might even be able to be of some assistance (OK, maybe that would be a bit of a stretch). Over by the first bed in the medical module, a heaving crowd had formed. Many of the staff appeared to be actively involved in holding down the patient, who was still invisible to me due to the collected throng. Although unable to see anything, I resorted to inferring details from the emanating tidal waves of unique verbal descriptives. These profane outbursts were released in spurts, as if to give us an intermission between shows or perhaps the time to appreciate their eloquence of composition and her mastery of English. Finally, once appropriate restraint had been applied with the help of a sedative, I was surprised to see that the focus of all the activity and source of our linguistic education was a very slight and not unattractive young woman who I doubt was a day over twenty.

She was a frequent ER visitor, a frequent flyer, and had told one of the nurses restraining her that she had had enough with life, or at least that's what she wanted everyone to believe. She appeared to have found a novel way to attempt to end it all.

After smashing the top off a beer bottle, she had taken the razor sharp, jagged lower portion and shoved it up into her vagina, mutilating herself. Clearly this was much more than just a simple suicide attempt, as there are, after all, far more efficient and less painful methods she could have chosen to reach her stated goal. Sadly, so many of these self-inflictions are just a symptom of a much deeper and more serious psychologic disturbance. In her case it turned out to be sexual abuse when she was young. She had lost a fair amount of blood, and the gynecology resident who came to see her informed us that she had a multitude of deep lacerations that needed to be stitched up, but for the majority there was nothing that could be done.

"It looks like mincemeat in there," he unabashedly pronounced, explaining his bedside exam findings to all nearby.

A little selfishly, I was happy that she was not in my module and that she was someone else's problem.

After having repaired as many of the lacerations as they could, she was sent off to psychiatry, where hopefully she could get the care she needed. If not, she would be back, and, most likely, one of these days she would be successful in reaching her apparent goal.

Back in 'my module', I sat out by the main desk and jotted down a few progress notes, trying to stay caught up with the paperwork. Not only was I always under time constraints (some naturally self-inflicted—wasting time in other modules!), but after a while, patients all seemed to meld together, and it became a challenge to keep them straight. I was always asking the nurses to help me recall which patient was which. With time and especially experience, I became much more adept at prioritizing and compartmentalizing each patient and their associated data. Learning this 'art' really helped later on when I had to round on 20 or so patients on the inpatient wards, while trying to keep them all straight.

As an intern, the medical information flew in thick and fast, and usually there was no repeat. We certainly did not have the time to memorize it, at least not right away, so many of us were in the habit of jotting facts and tidbits down in a notebook that we carried with us. Rapidly this book became thick, brimming with loose, well-worn pages chock full of anatomical diagrams, drug dosages, protocols, and pearls of information, some of which we assimilated by repeat utilization. These accumulations of notes became our 'peripheral brain'.

This method of learning and reinforcement has become obsolete; the modern resident now has an entire medical encyclopedia at

their fingertips: 'Dr. Google,' although perhaps not always readily
available in the middle of surgery.

While writing up the only patient that I currently had all results back on, I glimpsed out of the corner of my eye a nurse coming towards me. I kept on writing, trying to appear busy, purposefully not making eye contact and hoping that she was not looking for me. No such luck. She stopped right in front of me. I looked up with a face that I'm sure said, "And now what the hell have I done?"

Why all the guilt? Who knows? It was nothing new. I think it was just the result of being constantly demeaned and the perceived expectation that we should always be busy.

"Dr. Maxwell, could you come give us a hand. Please." She asked very politely, although it sounded more like pleading. Now I knew that was never a good sign. "We have a patient who needs his cast off."

I pondered the request for a few moments. The cogs were now busily turning in my head. A cast. That's ortho territory, I thought to myself. And, anyway, I was getting comfortable and actually making headway writing up notes.

"Don't you think you should give the ortho boys a call first?" I asked, in a tone suggesting that I didn't want to step on their toes. I was hoping that would be it, and that maybe after a little apology for disturbing me, she would leave me alone. Again, no such luck.

"We called them. They are all scrubbed in surgery. And . . ." She looked at me with sad, how can you refuse, puppy-dog eyes. I knew what was coming.

"They asked if you would do them a favor and take the cast off."

"But, if you are too busy . . ." she added, the words trailing off. She had struck my guilty nerve, and she knew it. Notes could always wait. How could I refuse such a request? I think it was a combination of the puppy-dog eyes and the helpless look that did it. I was a sucker, and that I knew. But they helped me out all the time when I needed it, so how could I refuse? Anyway, it was just a cast that needed to come off. How bad could that be?

"Well, OK. Where is he?" I inquired, thinking to myself that I was doing this favor for the nurses, not 'ortho'. After all, the 'ortho' residents were renowned escape artists, at least when it came to work. They had a reputation of avoiding work and especially if they could find someone else to do it for them.

I guess they just did.

"Over in 'Decontam,'" came the reply.

"Oh, great," I thought to myself. Maybe next time I should ask where the patient is first before agreeing to help. But I knew better. When someone asks for help, you just go. And I knew now that this was not going to be fun.

The decontamination room was not much larger than a small closet with a tub and a shower. It was here that the foulest of our patients were brought to be cleaned up, deloused, and literally hosed down. It was the epitome of low tech: a small, white-tiled floor shower, a scrub brush, and soap. This was not a room you ever wanted to visit.

Dealing as we did so often with a poorer cross-section of society, many of our patients had extremely poor hygiene, if any. Many had parts of their body that had not seen water and certainly not soap for many months. It was not unusual for us to have patients who came in with open sores crawling with maggots. The maggots, although revolting (and not looking any better), were for many a life saver because they cleaned the wound, eating only the dead tissue and leaving the healthy behind. This often is what prevented the wounds from becoming seriously infected.

"What is it this time?" I asked, really not wanting to know. After all, how could it be anything good?

"The guy has lice, all over," the nurse said as she descriptively crawled the fingers of her right hand up and down her left forearm. "And as for the cast, it looks as though he's had it on for months."

"Well, at least it's still on. The break should be well healed up by now," I thought out loud. "If the lice have not eaten it away."

In the decontamination room there was a man sitting naked in the shower stall, his yellowish hair in dirty, greasy clumps. Although appearing elderly, he was only 42. On his left forearm was the cast, surprisingly intact, yet it had long lost any resemblance of ever being a shade of white. It looked more like a large piece of antique clay water piping, perhaps sewer piping if the horrendous smell was any guide.

The odor that arose from his arm reached a new high of olfactory assailment. This was yet another time that I was fortunate to have an empty stomach. Anyone who has ever worn a cast knows how quickly and how bad they can begin to smell. Well, imagine that a hundred times over. Whatever might be growing or living under that cast was surely nothing that I wanted to get too familiar with.

I double gloved myself, cautiously wielding the cast cutter in my right hand as I held onto the patient's forearm with my left. What forearm? There was practically nothing left, just skin and bones rattling inside an overly loose plaster of paris shell. It would have slid off if it were not molded around the base of his thumb and wrist. Carefully I cut the cast down on each side, splitting it open like a clamshell, breathing shallowly, trying not to inhale any dust particles. Once 'bivalved', the heavily stained cast padding was peeled off his forearm. No maggots this time, just lice wriggling all over his arm and the inside of the cast. After examining him, I unfairly decided to leave him in the care of the nurses, who were much more tolerant and for whom this was a much more frequent sight. Sure, maybe now I was dumping on them a bit, but I had done my part. I was lucky, I thought, that I did not have to wash the poor fellow, but even so, I felt like now I needed my own decontamination.

A quick word about cast cutters would not be remiss here. As a patient whose cast has to come off, we are reassured that the cast cutter cannot cut the flesh. But is this true? A cast cutter does not cut so much as its toothed blade vibrates and separates the plaster of Paris. It can easily penetrate the skin, but hopefully the thick layer of cast padding and the conscientiousness of the remover prevent it from doing so.

As a medical student, I learnt the hard way the importance of padding, and lots of it, while we were practicing removing casts from each other. You could not really have too much, but you definitely could have too little. My overzealous cast-removing partner did not stop with just the cast and continued through its minimal padding right into the skin of my forearm. When he was done, I had a nice two-inch gash in my arm. Ok, so perhaps it was more of a deep scratch, but it hurt like hell, and anyway I needed to make him feel bad. Nevertheless, we all had a great deal more respect for the 'harmless' cast cutters after that.

Before long I observed our nurses checking in another 'customer'. He was clad in baggy, faded, beige paint-stained, worn denim overalls with a matching, unwashed, blue, mis-buttoned shirt. He sported a set of wide, dark brown suspenders that strained as much to keep in his gut as to hold up his pants. Perched on his head, partially obscuring his face, was a camouflage hunting hat, which he removed with reluctance. After completing her evaluation, his nurse walked over.

"What's that one? Anything exciting?" I asked, already pretty sure from slurred barely comprehensible responses, I had overheard, that it would be 'a nothing'.

"Nah, just a DFO ('Done Fell Out') drunk who forgot to take his meds and had a seizure," she replied, clearly not too perturbed, and pretty sure that she had the whole thing already figured out.

Sure enough, the story he told me was, all too common and one for which I could almost finish his sentences. He had a seizure disorder for which he was on 'Phenbarb' (Phenobarbital) and 'Diltin' (Dilantin). Commonly this disorder, as we saw it, was secondary to a penchant for imbibing excessive amounts of cheap alcohol. He was no exception.

Although he did not appear to be seriously injured, I was not so fortunate. I was again struck by the invisible, nauseating, 100 proof wall (of module one breath) that surrounded him like a starship's impenetrable defensive shield. He finally admitted with reluctant evasiveness to having been drinking and went on to explain that he had not taken any of his medications for a few days.

This was hardly earth-shattering news, and we began loading him up with IV Dilantin, while waiting for the expected low blood level.

We were all surprised when the result returned. It was unexpectedly high.

Immediately, we halted the infusion. I talked to him further. He was now a little more sober, and that helped.

Patients were instructed not to drink when on their anti-seizure meds, as most had experienced firsthand the disagreeable side effects when they didn't heed the warning. "The doc told me not to mix the pills with booze, so I didn't take any (pills that is, not alcohol)." Now this guy was no dummy. He did not want to abstain from drinking but knew that he needed to take his medication, so he loaded himself up with a number of days worth of anti-seizure medication at one time. His theory was that this would allow them the ability to drink for a few days, without issue. He had done this a number of times and had lost track (no surprise here) of how much he had taken. We observed him overnight, sending him home the next morning once his levels had fallen.

In addition to the routine 'knife-and-gun' club victims and those from unavoidable accidents, we saw people whose injuries were much more preventable and, sadly, not all had a happy ending.

That noontime, a couple had been driving down the freeway just a few blocks north of the hospital on their way to meet up with some friends for lunch, when the husband, who was driving, missed his exit. He decided it would be quicker to reverse back to the missed ramp rather than driving to the next one. While backing up, which he fatefully decided to do on the highway and not on the shoulder, he saw another car in his rearview mirror but thought that they would switch out of his lane when they saw him. The driver of the oncoming car did not expect to come across someone reversing in his lane and did not alter lanes in time, resulting in a collision. The paramedics were rapidly on the scene, and the couple were swiftly transported to us. The man, who had been driving, had very few injuries but was observed for a possible cardiac contusion as a result of his chest striking the steering wheel. His wife, however, was not so fortunate, as she hit the windshield and the dashboard with tremendous force and was pronounced DOA (Dead on Arrival) after snapping her neck.

Cockiness Kills

DAY 8 —Saturday again, one week later.

Arriving for work on the following Saturday, my stomach was still protesting a barely digested breakfast, wolfed down twenty minutes earlier. I was greeted, for a change, by a surprisingly quiet and pleasant calmness, as if an invisible early morning mist had softly enveloped the module. I took a cursory look around and happily thought to myself that perhaps this might be an easy Saturday. Tomorrow, Sunday, was my day off and for a few moments my mind weakened, and I easily let it wander.

Now, I was sleeping in, luxuriating in the tranquility of a morning without agenda, watching the (not so early) morning news while slowly savoring a strong cup of sweet aromatic Earl Grey tea. Milk and two sugars, thank you very much. I let my mind linger there for a moment. A delightful moment.

What on earth was I thinking? This was no time for daydreaming. This was Detroit Receiving, and this was Saturday—there would be no peace here, not on a Saturday. If there was one thing that was a certainty, it was that there was never such a thing as a quiet Saturday. Before too long it would get hopping—it always did. 'Days' were just the warm-up for the main event, which was of course, Saturday Nights at Receiving.

Walking around and taking inventory, there was a distinct, rare, and even a little worrying dearth of activity. Was this the calm before the storm? I opened the door to the resuscitation room to check it, and a streak of light sliced a swath through the dark, clean, empty room. It lit up the three unoccupied gurneys. It was quiet. Dangerously and deceivingly quiet.

Wandering back to the front desk, my eyes were immediately drawn to an all too familiar hanging piece of paper, its pastel pink contrasting against the dull, stained, whitish nursing carrel to which it had been taped. A consult request! Already! It had barely gone 6:30. Where did that come from? I had only just arrived; how could there be one so early? I thought and hoped that perhaps it was one that had been left hanging from 'nights' and had already been dealt with. I looked closer. No such luck. Was this to be an omen? Was this really the way this day was going to go? Starting with a consult right at 6:30 was never good.

But then, it wasn't really a new consult. This I soon discovered when I spoke to a somewhat reticent, embarrassed, and extremely apologetic nurse in the medical module from where the slip had originated.

The focus of this new 'insult' had come in a number of hours earlier, during the latter part of 'nights', certainly in plenty of time to have been seen. She explained that she had been specifically instructed to delay placing the request until after 6:30. Undoubtably it could have been dealt with on 'nights' when they had far more people.

However, when I found the true source of the delay, I was not in the least bit surprised. But it still really pissed me off. Now, it wasn't as if I was too busy. I was always more than happy to go take care of any patient that needed help, but I was still annoyed at the laziness of the resident on 'nights' who chose to dump it.

Dr. Jerry Hunter was the typical cock-sure orthopedic resident, tall with clean-cut, short, sandy hair, who thought of himself as God's gift to the world, or at least to women. I knew Hunter. We all knew Hunter. We had started together as interns, but he was on the orthopedic track. Rather than actually working, he would spend his days (or rather, 'nights') wandering around the modules. With his chin condescendingly high, he ran his fingers through his short, sandy hair, making sure not to miss the opportunity to view his reflection in every mirror, while flirting with every nurse he deemed worthy enough of his attention. He was currently doing his stint rotating through the ER trauma module, which to him was unnecessary, pedestrian, and plebian. After all he was going to be an orthopedic surgeon.

It is exactly this type of arrogance that repeatedly gets patients (not the physician!) in trouble. The providers who believe they know far more than they really do are a far greater menace than those who know little, acknowledge their shortcomings, and actually care. I summarize it to residents as: "Cockiness Kills!"

The consult request was for a 'pussed out' lip. An abscessed lip. It was nothing really exciting. I doubt that it would take me very long to take care of once I could get around to it. As expected, the calmness that had greeted me earlier had now evaporated and was replaced by a continuous parade of patients making themselves at home in 'my' module

I did not have time to see 'the lip' right now, but I would have to make time once I had the module cleared out a bit. This was always a dangerous tactic, as it might never slow down.

First, I needed to deal with a young man with a blood and vomit speck-led, filthy, ginger beard. His bushy appendage camouflaged his mouth but not its foul fetid breath. He was one of our 'solid citizens', tolerable as long as he kept his mouth shut. He frequented the module as if it were the most natural progression following an all-nighter at his local watering hole. He had become involved in (or perhaps instigated) a fist fight. But then to many of our visitors, brawling seemed to be a sport, a normal part of their Friday night activities.

The next stop of the night (or morning) after the brawl was usually a police-escorted visit to see us, which for many was the expected conclu-sion to their evening.

Along with his 'friend', in the next bed, they had both been severely assaulted, my bearded patient having also received two stab wounds in his upper abdomen. He was so rip-roaring, stinking (extra emphasis on the latter) drunk that he would not let anyone (and let's face it, no one really wanted to) get close enough to examine him.

The few times that I was able to briefly examine his abdomen, it was quite tender. More tender than I expected (considering his degree of inebriation). He had a couple of very deep, two-inch long wounds in the left upper abdomen just beneath his protuberant, emaciated ribcage. He remained stable and was not 'shocky'—just 'assholey', very abusive, and unbelievably smelly.

This type of patient required a great deal of attention, not necessarily difficult but still time consuming. He was not bad enough that we needed to rush him to the operating room (which was a blessing, for they were still catching up on the previous night's schedule) or lose him to the distant recesses of the CT scanner. But still, he was tender enough that I needed to entertain the possibility that the knife could have penetrated beyond the boundaries of his abdominal wall and perhaps could have struck an internal organ. He was top of my worry list. Although rock stable, he was too crocked to be of any real help. He certainly could not lie still for a CT, so that, for now, was out of the question. I knew that with time he would declare himself one way or another. I needed to wait, watch, and re-examine. Time would be our diagnostic aid.

This was just the beginning of the CT (CAT, computer aided tomography) scan era. The scanners were very slow (at least a half an hour per scan) and delivered nothing close to the image resolution to which we are now accustomed, let alone located in a remote area of the hospital. Not only were we learning and refining the process of taking the scans, but we were also all being educated as to what they could show us. Today, and with scanners frequently located right next to emergency rooms, a total body CT scan time is measured in seconds, something that would have seemed science fiction then.

However, the use of CT scans appears to have slowly (perhaps not so slowly) and insidiously replaced the role of a good physical examination. It makes me concerned that a physician as a diagnostician is becoming obsolete. Will physicians be replaced by computers, solid-state logic boards able to search the entirety of documented medical knowledge, completing algorithms in a fraction of a second, and along with advances in AI (artificial intelligence) soon be spitting out diagnoses? I certainly hope not. There are many things in medicine that defy logic, which is why medicine remains as much an art as a science. Technology is most effective when used as an adjunct to thorough clinical evaluation.

Our next patient was a man brought in as a code, a blood-stained bullet hole visible on the front of his faded blue Detroit Lions hoodie. He had sustained a gunshot to his abdomen, the special for the day. Following the same trend, he was extremely uncooperative and combative.

"You ain't fucking touchin' me, man."

This he repeated frequently, as he lifted his head and chest up, stiff and unnatural, perhaps like a vampire sitting up in his coffin.

"Stay the hell away. Let me go."

Although he appeared awake enough to understand that we were trying to help, he continued with nonsensical demands. So with his inability to reply to our straightforward requests, I finally capitulated.

We left him alone in the room, fulfilling at least one of his requests, returning our attention to the many other pressing issues in the module. Soon, as expected, we heard him loudly pleading for our return.

His tune had changed. He was scared yet stable and now was much more amenable to letting us help him. In truth, he was never completely alone, for I had left a student sitting off in a corner where they could observe him without being seen. He was never in trouble, and as so often is the case, when the gore and muck were cleaned away, the injury improved exponentially. The bullet had struck his abdomen tangentially but had not penetrated it.

It was starting to feel more like a Saturday as we soon received a man who had been stabbed multiple times in the chest. He was bleeding profusely and had labored respirations. He needed help. His breathing, however, had not yet deteriorated enough to quieten him down. He remained so combative that even the placement of an IV was impossible to accomplish safely. Once again waiting out of sight was the ticket. He soon tired to where he no longer put up any resistance and we could care for him. His chest X-ray showed that his left lung was completely 'down' (collapsed). I was now doubly impressed that he could manage such a verbal assault on only one lung. I explained that he needed a chest tube. He was not so enthused.

"Over my fucking dead body," were his exact words. However, he changed his tune once he understood that he might indeed receive his wish. After leaving him alone, he rapidly calmed down.

This trick actually sped up their care, allowing us to care for patients without any serious delay or harm. We did not have time for long discussions, such that we might have with someone sober. We just needed to get them fixed so we could get on to the next. We were there to get them better, save their life and get them home.

When I returned to see my shackled, vomit-laden, ginger-bearded man, he was asleep, placid. The only interruption was the occasional quivering of his lips and the gentle movement of his beard hairs as he exhaled, reminiscent of a light breeze passing over a field of long grass. It was hard to believe that this was the same man that I examined earlier.

I had hardly even begun my repeat examination, having just placed my right hand on his belly, when I awoke the sleeping beast. I was hit with another thunderous broadside of a clearly well-rehearsed repertoire of obscenities carried on his foul, alcohol- and vomit-infused breath. Yup, this was the same guy all right

He never complained about or appeared to be in significant pain (alcohol anesthesia perhaps), and about six hours had passed since he had arrived with an alcohol level of 350. Although not a record, it was still indicative of a significant alcohol load and his liver's ramped up metabolizing abilities. His bar sparring partner, in the bed opposite, was also secured with the favorite local DPD wrist jewelry. The police had decided not to hold either of them but they would keep them cuffed until they were more coherent. For now, I would keep them in my charge, where I could keep a close eye.

Directly behind the nursing desk lay another esteemed member of society, also shackled. So many of our arrivals proudly sported the latest in DPD jewelry. He appeared to be just awakening from his drunken stupor when I approached him after he had not cooperated on receiving X-rays. Noticing my imminent arrival, he decided to further test his vocal cords, perhaps unsure if they were injured.

"What the hell am I doin' tied down. I dun nuttin' wrong," he kept on repeating to himself and would not let up. The more he spoke, the happier I was that he was shackled.

"Why you treating me like an animul?"

He continued loudly.

"I'm a 'uman. Just like yous."

His antics were audible out in the hallway and down in the other modules, and before too long a small crowd had gathered to observe. Really, I think they were probably all just wondering, "what on earth was that crazy surgical resident up to today." With a pause that gave the mistaken impression of purposefully choosing his words, he continued.

"I'z bin 'ere all night, chained like this. I'z not a dog."

Accompanied by striking his hand cuffs against the frame to which they were attached, he continued.

"Get me the fuck outta here." Then in the next breath: "Gets me to a real 'orspital."

Even hours later, he had enough alcohol on board that every time he opened his mouth, everyone in the vicinity became instantly nauseated. It was chemical warfare. He was lying down for now, his head firmly pressed against a pillow soaked with blood from a profusely bleeding scalp laceration that he would not let anyone near. When we finally were able to go over him, it was his only real injury. Fortunately, with his head on the pillow, he had been placing direct pressure on it. Once sutured we gladly gifted him back to the police, who, at least for the immediate future, controlled his destiny.

I delegated a few suturing jobs to a 'stud' who had wandered into the module around midday, apparently "looking to help." This really was helpful, as it allowed me to see the consults, including the pussed-out lip that was still waiting.

Over-indulgence in alcohol has many undesirable side effects, besides the personal and social toll. But rapid cessation was also a problem. One of the most dangerous was the dreaded DT's (delirium tremens). This lays at the severe end of the alcohol withdrawal spectrum, and we usually only saw it in patients subject to multiple days of abstinence. Some of the more resourceful circumvented the issue by having friends or family members bring in flasks of their preferred beverage. In all likelihood it probably shortened their hospital stay, decreased its cost, and kept them alive.

Some progressive hospitals serve wine with dinner. Not only does it help relax patients, increase their appetites, and help them sleep, but it kept the DTs at bay. In the end it was certainly cheaper and more effective than benzodiazepines.

In only six to twelve hours, patients could experience mild symptoms of withdrawal including tremulousness and mild hallucinations. This could progress to withdrawal seizures (rum fits, as it was termed in the days when Britain ruled the waves with its well-rummed sailors) and then on to full blown DTs. We, of course, wanted to get the patients out before they had such symptoms. We would certainly hear about it if we took up a surgical bed with someone in DTs just because we were not able to get them out quickly enough. Once out, sure, we knew that they would be hitting the bottle in short order, and many would be back to see us not long after. No one ever took us up on our offer to help them dry out.

'Primum Non Nocere'

I MADE my way down to the OCU to check on patients I had been accumulating. It was easy to lose track. Some I had sent there, while others were left from the night before.

Entering, I passed a man sitting upright in his bed, lazily gazing off into oblivion. I did not recognize him, although I must admit to not looking too closely. A few moments later, out of the corner of my eye I saw him waving. He had recognized me and after making eye contact, he responded with a very slow, slurred, but comprehensible "Hiya, Doc."

Looking closer, I saw that this was Danny, one of our regulars. A most frequent of frequent fliers and someone I had met on many previous occasions. Sometimes our first inkling of his arrival was overhearing our staff greeting him.

"Oh, Danny, not again. Now what happened?" they would ask.

The nurses loved him, took care of him, and felt sorry for him. No matter what we did or how hard we tried to help him, he would bounce back to the ER, usually drunk and always with more lacerations to add to his already lengthy resume of scars. Over time we all came to know his story: how he had a son with whom he had not had contact for years, and how he had pickled his brain on alcohol and just could not seem to stop.

Danny was one of the regulars with whom I became familiar over the first couple of months. I must have seen him at least four or five times during my time there. No matter how drunk, he was always pleasant, and sadly his story was always the same. He would arrive intoxicated with cuts and bruises everywhere and explain that he had been beaten up and robbed. Once here, Danny, like the other alcohol over-consumers, was easily identifiable by their distinctive fluorescent yellow banana bag that hung, like a flag, from their IV pole.

The first time we met was at about 4:00 in the morning when I was an intern on 'nights'. A student had just finished sewing him up, and I was preparing to discharge him. He was all set to go as far as I could tell. The lacerations were all stitched up and looked pretty good (at least by Danny's standards). He looked at me with big, wide-open bloodshot eyes and a little stammer in his voice as he slowly mustered his question.

"Doc . . . please, aren't you going to send me down to the other room until the morning?" he pleaded. By 'other room', of course, he meant the OCU, and when I told him no, as I thought he could go home, the whining shifted up another gear.

"They always send me there and home after breakfast."

I thought about what he was saying, what he was asking me for. It was not for the world, although it might have seemed like it to him. What was the decision I was making? It was not medical; it was social. I was the one deciding if he should stay or go. If he should be dumped back, hungry, into the cold, wet night. Why not let him stay and eat breakfast? He wasn't doing any harm.

I realized then that for many we were often nothing more than a fancy soup kitchen—one with sleeping privileges and an expensive one at that. Being new and easily swayed by his pleas, I let him stay for his complimentary breakfast. Naturally this was perhaps a well-choreographed act and one that he had likely pulled on many of the newbies before me and doubtless many since. I never felt bad about it, as when he left, he was always pleasant and genuinely thankful, which was a refreshing change. Yet I always felt pangs of guilt when sending him back out onto the cold, wet, and lonely streets.

By early afternoon our EMS must have decided that things were a little too quiet and wheeled in more business. Their 'delivery' was a man close to my age (these always seemed to hit home the most) wearing a blue denim western-style shirt, blue jeans, and a very worn and cut pair of light brown cowboy boots. His outfit, more suited to a Texas ranch hand, was in complete contradistinction to his name and matching Italian accent. He was completely caked in a mixture of blood and dirt, making identification of specific facial features challenging. He arrived securely strapped to a slightly warped aluminum backboard, secured so well that NASA could not have done a better job if they were preparing to launch him into orbit. His head was immobilized between two bricks, strapped down with wide cloth tape across his forehead, and secured to the board.

He had been driving his car on one of the city's too common Swiss-cheese, pot-holed surface streets, when he was rammed at an intersection. Not just once but multiple times by a much larger vehicle. An accident for sure, but accidental, perhaps not.

We were further appraised as to how his car had been tightly wrapped around a telephone pole and that his rescuers had to use their hydraulic 'jaws of life' to extricate him. Our EMS colleagues were always excited when they got to use their massive pincer cutting tool, comparing its ease of use to that of a can opener.

He responded to our questions with only the briefest of mumbled evasive responses. For whatever reason, he did not divulge any details as to how or why this 'accident' had taken place. Whenever we broached the subject, he became nervous, apprehensive, and even a little agitated as he tried to change our focus. It all felt like something out of a movie, and we knew how they ended. We decided it was easier and wiser for us to stay in the dark.

While asking routine questions, I began using hydrogen perox-ide-soaked sponges to clean the blood from his face, enabling me to see the extent of his underlying injuries—and him. There were tiny fragments of windshield glass imbedded everywhere. His forehead was peppered. I tediously plucked out the stubbornly entrenched shards. Extending two inches from the left side of his hugely swollen raspberry of a nose were two very jagged lacerations that would take some time to repair, and above which he fought to keep his swollen bloodshot eye open. Every cut was filled with muck and grit, which if not removed might result in permanent discoloration, like a cheap tattoo.

He responded to every question with a new complaint. Pain in his shoulder then ankle and foot. This could go on all day, I thought. Was he stalling for more time, waiting for something, or someone or just too scared to leave?

Surprisingly his whining lessened slightly once he was lying on sheets, but we still needed to get him undressed, which proved no easy task. His clothes were rain-drenched, his jeans stuck, as if glued to his legs. We lifted his legs and his hips slightly off the stretcher and then, one to a leg, peeled his jeans off.

During my exam, when I pushed on his chest with the palm of my hand, he flinched and not just a little. He almost jumped off the cart. He must have had broken a few ribs. It was at this same time that the nurse reported that his pulse had now become erratic. His rate had not changed much—it had just become irregular. The EKG confirmed that his heart was in atrial fibrillation, a condition where the top chambers (atria) of the heart are not contracting properly. The most likely cause was a cardiac contusion—a severe bruise of the heart as a result of it being compressed between the breastbone and the spine—as his chest smacked against the steering wheel. Before sending him to X-ray, we began a second IV and hooked him up to a monitor. We also slipped in an NG tube that he was not thrilled about, but it gave us loads of additional information. Not only did the tube empty the stomach and let us know if there was any blood in there, but on chest X-ray we would be able to see if the tube altered its natural course, revealing the possibility of a traumatic aneurysm pushing the esophagus away from its normal anatomical path. Soon he began complaining of discomfort in his left eye, asking if he might have some glass in it. Was he, again, just trying to redirect the conversation? But then, he certainly had a point. There were fragments of glass everywhere, and his left eyelid was huge.

Investigation of eye complaints following trauma was routine, and although I had minimal experience before I began in the ER, I rapidly became quite competent at it. The tiny, sharp, windshield fragments were notorious corneal lacerators, and I learnt not to be squeamish when moving the eye around, lifting up the eyelid, and turning it inside out to check under it.

Trying to check his eye under the swollen eyelid was a challenge. I could not see any overt evidence of trauma, but he would have to go through a much more detailed evaluation before I could be satisfied that there were no issues.

We did all the regular screenings, and there appeared to be no damage.

Before too long he found something else to complain about, this time his neck. With all the complaints he appeared was 'concocting' for us, it was clear that the real pain was not in his neck at all, but ours. He was already in a 'Philly' collar and perhaps that was contributing to the discomfort, or maybe it was the newly inserted NG tube that he hated. Anyway, he would need to stay in the collar until we had all the X-ray results back, which could easily be a couple of hours. This guy was clearly extremely lucky so far, but I still really wanted to know the 'skinny' on what had happened.

When there was a slight lull in the action, I decided to head off and see the consult that I had been procrastinating about since it was dumped on me early that morning. I know I should have tried to get there earlier, but I just couldn't seem to get free from the endless 'conveyor' of patients. Now I had no excuse.

The gentleman, whose age was difficult to gauge, had a deeply tanned and pock-marked, cratered face, evidence of a harsh acned adolescence. I soon discovered he was also a frequent flyer, well known to our staff from multiple previous visits, mostly to have lacerations repaired. He was here now with a fat, ballooned-out lower lip, surrounded by a landscape of scars and lacerations in various stages of repair. His lips were a shiny purplish blue, adorned with whisker-like white sutures, straining to resist the swollen repair.

The wound appeared clearly infected. However, before I went digging, I injected some lidocaine in and around the angry edges in an improbable attempt to anesthetize it. This naturally only made him threaten me with further bodily harm. Sadly we became used to this kind of gratitude from many of our patients. Using the tip of a hemostat, while trying my best to distract him, I swiftly yet gingerly separated the wound edges, knowing he might lash out at any moment. Cutting the stitches allowed the foul-smelling, thick, beige-grey pus an escape route.

Once completed, it did not really look all that bad. However, I was sure that it would be short lived and would not stay that way for long. It was not in his DNA to follow instructions, especially those advising him to stay away from further conflict. Luckily, despite extremely poor hygiene and his propensity for recurrent injury, the wound would undoubtably heal fine, and he certainly was not one to worry about a little scarring.

Heading back to home base, I stopped off in X-ray to check on the films of our western-clad, motor vehicle accident (MVA) victim. His films revealed a C6/C7 anterior subluxation, a fracture of his right fourth rib, and a few other findings to heighten my adrenaline flow. The chest film appeared to show a widened mediastinum (the portion of the chest directly above the heart) and a pleural cap (sliver of opacification above the apex of each lung, usually from blood). These findings, especially in view of the mechanism of injury, were suggestive of a traumatic tear of the aortic arch—a potentially fatal injury. If present, the treatment was immediate surgery, and it was a huge one at that. We sent him for an emergent aortogram (a contrast study of the body's largest artery), which luckily was normal.

This time-consuming procedure has now been completely supplanted by use of rapid CT imaging.

Rib fractures run the gamut from completely innocuous to life-threatening. We were taught early on to admit everyone who we didn't think had the ability to cough and take deep breaths well enough by themselves. These fractures were very painful, and many needed a strong analgesic or a rib block in order to breathe deeply enough to fend off pneumonia. This was the dreaded and sometimes fatal sequela, especially in the multiple-injured, elderly, or debilitated.

His most serious and potentially disastrous injury was his cervical spine subluxation. Here the sixth cervical vertebra (in the neck) had moved forward relative to its neighbor stacked below. Should it continue to move, it could easily impinge on the spinal cord causing any number of possible neurological injuries from simple nerve dysfunction in a particular muscle group to complete quadriplegia.

We immediately placed a consult to orthopedics, who were on call for spine injuries, a rotation they split with neurosurgery. They responded quickly, bringing with them a specialized frame bed from the spinal cord unit. This highly padded bed was capable of gently rotating from side to side to equally relieve pressure over the entire body, while the head and spine were kept in line by traction. The ortho resident went to work placing him in skeletal traction.

Watching this was definitely not for the faint of heart, as a pair of stainless steel (Gardner-wells) tongs (which looked like they could have been used to lift blocks of ice in a previous life) were attached directly to each side of the skull just above the ears. A shiver ran down my spine as I watched. The resident made tiny cuts and inserted a screw into one side of the skull. I have seen plenty of gore and unsightly injuries, some that even make my stomach churn, but there is something that just seems fundamentally wrong about watching bolts being screwed into the side of someone's head, especially when they are wide awake. I think it just reminds me too much of Frankenstein. Maybe medicine hasn't come that far after all. Then it was my turn, my side to screw in.

My brain got ahead of me. What would happen if the screw went in a little too far? Perhaps the bone was thinner than usual. Would there be a crunch? Would the skull cave in? How did I know when to stop turning the screw? What if I go too far? Do I just back up a turn? I knew it was more than this that was bothering me. In all of medicine, when we performed procedures, trying to help people, those same interventions could cause irreparable harm, even death. It made me acutely aware of how little medicine I knew and highlighted the most important of medical aphorisms. *Primum non nocere:* First, do no harm.

We attached the tongs through a series of ropes and pulleys to weights that hung off the end of the bed. A constant force could now be applied to the skull to keep the spine in column until it was able to heal or be surgically repaired. My chief decided that we should admit him to our surgical service for observation and coordination of his care. We all detested baby-sitting duty.

A Heart Attack

WHILE I was busy writing up progress notes, Bill, my fourth-year chief, came by. Tall, lanky, with dark curly hair, he was a lackadaisical but kind fellow. He got on well with everyone, it seemed, except the Attendings. Apparently, they considered him a little too laid back, lazy maybe, and not living up to their estimate of his potential. Recently, however, I had noted a significant change, as he appeared to have matured dramatically over the space of the dozen or so months since my intern year. He was the perennial jokester, never one to take things too seriously, and we all thought he was the ideal 'senior'. He made being an intern tolerable and gave us a sense of, "Well, if he can do it, maybe we have a chance." But now that was all in the past. He had made a complete turn-around, and we all thought he must have been talked to, perhaps even given an ultimatum. Now, don't get me wrong, he was still a great resident to work with but gone was the fun, laid-back Bill I had previously known. He was now all business and took his responsibilities seriously, as naturally a chief should.

He had come by to check out the 'hits' that his service had received so far that day. I unfolded progress note from the top pocket of my scrubs and started to go through the admissions scribbled on it, including the stab wound to the abdomen we had been observing since the morning.

The list was not long, but I still needed him to see them. While making our way down to the OCU, the overhead speakers crackled to life.

"Surgical code one to resuscitation. ETA three minutes," it announced, almost in a mocking tone intimating, "And you thought that you were going to get out of here on time today! No chance!"

We stopped in our tracks and were looking at each other, when Bill finally broke the second-long silent deadlock.

"Well, I guess we'd better get over there. We'll see these later," he announced unenthusiastically.

Although I really needed him to see the patients, they would have to wait. I would have to wait.

We swiftly came about (with almost parade ground like precision) and headed off to 'resuscitation'. Slowly the adrenaline increased, and I felt a tingling, nervous, anticipatory warmth penetrate through me. This was my first surgical code of the day.

We were not the first to arrive—far from it. There was already a crowd of nurses, students, and pharmacists jostling for position around the empty gurney. They all appeared to be contending for the 'the most prepared' prize—well, that is if there was one. Luckily, there wasn't.

It was just after 4:30, less than two hours until the next team relieved me. What better way to help pass the time than a good code? Maybe we would get a case.

Over at the head of the gurney, I opened the top drawer of the cart and checked the intubation equipment. Endotracheal tube. Check. I flipped open the laryngoscope. Light on. Check. Get my nerves under control. Check, check and check again. I turned to our code nurse and asked if she knew what was coming in.

"Stab to the left chest. Blood-pressure 50. MAST pants," came the calm, short, incisive response. She was an experienced nurse, and her confident calmness helped all of us remain composed and focused. She had been doing this for years and likely had seen more even in the last year than I ever would.

I, for one, hoped it would be something good. But then good for us was never good for the patient. We were ready: needles, IVs, and endotracheal tubes in hand, and anything else that we might possibly need never too far away. Bill spent a few moments to page Dr. Wilson, the Attending that night. When he was 'on', he always wanted to be informed right away of a code. Little did we know at the time that this was probably the best decision that Bill made that day (and maybe much longer).

Shortly after the pronouncement of "Surgical code now arriving," the EMS team was rushing the patient down the hallway towards us, the patient's head way down in the shock position, one of the team bagging him, others helping to push. As they wheeled him in, we all flew into action in our explosive, well-rehearsed, choreographed routine. I immediately went to the head of the bed, and while quickly going through my primary survey, spoke to the EMTs, attempting to get a history.

There was no talking to the patient as he was completely unresponsive. Swiftly he was lifted onto our gurney.

"We got a pressure of 60/0 in transit, but that was it," one of the EMTs responded. "Nothing since."

In seconds he was stripped of all his clothing, including the more obstructive than beneficial MAST (medical anti-shock trousers) pants. Bill immediately started a left subclavian line while one of our 'studs' attempted to insert a peripheral line. He was breathing extremely shallowly, and listening to his chest, I could not hear a thing on his left, the same side as the stab. Not wanting to wait for his breathing to deteriorate further, I immediately set about intubating him. This for some reason I found somewhat problematic, having great difficulty visualizing his vocal cords. It might have been just my nerves, but it took me a few seconds before I was able to slip a tube in, and then after quickly taping it, passed it off to the respiratory therapist to continue ventilating while I went ahead and placed a chest tube on his left side. While all this was going on, Bill and I exchanged few words. We both knew what needed to be done, and we divided our duties seamlessly. It was clear from the location of his injury and lack of breath sounds that he must have a collapsed lung and a whole lot of blood in his left chest. Looking at him more closely, I saw now that he had markedly dilated neck veins, something that I might not usually have picked up on except that they were huge.

Low blood pressure, a stab to the chest, massive neck veins: it all led to one conclusion. This man must have a cardiac tamponade from the stab injury. The knife must have struck the heart.

Now my heart was racing. What to do next? I needed to stay calm, stay focused. We already had a couple of decent IVs, in and we were starting a third. Soon I started to feel a little more in control, as with all the fluid we had his pressure back up to 70. But when I put the chest tube in, I only got 50 ml of blood out. Where was all the blood? This was definitely not what I had expected. I thought that there would be a chest full, a liter at least. While inserting the chest tube, the nurses lubed up and slipped in an NG. Not only would it empty the stomach making it safer for anesthesia, but it would tell us if there was blood in the upper gastro-intestinal (GI) tract. Perhaps even more importantly, if we had to open the chest and cross clamp his aorta, this normally pulsatile, but now empty and flaccid vessel could be distinguished from its equally flaccid esophagus by the presence of the tube.

Surprisingly my chest tube made little difference. As I was tying it in, I attempted to think of what was going on. In all the commotion and accompanying stress, I had completely forgotten about the enlarged neck veins. I was far more concerned that my tube might not be in the right spot (I must have screwed up), and that was why it was was not draining much.

Suddenly as if someone had flipped a switch, the room fell silent. I turned to see Dr. Wilson gliding into the room, with all the panache of Darth Vader walking down the ramp of his Imperial Shuttle. (Sadly, the orchestral accompaniment was absent.)

Dr. Wilson, our chief of trauma surgery, had a system-wide reputation for his very aggressive treatment of trauma victims. But then what other way should one be in a trauma center? This was not a place where procrastination benefited anyone.

He was an imposing, athletic man, appearing younger than he really was, with a constantly tanned face residing under the cover of thick, slightly slick, dark brown hair. He, more than anybody, fit the TV persona of the fast-paced, cool under pressure trauma surgeon. He wore dark green scrubs (not the faded ones which we were allotted) topped by a wrinkled long white coat with his name in bold red under the hospital's logo. Balancing a stack of papers in one hand and a Styrofoam coffee cup in the other, he was constantly on the move, dashing from one case or meeting to another.

"What've you got?" he asked simply, swiftly rounding the patient, carefully looking, intently listening, his eyes sweeping the room like radar. The consummate clinician, he was constantly gathering and processing information.

"Single stab to the left chest," Bill interjected, trying to sound under control. "He came in with MAST pants and not much for a blood pressure. But it came up to 70 with a couple of liters of fluid. He has marked JVD (jugular venous distention: enlarged neck veins)."

"Not much out when you put the chest tubes in?" Dr. Wilson asked somewhat rhetorically.

"No, just what we have in there now," I said. Not really understanding the implication of his statement.

Dr. Wilson looked down at the practically dry Pleur-evac. Then, apparently having quickly made a decision, continued, "OK, let's get him over to the operating room now," he said, or rather commanded. "Go straight back." There was a momentary pause as we looked up with slightly vacant looks, wondering how he had so rapidly made his decision.

"Now! Let's go! Now." His tone shook us out of our temporary paralysis.

Dr. Wilson briskly left the room.

It had barely been five minutes since he had been wheeled in, and now we were off to the operating room. There was no time to lose if he was to have any hope, and there was only a slim one, of surviving.

The trip was a quick one but unfortunately not straight. It was quite a trick to maneuver the gurney at speed (and no one took this kind of trip slowly) around the 90° bends and narrow doorways, while trying to keep all the necessary life sustaining paraphernalia on the cart, let alone connected. It was amazing that we didn't lose more IVs or other tubes; we did lose some. As he was being whisked back past the front desk, the lavender attired OR team, in their blue-paper head and shoe covers, seamlessly took over as expertly as the passing of a baton during an Olympic relay.

I wrote up a brief history and physical before dashing back with it. Brief is exactly what it was, for we had no lab work back and we never had the chance to get any X-rays. There was just no time. He had no time.

Middle-aged Black male brought in as a Code one by EMS. BP 50. In MAST pants. SW to the left chest. No BP arriving. No verbal response. GCS 8. Breathing spontaneously but labored. Pt. intubated. Sounds decreased on left. JVD. Bilat. L chest tube placed. 50ml gross blood out. BP increased to 70 with 2 L of fluid. To OR, for thoracotomy.

I wanted to see first-hand what they were going to do, even though I knew I wouldn't be scrubbing in, just observing. As a second year, the module was my primary responsibility. I relinquished my note to one of the nurses and hurried back, grabbing a couple of the thin pale blue shoe covers on my way. They stubbornly resisted, then tore as I impatiently stretched them over my blood-soiled shoes. With them half on, I set off briskly if not somewhat uncoordinatedly back to the room, fumbling to put on a cap and mask.

Through the round window of the room's door, I could see that they appeared almost ready to start the case. There was certainly no time wasting. Balancing on one foot, I slipped the remaining shoe-cover on and fumbled into the room.

As I entered I felt as if I had been suddenly caught in the pedestrian rush hour at Grand Central Station. There were countless personnel running around everywhere. Most I did not recognize, but then I was still relatively new, and anyway, they all had masks on. At the head of the table, the anesthesiologist, who already had the patient 'out', was preoccupied explaining ventilator settings and drugs to a resident. He was rattling off names so fast that it sounded more like a commuter railway announcer listing the upcoming stops. It all appeared chaotic, although in reality it was a very controlled and organized chaos.

Dr. Wilson and Bill quickly had the skin of the left chest painted brown with antiseptic then draped it all out in with large disposable blue sheets. One sheet separated anesthesia from their surgical world: the ether screen. Above it was a foreign country for most surgeons, and as such we took little notice of the goings on there.

The scrub tech shuffled around her back table, making sure that she had all the instruments that she could possibly need (a tall order), neatly organized and within reach. It was her job to be ready for anything and everything, for in trauma that's precisely what was needed and expected. In cases such as this, a scrub nurse who 'knew her stuff' was invaluable, if not absolutely indispensable. She had one of the hardest jobs in the room as she attempted to keep pace, often with multiple surgeons. More than anybody, she was responsible for the smooth running of the surgery. They might not always (pretty much never, from what I saw) get the credit, but they certainly got the brunt of the surgeons' wrath for errors or delays. They were expected to be tireless, efficient, knowledgeable mind-readers. Some had worked with particular surgeons long enough that they knew their individual needs and idiosyncrasies. More importantly, they knew how to keep the surgeon calm and on task. Often they would have the instruments ready before they were requested. As all experienced scrub nurses will tell you, they gave you what you needed, which is not necessarily what you might ask for.

With the drapes on, all was ready, and like a conductor getting ready to guide an orchestra through his 'magnum opus', Dr. Wilson rapidly took his place across the exposed painted chest from Bill. The nurse passed the scalpel to Bill's outstretched hand who looked up at Dr. Wilson expectantly.

"OK let's go. Fifth interspace."

Bill began his cut way up towards the left axilla, sweeping it down under the left nipple and following what he hoped was close to the course of the fifth rib. Even with such a huge incision, there was minimal bleeding. This was never a good sign but expected due to the patient's blood pressure still being 'in the toilet'. We were trying to correct this, squeezing in blood and crystalloid as quickly as it became available. I tried to make myself useful, and I took charge of getting the blood in, standing obliquely off the foot of the table, which also allowed me the opportunity to clearly observe the surgery. Bill cut through the intercostal muscles using the electrocautery, stopping only occasionally to coagulate larger perforating vessels as they found renewed strength with the increasing blood pressure (a good sign?). A few seconds later they entered the pleural cavity, the space between the lung and the inside of the rib cage, normally occupied by the inflated lung. The space was filled with some blood but a great deal of clot, collapsing the lung. The chest tube I had just placed in the ER was already clogged and useless. They cut the stitch and removed it.

"Rib spreader," Dr. Wilson commanded, although it seemed more of a statement announcing that the chest was now open.

"Let's get this opened up wide and these clots out of here," he said. Sticking his oversized hands into gap, he helped to pull the ribs apart, while a large, dull, steel rib spreader, scratched from years of use was slipped between the ribs and cranked open.

"Can someone get some light in here. I can't see a damn thing," Dr. Wilson barked.

Bill continued cranking open the chest but had to stop before it was fully open, complaining that there was just too much resistance. We could hear the ribs cracking.

"Extend your incision, damn it," Dr. Wilson told him. Then after a slight pause, just as Bill was about to cut, he added,

"And for God's sake watch out for the mammary, will ya?"

The twin set of internal mammary arteries run along the inside of the rib cage, on either side, a couple of inches away from the sternum (breastbone). They are relatively large and are now preferred by cardiac surgeons to leg veins as a coronary artery bypass conduit.

All I could see from my vantage point, squeezing the saline bags at the foot of the bed, was a bloody great hole surrounded by blood-soaked blue towels. There was blood and blood clots everywhere. Bill inserted his hand and scooped out large dollops of bright red gelatinous clots, which he dumped unceremoniously into large stainless pans. Yet in seconds the chest cavity was full again.

"Let's pack it and check the lung," Dr. Wilson suggested.

Grabbing a bunch of large lap (laparotomy) sponges, Bill shoved them into the abyss of the open chest so they could examine the young, light pink, spongy lung.

Looking over the other screen, seeing the massive amounts of blood and clot being removed, Anesthesia dispatched a medical student to the blood bank to see about the blood. They needed more blood, a lot more blood. He soon returned, but not with good news. There was no more type-specific blood available for our patient. Fortunately, our patient was type AB+, which meant he was a universal recipient and could receive blood of any type. We ended up transfusing him with type B blood and bucket loads (it seemed), such that by the end of the case he had received 26 units.

Bill grabbed a couple more lap sponges in his right hand, and once again began to remove handfuls of clot, as if bailing water from a sinking boat, his left hand holding pressure against a mass of bloody sponges. For the time being, with the mopping up going on and the patient receiving 'buckets' of blood, all seemed to be under some control, although the generalized frenzy in the room had not diminished. Most of the blood appeared to be welling up from behind Bills left hand, an area far behind the heart, naturally the hardest place to get a good look at.

Dr. Wilson grabbed the lung with large triangular shaped Duval clamp that he took from the back table. This is not something that we, mere mortal residents, would ever dream of doing, as we would likely get our hands slapped or 'amputated' by the scrub nurse. Elevating the lung slightly, he manipulated and checked all sides, looking for injury. There was none. Now with the lung retracted, they were able to get a better look at the pericardium and saw a small cut from which flowed a small yet steady stream of blood. Could this be the source of all the bleeding?

The pericardium is a thin, strong, fibrous bag that encases the heart. It normally contains a small amount of clear fluid, lubricating the continually contracting cardiac muscle. His, however, was markedly abnormal, bluish and tense with blood. This prevented the heart from relaxing properly, impairing its ability to fill (cardiac tamponade). No wonder his neck veins were so enlarged.

With all the help both above and below the ether screen, our patient was faring a little better, his blood pressure (albeit with the help of a large amount of fluid, blood, and drugs) had finally risen above 80.

Knowing that the pericardium had been injured, the next question was what was the condition of the heart? We had a pretty good idea that this was where the problem lay. Bill went ahead and made a longitudinal cut into the tense blood-filled sac, making sure to miss the phrenic nerve as it ran along its surface to the diaphragm. The size of the hole in the pericardium was deceiving, as once it was enlarged, all hell broke loose. A jet of bright red blood squirted high through the incision and into the air. Artesian well meets Old Faithful. The dam had busted loose, and the injury was exactly where we (or at least Dr. Wilson) had suspected. It was a stab to the heart or more precisely, to the left ventricle, its main pumping chamber. The injury, naturally, was at the back of the heart, the hardest place to get to, let alone fix. We never did figure out how the cut got to be back there. Now, with every heartbeat, he was losing an amazing amount of blood, as it was forcefully ejected, no longer being partially contained by the pericardium.

I was constantly amazed by how powerful the heart really is. Naturally, it needs to be strong enough to pump blood to the farthest reaches of the body and never takes a break (at least that's the goal). So it shouldn't surprise me that it can squirt blood over our heads and across the room.

Before long, despite heads-down preoccupied, they became aware of their anesthesia colleagues above the ether screen. There was suddenly a frantic increase in activity (never a good sign!).

"We have no blood pressure." A voice cracked with urgency from the head of the table.

"Well, no shit," I thought to myself. "Have you seen the amount of blood coming out?" I wondered how soon more blood would arrive.

There was no response from the two surgeons, and it almost appeared that they had not heard anything as they continued on.

A sustained, tightened wrinkle on Dr. Wilson's forehead revealed to the attentive that the statement had not fallen on deaf ears.

"Just keep on pumping in blood as fast as you can," he finally said, as he dove his hands back into the chest cavity, attempting to stem the bleeding and help get the blood pressure back up.

"He needs volume, lots of volume," he added, his tone clearly escalating in concert with his frustration at having to alter concentration to tell anesthesia what to do.

From my vantage point, I could see that the patient was in trouble, big trouble, as even his cardiac rhythm, represented by the fluorescent green EKG tracing, had become increasingly erratic. I continued to do my tiny part, squeezing the IV bags, pumping in as much fluid and blood as I received. I really wanted to scrub in, but I knew I couldn't, and anyway, there was little I could do that would be of any use. I was far more useful pushing fluid, and I also got to observe, not just the surgeons but the well-orchestrated machinery of the operating room in full battle mode. Luckily the module was staying pretty quiet, and there were no urgent patients to be attended to. I hoped I was good for at least a half an hour or so.

I was riveted to the scene unfolding in front of me and almost had to pinch myself to realize that it was real. This was not a TV show. Here, a patient's life was teetering in the balance. He was trying so very hard to die, yet it was up to the talented hands of the two surgeons to not let that happen. I was nervous yet excited, anxious, and uncertain, curious as to what was going to happen next. I was fixated. What on earth must Bill be feeling? What a crazy responsibility he had. I was immediately struck by the realization that soon it would be me standing under the harsh bright operating room lights, a bloody heart in my hands. Part of me felt exhilarated, yet another part absolutely terrified.

Bill and Dr. Wilson waited with their hands frozen in the chest. They dared not do anything until the patient was more tanked up. He needed more fluid and a great deal more blood. Because of the nature of the injury they had seen, they knew they would lose a lot more when try-ing to repair it. The room remained unusually silent. There was no idle chatter, but after a painfully long few minutes, the tracing on the EKG monitor perked up a little and even began to sound more normal. They had bought some time, and it was time as well as a whole lot more blood that they needed the most if he was to have any chance of making it off the table alive.

Their hands were packed tight against the heart, attempting to stem the loss of the precious oxygen-carrying fluid. I tried to imagine what their hands must have felt like. Every minuscule relaxation of pressure, as they tried to find a more comfortable position, was accompanied by a torrential gush of blood. Their fingers were likely turning white in their bloody gloves, painfully cramping as they held pressure. They just wanted to let go but didn't dare. They couldn't. They held on despite the immense discomfort. Their patient's life depended on it.

Besides Dr. Wilson, Bill, and their scrub nurse, a fourth-year 'stud' had joined their inner sanctum. He was put to work, holding a broad, flat, stainless steel retractor shoved into his hand and then manhandled into position to hold the lung 'gently' out of the way. (After all, isn't that what students and interns are for?) The student, scared to breathe for fear he might move, was working blind, his arms stretched uncomfortably over the edge of the open chest, attempting to maintain his position. He leant back slightly. There was absolutely no room for an extra head.

A few moments later there was a palpable excitement in the room, the background chatter momentarily escalating, as Anesthesia informed us that they were finally able to record a blood pressure, even if only barely. We knew that there was still a very long way to go.

Carefully Dr. Wilson lifted the heart up to see if they could find the exact spot where the injury was. After rotating the heart slightly, they found it: a one-centimeter laceration along the back wall of the left ventricle. This was certainly not an ideal spot for a repair, but then was there ever such thing as an ideal place in the heart to get stabbed? I guess that depended on your point of view. Every time they attempted to expose the injury not only did they get a spurt of blood in the face, but they kinked-off the great vessels, dramatically impairing the heart's ability to deliver blood efficiently. For the 'umpteenth' time, they cleared the blood out of the way so they could attempt to repair the gash. Dr. Wilson looked up at the 'scrub'.

"Let's have a 4-0 non-absorbable suture on pledgets," he commanded.

"Mersilene okay?" the scrub nurse responded.

"Yes. Fine. Let's have it," came a short, preoccupied, and impatient reply.

The scrub nurse carefully slapped the handle of the needle driver into an outstretched hand. The entire room once again fell silent, well, at least silent of human sounds. It was as if a quiet-on-air sign had flashed on the wall, with the only noise remaining being that of the mechanical respirator in concert with the high pitch monotone of the EKG monitor and the coarse, continuous slurping of the suction. It was not long before this magnificent trio was again interrupted.

"We've lost blood pressure again," came an unwelcome voice from above the blood splattered ether screen.

"OK. Let's keep giving fluids," Dr. Wilson responded unemotionally. Then pondering for a second, he continued in a tone as if it was some new revelation, "And keep giving blood. Lots and lots of blood."

Once again the fluorescent green tracing on the EKG had deteriorated to an incomprehensible bunch of squiggles with the occasional normal cardiac trace, as if to remind us of what normal looked like. Tensions mounted, and the expressions on everyone's faces revealed the understanding that we were fighting a potentially futile battle to maintain this man's blood pressure—and life.

A few moments later anesthesia decided to give another update. They spoke to the surgeons still holding pressure, and as if revealing new information, explained that the blood pressure was still zero and how hard they had been trying.

Dr. Wilson had by this time become visibly agitated. They were really testing his patience.

"Please don't keep on telling me the same thing. I heard it all the first time. Just fix it, damn it," he snapped. "He doesn't need any excuses. He needs a damn blood pressure."

Bill was handed a Mersilene suture by the scrub tech.

"Let's be sure and use pledgets," Dr. Wilson told the scrub, or rather reinforced what he had already asked for. Because of the tendency to tear through heart muscle while being tied, small, quarter-centimeter Dacron squares (pledgets), were used to buttress the stitches. Bill attempted to place a suture through a pledget, his hands now visibly shaking. Clearly he was feeling the pressure. With increasingly impatient coaxing, he finally succeeded.

"Here let me put it in from my side," Dr. Wilson said, taking the suture from Bill. "I have a better angle."

Trying to sew the heart was hard enough when it was cooled and slowed as during open heart surgery, but here it was beating hard and squirting what little blood it contained everywhere.

The 'stud' was sucking the blood out of the open chest cavity as fast as he could, trying to keep the field clear. However, in just a few seconds of increased blood pressure and with a couple of cardiac contractions, the chest filled right back up again. Dr. Wilson carefully placed the first stitch into the cardiac muscle himself; he did not tie it, but instead he put a clamp on the suture and continued to the next one. Each suture in turn was clamped, and once they were all in, he began to cinch each down in turn.

With yet another stitch placed, it appeared that things were really coming along. So thought Dr. Wilson, who looked up at anesthesia expecting them to give him an '"Attaboy," as the patient's blood pressure stabilized, but instead his eyes were met by a blank, cold stare followed by the uttering of two spine chilling syllables.

"V-tach," they announced in unison. The words hit everyone in the room like a sledgehammer. Stunned, the whole room appeared to be frozen, like a scene paused by a remote. How was this possible? The wound was repaired (well almost), the bleeding was under better control. So please not now. Not when he was so close.

"Giving Lidocaine," came an almost immediate response from yet another distant voice above the ether screen. There was no answer from Dr. Wilson, who just kept going. There was still some bleeding to deal with, and with the reduction in blood pressure, this was their opportunity.

The proceedings at the head of the patient were reaching fever pitch as the level of tension was only matched by the crescendo of high-pitched chatter.

A few moments later his heart stopped completely, and the EKG tracing went flat (asystole). As soon as that was announced, Dr. Wilson took the heart between his hands and began internal compressions, trying to restore and maintain some circulation. Anesthesia pushed a few more drugs (atropine, epinephrine, and sodium bicarbonate), and there was some response as his ventricle went into fibrillation. This fibrillation is a critical and often fatal cardiac rhythm that arises due the inability of the ventricular muscle to contract synchronously. It would be similar to an orchestra trying to get through a difficult portion of a symphony without a conductor helping the musicians know exactly when to play. This resultant lack of coordination led to ineffective pumping and a lack of effective circulation.

"Get the crash cart," I heard someone say from deep within the huddle around the table. Without asking, the team knew what needed to be done. Momentarily the scrub nursed announced.

"Paddles charging."

"One milligram of epinephrine." Dr. Wilson's voice rose with authority above everyone else, and swiftly a pre-filled syringe of 'epi' was placed in his open palm. He grasped it, looked at it briefly, checking that he had been given what he had asked for and immediately plunged the needle into the quivering myocardium (heart muscle).

"OK. Let's go ahead and defibrillate," he stated, not even raising his head.

The scrub nurse passed Bill the internal paddles, which looked like a couple of long, flattened, wired-up serving spoons. They were placed directly against the heart (hence, internal) as opposed to the more familiar external ones placed on the skin of a patient's chest. The blood was again quickly sucked away as the paddles were adjusted.

"Clear!" Bill announced loudly, his meaning clear: get your hands out of the way or you're going to get zapped when the defibrillator was triggered. He triggered it, the heart responding with a visible jolt. All eyes were on the monitor. The signal on the monitor continued its flat irregular trip across the screen. Our hearts sank as we saw no change. His heart remained in fibrillation.

Anesthesia informed everyone of what we already knew.

"OK. Repeat it," said Dr. Wilson. Once again they went through the identical preparatory steps, and Bill defibrillated a second time. We waited, seemingly forever, but this time we were rewarded as the rhythmical, cyclical, tracing returned to the EKG monitor. Amazingly, he had returned to (a normal) sinus rhythm.

"Good," came the simple monotone response from Dr. Wilson, as he proceeded to get back to the task of completing the ventricular repair. As well as suturing the heart injury, they also had to ligate (tie off) a small branch of one of the coronary arteries that was sliced in two and likely had contributed significantly to the bleeding. Hopefully it was only a peripheral branch that once tied would not cause any major problems.

It was now already way after 6:00, and so reluctantly I returned to the module to prepare for sign out at 6:30. I went over the few new cases with my medical student. I had been fortunate that it had not been too crazy during my time away. I got everything squared away, the only real issue being the patients that I had sent down to OCU. I wanted to get back to the OR and see how things were going, so I went over my list with our module nurse so that she could inform the incoming team.

Not wasting time, I was soon making tracks back to the operating room and bumped into Rick, the fifth-year, 'Visiting Professor', on duty that evening. I explained to him briefly what I had to sign over, as well as the case in the OR, and with little more than a nod, he immediately started to head on back with me.

While away the patient had both arrested and had been successfully 'jump started' (defibrillated) several times. By the time we arrived, things had really started to look up. The cardiac laceration was closed, and he had a recordable blood pressure, and a good one at that.

"Let's get this all closed up and get him up to the unit," I heard Dr. Wilson say as I re-entered. Those few words sounded amazing as they appeared to reverberate around the walls. The relief was palpable. For a second, I thought everyone would break out clapping.

"Would you like some help?" Rick asked, entering the room ahead of me.

"Why don't you scrub in and close so that they can go off and get a bite to eat," Dr. Wilson proposed.

Rick was not thrilled at the suggestion but was always glad to help.

"Sure, I'll scrub in and assist. But if they open the chest, they close it." With that settled, he went off and scrubbed.

I was a little surprised that Rick had just spoken to Dr. Wilson that way. But he knew Rick was right, and as chief resident, he was entitled to his say. Besides, Dr. Wison knew that he needed to support his chief's decisions.

With the pericardium partly closed, they again, and hopefully for the last time, cleared the clots out of the chest and inspected the lung surface. They found a small through-and-through injury, which was bubbling blood with each ventilator breath. Bill quickly oversewed it, making it airtight.

Silently, without fanfare, like two ships passing at night, Rick scrubbed Dr. Wilson out. Closing the chest was all that was left. After inserting a couple of large chest tubes, they reapproximated the ribs and then sutured each muscle layer of the chest together. It looked at this point that he might actually make it. So, once again, I headed back to the module to complete sign-out.

What I had witnessed during the exhilarating last few hours was nothing short of amazing. A miracle of sorts? It was the first time I had seen surgery for a stab to the heart, let alone witnessed someone actually surviving it. There was so much to learn from this case, so much that I needed to store in my memory banks. Once again, the quick decision making by Dr. Wilson had given this patient his real chance for survival. That was the most important lesson: the decision to go and not procrastinate.

Indeed, he did make it. The operation had lasted around two hours, finishing just after 7:00 that evening. He was transferred directly to the surgical intensive care unit (SICU), still in critical condition but stable compared to where he had been a couple of hours earlier. He remained on the ventilator in the SICU for a few days while issues with blood pressure and cardiac arrhythmias were dealt with. Soon he was breathing on his own, eating, and a few days later was discharged. He walked out of the hospital nine days after receiving what would uniformly have been a fatal injury.

Cigarettes Kill

I LOOKED around for some toothpicks to help wedge open my eyes. Immediately I knew that I would regret having gone out for dinner so late the previous evening, even if it was for Mexican. Going out to eat at Xochi's in Mexican Village was always memorable. Beside sleeping, eating was one of a resident's favorite activities. I neither required a meal card nor had to stand in line with my plastic cafeteria tray wondering if I would have time to wolf it down before my pager went off. It was also a chance to wear real clothes. Only on television was it cool to go out wearing scrubs. In the real world, wearing scrubs out would likely result in dismissive glances from other patrons wondering what institution had let you out. This was my chance to be a participant in the real world, so I did not squander my opportunity and took full advantage of the rare night out. Naturally there was a price to be paid. There always was.

In reality, it wasn't so much the lateness of the evening as the earliness of the morning, mixed with some of Xochi's delicious margaritas, which was the real issue. I should have been accustomed to the short nights by this time. I never did.

The incessant, high-pitched buzzing whine of my alarm burrowed its way deep into my brain's auditory cortex. Slowly opening my eyelids, it took a few seconds for the blurry florescent green digits of my clock to become focused. Five, three, zero. Of course, I did not even have to look.

My alarm always went off at 5:30. Every day the same time, yet every day it seemed to arrive just that little bit earlier. I pondered for a few moments in my semi-awake state whether or not I should hit the snooze button. I wished it could be rigged with an electric shock to jolt me to my senses in case I was that foolish. I knew better.

There was only one way to take care of my predicament, and I rolled from my old, lumpy, hand-me-down mattress that had survived medical school and the voyage down from Montreal. I fell a whopping six inches on to the hard, cold, uneven, varnish-peeling floor of my fourth-floor apartment. I dragged myself up, mentally kicking and screaming, fighting the urge to return supine. I wondered what the hell I was doing, while making my way into my tiny bathroom where a rapid reanimating deluge, in my closet-sized, chipped white tile shower, worked wonders at stripping away the stubborn remnants of my sleep deprived lethargy. A shower always did the trick, returning me to at least a semi-functional state such that by 6:00, I was showered, shaved, cerealed, and out the door.

Seconds later I was behind the wheel of my cool (at least, I thought at the time), very dusty, a tad rusty but usually trusty, dark blue Dodge Omni 024, heading down a deserted Jefferson Avenue towards the Medical Center. Not a day went by that I didn't pat myself on the back for having moved to Alden Park Towers an apartment complex on the Detroit River closer to the hospital. I was at least 20 minutes closer than my previous abode on Wayburn, one block off Alter Road, the 'DMZ' between Detroit and Grosse Pointe. This meant at least 40 minutes more sleep, which I rapidly came to appreciate was a most precious commodity. I was between seven and fifteen now minutes away depending on if I hit the lights just right. Not a bad run this day. Only eight.

After exchanging 'greens', I walked into the emergency room still wiping the sleep from my weary and likely bloodshot eyes. I tried my best to look awake; the shower's effect was already wearing off, and adrenaline was not yet kicking in. Most of my fellow residents would, on their watch, be busy downing at least their second cup of coffee by now, but then, I was never the 'Java' type.

Nestled around nursing desk were a listless bunch of nurses, residents, and medical students eager to escape, appearing more like gang members loitering on a street corner than medical professionals. They were all waiting for me. Maybe I should have felt honored. I didn't.

An inner-city trauma ER like ours was always much busier at night and staffed appropriately, so there was always a good crowd waiting for sign-out. They knew that they couldn't leave until it had been completed, but that also meant that occasionally they were quick to leave me with half worked-up patients or ones that weren't worked up at all.

As I made my way past the group, I actually thought I was doing quite well with my attempts to stay awake. This fantasy was soon shattered when I entered the module and was assaulted by the invisible, yet solid as any stone wall, odor barrier. Only those with severely dysfunctional olfactory organs were exempt. "Welcome to 'module one', and hold on to your stomach," it announced resolutely.

Invisible it might have been, but harmless it definitely was not. The putrid mixture of cheap alcohol intermingled with other disagreeable, if not plainly repugnant, biological odors was enough to cause peristaltic reversal in even the most cast iron of stomachs. It was not the best timing, as I was still trying to put the effects of an overindulgent evening behind me.

"This was no place for a sick person to be," I thought, as I fought back another wave of nausea. Sadly, with time, we all became accustomed to the stink. It became just part of the job, part of our everyday environment. Maybe we became immune to the unpleasantness like those who clean out sewers or septic tanks.

The module was packed, crammed with the remnants of a typically busy Friday night. Many had come in much earlier, some even the previous evening—perhaps even during the time I had been digging into my delicious sour cream and white sauce covered chicken chimichangas washed down with divine lime margaritas.

No sooner had I arrived then we started in on our sign-over, parading from bed to bed around the module. We weaved in and out of each curtain cordoned area, a long winding snake of residents and students. The night crew sequentially went over each patient that remained. I started keeping count. Three patients ready for discharge. Good, that's three less that I would have had to worry about.

Soon after we finished 'sign out', a 'medical code blue' was called from our adjoining (medical) module. Never wanting to miss out on some action, we (our team had now evaporated to myself and a medical student) immediately headed over to see what was going on.

We were met with pandemonium. It was so jammed full of people that it looked more like a rugby scrum than any type of medical emergency. There were residents and students swarming everywhere in a frenzy of evidently ineffectual activity. At the center of the chaos was the focus: a man who was suspected of having suffered a subdural bleed and had arrested. The feverish activity continued as the various members of the mob surrounding him took their turn at performing the futile CPR. Slowly, one by one, people peeled away until there were only two remaining, one performing CPR and one ventilating.

Observing the fiasco, my fleeting amusement was rapidly replaced by distain as I wondered why we were torturing this man whose outcome was determined long before he had arrived. Thankfully, after discussion with the family, the futile resuscitation efforts were terminated.

In the end, we all could appreciate the bigger picture and allow him to complete his life's journey.

In surgical training, as with many medical specialties, we are taught to fix people, to cure them, to rid them of disease. Failure is never an option. This, of course, is exactly the attitude you want if you are the one under the knife, and it was repeatedly drilled into us during our surgical education and no more so than at our infamous M & M (morbidity and mortality) conferences. But this causes us to forget or ignore one of the most important parts of medicine and indeed of life: dealing with its end, with death. Not every ailment can be cured, not every injury repaired, and not every patient can have a successful outcome. This is the nature of the frail, unforgiving human shell which we inhabit.

As physicians, we are notoriously poor at dealing with death and end-of-life issues. It is one area where there was little if any formal training. It is the very antithesis of surgery training, yet it is the common denominator of everyone living.

It is okay for us to have tears in our eyes and a lump in our throat when things do not go as planned, we have a bad outcome, lose a patient (a terrible euphemism), or diagnose a terminal disease. It is at these times that a family needs to know that we understand a little of how they feel and are able to empathize with them. But this means that we must allow ourselves the danger of showing emotion and exposing our humanity. The expression of such sentiment is subtly discouraged and suppressed during (surgical) training and for good reason. Emotions frequently lead to poor decision making, which lead to poor outcomes. Therefore, we are trained to keep them in check.

We can learn a great deal from nurses who, due to their more holistic education, are often far better than physicians at discussing end of life issues. Their focus is always to care, even if it does not always mean to cure.

Today was a 'consult' day, and there were an unusually high number of requests for our evaluation and opinion. I switched into overdrive mode in order to juggle caring for my module patients and getting all the consults seen. I spent most of my day running between the medical modules (modules two and three) and down to the OCU to see them all. I spent very little time in my module, which made for a pleasant but busy break. This was possible because I was fortunate to have the help of Dr. Stratton, a pleasant, competent, and always willing ER physician. An in-house trained full-time member of the Department of Emergency Medicine, she helped me with the day's load. There were always patients waiting, some for X-rays or labs, others to be stitched up. Every day was a juggling act, during which we attempted to keep the 'module' patients moving through and at the same time being sure that the consults were seen.

My first two that day were for pancreatitis, both from alcohol use, or rather over-use. The pancreas is an organ that resides deep towards the back of the upper abdomen where it curves over the spine. It hides far behind the lower portion of the stomach, closer to the back than the front of the body. One of its many functions (besides insulin production, for example) is to produce and secrete enzymes in response to food entering the intestine, where it helps to convert it into the absorbable fuel that our bodies need.

Pancreatitis typically causes severe pain, and in metropolitan areas it is most frequently associated with heavy alcohol usage, often binge drinking. It can run the gamut of being mild, getting better after a few days, to much more serious and even fatal.

It is an organ for which we (surgeons) rapidly learn to have the utmost respect. We experience first-hand just how difficult an organ it is to operate on, as well as the significant morbidity and mortality associated with trauma to it. The pancreas can't take a 'joke', we would say, or more frequently, "Don't fuck with the pancreas." We all had experienced patients who, after being admitted with what we thought was straightforward pancreatitis, rapidly deteriorated and succumbed to the ravages of this sometimes-devastating disease.

Both patients were in severe pain, and both also knew their diagnosis: they were 'frequent flyers'. One of them, "Willie", like Danny (page 117), already appeared to have gained elite status being admitted so frequently. We appeared to have become his de facto primary care givers, and he was yet another patient with whose medical record the staff had become intimately familiar. Each time he came in, his pancreatitis tended to be a little more painful, each time a little more serious, and each time he would promise us that he would not drink again. It was a promise he never kept.

He knew the routine. They all knew it. They would need to get the 'nose-hose' (nasogastric tube) before receiving any narcotics for pain relief. Some would even ask, almost beg for it (so you knew they were really hurting). They knew that this was their route to pain relief. As an intern, they would try to con you into giving them narcotics without the tube. "Oh Doc, Doctor so-and-so says I just need the medicine and I'll be ok." This might work when as novices, we had not dealt with the 'urban pancreatitics.' However, we soon learnt, as our seniors let loose on us and the Attendings on them. (Remember: shit always flows downhill, and we were at the bottom.) The experienced knew how to get what they wanted out of the newbie interns.

The pain was so severe that patients would go to almost any length to obtain relief, even going as far as placing their own NG tube. Lying in a hospital bed for a week or more with a plastic tube stuffed down your nose was no holiday, and it could drag on for much longer in more resistant cases. They rarely complained when this was their avenue to obtain pain relief. Moreover, they had a warm clean bed to sleep in, caring nurses to look after them, and even a functioning TV to watch!

Each attack did incremental, irreversible damage to the organ from which some failed to recover. The majority of our patients never posed much of a diagnostic dilemma, for they would frequently offer up, "Doc I got my panc-ritis (or something similar sounding) again." Invariably they knew the signs, and almost all of the time were right on with their self-diagnosis.

Between extra-modular excursions, I needed to check back and keep tabs on the goings-on in the module, which was always my primary responsibility. I needed to know about every new arrival. Dr. Stratton was a lifesaver, allowing me to efficiently deal with all my responsibilities.

The one consult that we all dreaded, although detested was perhaps more accurate, were those for GI bleeds. They were always sick, messy, and time-consuming. Messy, literally 'bloody' messy, was an understatement. As surgical residents we are not supposed to be put off by a little blood or even a lot of blood, and for the most part we weren't. But the GI bleeder, well, that was altogether a distinctly (and not in a good way) different beast. Patients came in vomiting large, sometimes massive amounts of 'altered' blood (blood that has been sitting in the stomach for a while and degraded by gastric acid). But it never just ended there. That would have been just too easy. As the GI tract has two openings, it was not long before the blood, which is a very effective cathartic, continued on its way through to the colon, mixing with stool and resulting in a forceful, almost explosive, evacuation at the other end.

This combination of vomited blood and blood mixed with excrement is an onslaught on the senses not soon forgotten. In these patients, the odor, the gut-wrenching stink, is so hideous that we could smell the patient long before we were ever officially consulted.

Just like with the pancreatitics, overindulgence in alcohol was the most frequent cause for these 'bleeders'. Our first priority was to determine if they were still bleeding. This involved placing a larger-than-normal tube, only just a touch smaller than a garden hose, down into the stomach to wash out the clots, while transfusing and correcting electrolyte abnormalities. We poured in 'clean' odorless, blood, and just as fast, the dark, foul-smelling, concoction poured out. It was frequently futile.

Not everyone we took to surgery required a cut, as in my next patient. Although complaining of chest pain, this young man was triaged to our module after saying that he had swallowed a needle. His story was that after he had 'shot up' (injected drugs), he placed the needle between his teeth while deciding to attend to a commotion outside the door of his apartment. During the ensuing discussion (shouting), he realized that the needle was no longer between his teeth but had been sucked into his lungs. An X-ray soon corroborated his concern. The sooner we got it out, the better. It was not too busy, and because of Dr. Stratton's help, my day chief offered me the case.

The clear plastic endotracheal tube that anesthesia had slipped between his vocal cords was our access to the recesses of his lungs. It was large enough that the patient could still be ventilated while we were passing and manipulating the 6mm-diameter, flexible bronchoscope into his lungs. I gently advanced the pencil thin endoscope with my left hand, my right manipulating the controls, while looking through an eyepiece. Slowly, millimeter by millimeter, I progressed until the needle came into sight, its reflecting metallic needle body toward me while its pink colored hub lay further down the bronchus. It was backward, the way it had been in his mouth when aspirated. I threaded a flexible biopsy forceps down the tiny 'working' channel of the bronchoscope, until I could see its jaws. Our scrub nurse controlled the jaws, closing them on my request (unlike modern endoscopy suites, there was no video screen for the nurse to observe), but our timing failed us, and we missed on multiple attempts. The needle would move in one plane with every respiration and then more rapidly in another, counting out each heartbeat like a metronome. After finally grabbing it, we just needed to pull it out without losing it. Slowly, I first pushed to release it, then I pulled it out as I withdrew the bronchoscope. I felt a little like I had landed a prize fish, and it was even sweeter as I did so without having to ask for help from my chief, who stood quietly (and patiently) by. Hopefully the patient would think twice (even once would do), the next time he was overcome with an urge to stick a needle in his mouth.

I must not have heard the next code when it was initially called overhead, for it was actually the smell that first got my attention as I headed back from the operating room.

What was that smell? My nostrils flared slightly as they registered their first whiff. It was vaguely familiar. It was a smoky, almost sweet smell, which at first escaped all my attempts to place it. It smelled somewhat reminiscent of barbecue, but then, that would be impossible, for the cafeteria was far away. My subconscious recognized the smell, yet somehow it knew that I did not want to. It was not a bad smell, but it was definitely out of place here. In a restaurant I would be tempted to inhale deeply, allowing it to linger on my taste buds, savoring it. But no, not here. It was not right to smell this here. I followed the smell (I might even say, aroma, until I discovered its origin) to its source: the resuscitation room.

Once I discovered the source and the visual and olfactory cues made their neurochemical connection deep in my brain, it no longer generated a pleasant response. Actually, it was awful. It was the pungent, nauseating, smell of burnt human flesh.

Burns, especially severe ones, were a frequent occurrence. Some were accidental and some intentional. Some were caused by the victim and some by others.

When I could finally part the crowd that had congregated, I was able to get a better view of our victim. He barely looked human, more like a heavily made-up character from a *Night of the Living Dead* movie. It was almost too unreal to be sad.

At first glance I could see that his entire left arm, which was protruding at an awkward 90-degree angle to his body, was black, charred, shrunken, and stiff. It was burnt all the way back to his shoulder. I looked at his hand. Well, there was no hand, at least not a real one, just charred bones, a skeleton of wrist and fingers, white knuckles protruding through the remnants of charred skin. On his forearm, a few fragments of cooked flesh still hung on tenaciously, resembling pieces of overdone steak. Virtually all the skin had been incinerated, the fat boiled away, vaporized, leaving only a few areas of underlying muscle that had been scorched to a crisp.

The only semblance of recognizable structure was far up on his upper arm. Here there was actually some intact skin, although what was left was deeply burnt. This continued onto his shoulder and did not stop there, as it involved the entire left side of his face. There was little blistering separating the left from the right side of his face; it just went from dead to live. It was an eerie dichotomy; the right side of his face appeared to be normal, whereas his left side was completely paralyzed, dead—charred flesh adherent to burnt discolored bone. Where a left eye should have been, there remained only an empty burnt-out socket. There was not even an eyeball remnant. He was truly a real-life 'Phantom'.

Despite this devastating injury, that went from bad to worse the closer we looked, it was truly amazing that he was alive at all. Yet he was. He was alert and responded to our questions, and not once did he complain of pain. But how could he not be in excruciating pain? I thought, my eyes scanning his body. His entire left flank extending down to his hips had fragments of burnt clothing still attached to the underlying 'cooked' fat layer. There was no skin there either.

It was strangely surreal to have someone answer questions with just half a face, and I almost had to pinch myself as he spoke to remind me that this was real.

This is real! Get over it. Quit staring and do something. Figure out what you are going to do about it. My inner monologue was giving me a good dressing down, forcing me to focus on what was important. But the smell, was so overpowering, and it had attracted, as these things always tended to do, a significant crowd of gawkers, who paraded through as if at a wake or a circus sideshow. I slammed the doors; we needed to focus.

He had been found lying on the burnt remnant of a mattress in an otherwise empty room in a crack house following a fire, not too far from the hospital.

He remembered injecting a drug concoction (what it actually was, he did not recall) and lighting a cigarette. We concluded that as he got 'high', the cigarette must have slipped from his relaxed fingers, lighting the mattress. Surprisingly neither the blistering heat nor the charbroiling of his arm down to the bone woke him, and he only 'came to' once the drugs had begun wearing off and help had arrived.

Closing the resuscitation room doors had minimal effect, and the crowd in the room continued to swell despite all our requests. In the end we were too busy and the patient too sick for us to worry about it. Most had come out of morbid curiosity more than from any intent to help. There was not much more that we could do here, so once we had blood drawn and IVs in, we wrapped his exposed burns in saline-soaked, coarse 'burn' gauze and made arrangements for his transfer to the burn unit. I didn't envy the intern on 'burns' that month, as we knew that this guy would be a lot of work, keeping the intern busy for the rest of the day, the night, tomorrow, and for the foreseeable future. Although the patient seemed fine now, we knew his future was bleak. No matter how hard anyone tried, without the skin's protective barrier, bacteria would invade, and overwhelming infection would take over. The odds were impossibly stacked against him.

At a minimum, he would need an amputation of his left arm, probably even the shoulder. But then what? Where do you stop? The face? The cheek? The eye? They were also all gone or dead.

As with most patients transferred out of the ER, we heard little follow-up afterwards. Once in a while we might receive snippets of information from the Plastics or burn resident when our paths crossed.

A few weeks later at our weekly Saturday morning M & M, this same unfortunate man was presented by the Plastics fellow who was the chief on the burn service at the time. This Fellow was universally liked by all of the Attendings, having graduated from our general surgery program the year before. I had first met him when I came to interview, and it was his infectious enthusiasm for the program that encouraged me to rate it high on my match ranking. It appeared to us that he walked on water and could do no wrong.

"This poor man underwent numerous surgeries, some extensive," he summarized "including amputation of his entire left upper extremity and extensive facial reconstruction." By projecting a picture of the terrible injuries onto the auditorium's large screen, he had everyone's undivided attention. He was part surgeon, part showman, and reveled in the spotlight. "In the end, when in the burn unit ICU, he unfortunately, sustained a cardiac arrest, and while he was being shocked, his dressings caught on fire. After continuing for a while, the code was called." He then went on to add somewhat flippantly, "He appeared to succumb to recurrent disease."

The audience, who had stayed 'pin drop' silent up to that point, broke out in a combined subdued chuckle. At the podium he managed to keep a straight poker face, and there was no further discussion or questions from the stern faced, front-row seated critics. He had once again side-stepped what would, for the rest of us, have been a prolonged and painful interrogation.

Of course, his statement was only partly true. The unfortunate man was already dead when in full cardiac arrest prior to catching fire during the attempted resuscitation. Sometimes our flippancy is just our way of trying to deal with a terrible situation, in this case an injury whose outcome was sealed the moment the cigarette ignited his mattress.

Within our hospital we were lucky (or unlucky—it really depended on your perspective) to have a full-fledged burn unit that accepted all comers, burns of all severities, both from our own ER and especially from other hospitals.

We (the surgical residents) all had to rotate through the unit during our first year. Although it was never rated as one of the more favored rotations, it was certainly memorable, if not highly educational. It was a busy, tough, unforgiving, and frequently sleepless four weeks. This was not so much because the work itself was difficult as it was the stress of dealing with the suffering patients, compounded by the fact that we had absolutely no idea what we were doing. The hours did not help. We were there day and night. We moved in at the beginning of the month-long rotation and moved out at the end. We were the doctors in the specialized burn unit, the 'experts'. In reality, we were ignorant interns who knew next to nothing about burns . . . at least we thought so (and for the most part we were absolutely right). We were learning, or supposed to be learning, from our nonexistent more senior resident.

The senior burn resident was a Plastics fellow and was rarely around—pretty much never. They did not go into Plastics to do burns. None of the 'Plastics guys' did. They hated burns, and that sentiment was not lost on us as they also were just doing their mandatory time. They wanted to be in the operating room doing 'fun' surgeries. The burn unit was a chore, never a priority.

As always, we were saved by the nurses, from whom we learnt the majority, if not all, of our burn care. There was no one else. This was nothing new, for in all our rotations we learnt so much from them. But nowhere was this truer than in the burn unit, where they were the real de facto experts. They showed us how to dress wounds, what type of dressings to use, and when and where to use them. As much as we perhaps did not enjoy it, burn care education was an integral part of our surgical training. But it was more than just burns and wounds, as we learnt reams about caring for the critically ill patients in our dedicated burn unit ICU.

Dealing with patients with the massive burns was minor compared to the heart-wrenching sadness of caring for the screaming burnt kids. Rounding and caring for them all day every day was both depressing and uplifting, as we watched young kids, some with massive burns, express their relentless fighting spirit to never give up. The survivors, however, were often left severely disfigured both physically and mentally

But where was the Attending? You might well ask. They were even more invisible than our aloof chiefs. They showed up for a few minutes a day to do rounds, really just to pimp us and to make us feel like crap for being so ignorant and dragging them away from what they would rather be doing, which was essentially anything else.

It was a residency within a residency. There was so much to learn and not just about burns. It was a practical education in physiology and what occurs when the protective barrier of skin, which we all take for granted, was violated or absent. What fluid to give? How much fluid to give? Should we give crystalloid? Should we add colloid? This was the biggie, as in the burn unit we used buckets of albumin, yet on other rotations we would be 'hung, drawn, and quartered' for even considering it. The rotation involved very little of what we would really term surgery. What we usually had to deal with were burn wound excisions (a literally 'bloody ugly' procedure), where the top layer of burnt nonviable tissue was removed in thin layers down to healthy bleeding tissue. This was then followed by skin grafting of an extremely thin sheet of non-burned skin, which was secured over the excision site.

Burn surgeries were always bloody, requiring frequent blood transfusions, and because of the loss of the skin's normal thermal barrier, there was tremendous heat loss. Consequently, the burn unit's dedicated operating room was always kept really hot, dripping sweaty hot. At the end of any case, we were all so drenched in sweat that we appeared to have showered in our scrubs. But this 'in unit' operating suite meant that we did not have to transport these sick patients to the main operating rooms, even for the occasional more extensive surgery.

The next day, Sunday, was my day off.

L & L

DAY 10 —"Where the hell's our replacement?"

Those few endearing words were my greeting as I turned the corner to enter 'module one' on Monday morning. The module was full—bristling, busting-at-the seams full. The words hit me like a sledgehammer. There was no good-morning-it's-great-to see-you. It was all business. I took a quick glance around and understood a little better the sentiment, for not only was it full, but there were beds doubled up in many of the single patient spaces. There were patients everywhere, every available space was occupied, even the hallways were backed up with carts. I needed to get my game face on and switch into high gear right away. There would be no warming up today. What the hell went on last night? I wondered. It looked like the aftermath of a true battle.

Next to the nursing desk stood one of our emergency medicine residents, who had been doing her stint of 'nights'. She looked drained, her long black hair rumpled, forehead sweaty, and there was even a hint of discolored bags drooping beneath her exhausted young eyes.

"Let me show you around so I can get out of here," she said, always one to get straight to the point and apparently not one to hang around, either.

"Let's wait till everyone is here," I replied, curbing her misplaced enthusiasm but mainly realizing that there was no point in starting until everyone who had information (i.e., the entire team) was present. I knew she was frazzled and wanted out, but she certainly did not know the scoop on all the patients, which is what I needed.

Once everyone showed up, we began rounds, the morning parade of information exchange. We worked our way around the module, and I took note of the 'damage' that I would need to deal with. As if revealing a prize, a green dividing curtain was pulled back, and then each subsequent patient was presented. Behind which curtain, I wondered, would the next disaster be lurking, waiting to bite me, if I didn't remain vigilant?

When working 'days' in the trauma module, it was critical to pace ourselves and not get behind. After all, I was it. This was confirmed by a small blackboard outside the module that listed the personnel for the day. There, the words 'Maxwell's House' were chalked up; the staff was trying to add a little humor as it announced that, indeed, this was my module that day. Perhaps not exactly 'the buck stops here', but that was certainly the way it felt. Part of me was proud, yet another part just wanted to go and wipe it off, as it definitely did nothing to alleviate my already elevated stress level. Sure, sometimes I might have a student to help out with suturing lacerations and other 'grunt' work, but the decision-making and the responsibility was still all mine. Basically, it meant that my ass was on the line, perhaps even my place in the program, if I screwed up.

On the left, just inside the now faded once white melamine half wall that separated the module from the nursing desk, one of the first years from 'nights' hurriedly took the lead and began presenting, speaking as if the patient directly in front of us was hidden behind a clear soundproof screen. This was the classic way patients were presented during rounds at teaching institutions. Inadvertently, sometimes they were treated as if they were not really there or certainly did not understand what was being said about them.

It began: "This is a 27-year-old man who sustained gunshots to the left shoulder and left leg." His tone was slow, monotonous, as if he was ordering from an uninteresting menu that he knew by heart. But wait. This man just got shot! Shouldn't we all be a little more animated? Our presenter was tired, exhausted after a crazy night. He was ready to go home and gave us the information deadpan, Sgt. Joe Friday style ('just the facts'). He did not give us much in the way of details, but as I found out later, the man had been in a fight with his 'good friend' and had exchanged shots on the street outside his house. Fortunately, neither were marksmen, but then they didn't need to be to cause serious injury.

"The slug went in high in his left shoulder and is lodged posteriorly, almost in the middle of his back. His first chest X-ray was perfectly normal," he added.

Another lucky escape. But what about the other bullet?

As if reading my thought, he continued. "His left leg sustained the full force of a second bullet, which went through and through the calf."

While he was talking, we pulled his sheets back. His calf was bleeding profusely, and dark blood was rapidly seeping through the thick layers of gauze bandages. We took these down to examine the leg. The bullet had struck the soft tissues of his left calf, causing it to swell massively. There, on the swollen, shiny, and very tense upper medial calf was a dark red, oozing, circular entrance wound surrounded by a small circle of discolored, darkened skin. His pain increased exponentially with just the slightest upward bending of his foot. Once again, the mind-reading intern was way ahead of us.

"Dr. Ledgerwood came by with Keith (the night chief), and they are taking him as soon as possible for a fasciotomy."

Well, that takes care of that one, I thought. Wrong! The 'shit' was only just warming up.

During a fasciotomy, two extensive longitudinal incisions are made, one on either side of the leg, and through each of these, two deeper incisions are made to release the pressure building up in the four calf compartments. These swollen muscles, under internal pressure from the injury and bleeding, bulge through the incisions like rapidly rising bread dough, but now with the pressure released, perfusion is reestablished. It may look ugly, but it's a small price to pay to keep a leg.

Before being released to go to the operating room, a true upright chest film (as opposed to the first one, which was performed supine) was obtained, which revealed that the bullet had, not surprisingly, left him with a souvenir from its destructive journey through the chest. The night team had placed a chest tube for the resultant collapsed lung.

Dr. Ledgerwood, the attending from the previous night, was in a pretty foul mood that morning, which wasn't all that unusual. She appeared constantly unhappy with things here in the module. As we later discovered when we had a couple more years under our belt, this apparent dissatisfaction was orchestrated mainly for our benefit. We were never to become complacent enough to think that what we had done was good enough. There was always another level that she expected from us, and she believed it was her duty to make sure that we got there. Luckily, she was not upset with me (so I thought) for a change but with the shambolic state that the module had been left in from 'nights' with so many patients having not even been seen.

As far I was aware, the patient in the first bed, waiting for the fasciotomy, was ready to go, except that an X-ray revealed his chest tube was not in far enough. I rapidly adjusted it, making sure the last hole was now in the chest, and yet another X-ray confirmed it. Everything was good. But was it?

Not long after, Dr. Ledgerwood stormed through the module wondering what was delaying her patient. She also had been up all night operating. I knew that the nurses were getting him ready, so I went to tell her that the chest tube was now confirmed to be in a good position. She appeared deaf to my statement (a common practice of all Attendings interacting with us lowly residents) and not the least bit interested in what I had to say. She began shouting, first at the nurses and then at me, demanding to know why the patient was not already in the operating room and telling me in no uncertain terms to get the patient there right away. I was in midtrack, halfway between another patient and nursing desk when Dr. Ledgerwood began walking out of the module, stopping when she saw that it was the nurses bringing the patient, not me.

"Well, Dr. Maxwell, it looks like I'll just have to take the patient myself if you can't do it."

I'm not really sure what that was all about, except that she obviously was not having the best of days (and it was not even 7:00 a.m.). Yes, of course I could take the patient over just as well as the nurses or anybody else. Did it really matter who did it as long as it was done? Of course not. This was just another way for our Attendings to demean us, which many loved to do in front of the nurses. Besides, I also had a module full of patients to take care of, and Lord knows I would hear about it (from her especially!) if they weren't. I knew that this was no time for excuses, so I dropped what I was doing and lent a hand to the nurses as they began wheeling the patient over to the OR. If you did not keep them (the Attendings) happy, there was no recourse, and it just made the rotation unbearable. For some it became their signal to look for another profession. This was no different from being dressed down by the platoon sergeant during basic training. It never had to make sense. There was only ever one acceptable answer: Yes, Doctor. This surgical 'boot camp', however, lasted two years rather than six weeks. Its effects, however, good and bad, would last a lifetime.

She may have been an excellent surgeon, but along with her partner, Dr. Lucas, they were two of the hardest surgeons to please. Not that it was necessarily our job to please them, but it was certainly in our best interest to learn as much as we could from them and preferably with the least amount of pain. However, they were two of the best teachers, so perhaps in a strange self-flagellating sort of way, we wanted to please them.

Of all the Attendings that we worked with, these particular two devoted the greatest amount of time to resident education, yet it was not always in the most endearing fashion. In the operating room there were none better. She was a superb technician and a gifted teacher. If she was having a good day (which seamed rare to us), then she was a delight to scrub with.

She was one of only a few female trauma surgeons at 'Receiving'. Nationally she was renowned for her work in surgical trauma care, and locally she was known as someone not to be messed with and certainly never to be crossed. Standing around five and a half feet tall, she had a slight build with a mop of curly grey hair that gave her an air of experience beyond her years. She had a penchant for brightly colored jackets (especially red) and walked with a characteristic wide gait swagger, as if she was returning from a gunfight at the O.K. Corral (and that was what it felt like to us).

When she spoke, all listened. She was a woman of few words except after a glass or two of wine. If, on rounds, she agreed with your proposed plan, she would respond with a simple slow and monotone, "G . . . o . . . o . . . d." This came out almost like a New Yorker (although she was actually from the north-west) trying to imitate a Texan and was as close to a compliment as you would ever get. If she did not completely agree, but yet you were not necessarily wrong, she would simply say, "Oh . . . Kay," the letters O and K strung out with at least a couple of seconds between them.

Her style of speaking, especially to her to patients, was so unique that we frequently found ourselves subconsciously (or even consciously) copying her expressions and mannerisms. Maybe it is true that imitation is the highest form of flattery.

Many attendings at that time allowed the chief resident on their rotation to operate at night unsupervised but not Dr. Ledgerwood. She could always teach you something, and she knew it. She realized that you were there to learn and that she was there to teach and as such took her vocation very seriously, even if it meant she had to forgo her sleep. But that meant she was not so much fun or forgiving the following day!

To this day I still recall performing my first splenectomy for trauma with her. (Splenic salvage was not yet mainstream and certainly not for the types of injuries that we routinely saw.) It was late in my second year, and she really came down on me like a ton of bricks for being so slow and indecisive. This was my first splenectomy, but that would have not made any difference, as excuses were not tolerated. I learnt quickly not to dawdle, not to be indecisive. Expeditious and efficient, yet careful and calculated, that's what she taught me.

She had a reputation amongst all of us for being able to do an entire operation as the assistant, yet all the while making us feel like we had done it on our own. But then I guess that is the job of all good teachers. This was 1985, and still the days of the long incision open cholecystectomy (gallbladder removal). She would cleverly dissect out the gallbladder anatomy with the thin-tipped surgical sucker, letting us take the credit. (She could probably write volumes on 'Surgery with the Sucker'.)

Laparoscopic Cholecystectomy did not really become mainstream until the early- to mid-1990s, after I had entered practice.

She worked with her more senior partner, who had also been her Attending when she came through the same program a number of years earlier. Dr. Lucas, her 'pardner', as she called him in her pseudo-Texan drawl, was also a nationally known figure on the trauma scene and was likewise both respected and feared by all. Tall, trim, and silver haired, he was almost always to be found dressed in a somber but smart blue three-piece suit. He was known amongst us all as the 'Grey Fox'. His presence in a room instilled fear and respect in those that knew him and soon it would in those who didn't. He had the characteristic surgical ego and would not waste his time or breath talking or explaining something to anybody who he did not believe to be worthy of his efforts. Doing just one case with him, no matter how simple it might be, would make you feel as if you had just completed the most intricate of brain surgery marathons. You were mentally exhausted, tired from the constant pimping, yet much more knowledgeable for the experience.

Whereas Dr. Ledgerwood wielded the sucker, Dr. Lucas was the master of the 'right angle' clamp. He would single handedly perform the cases as the assistant using his favorite 'right angle', carefully dissecting the tissue and then encouraging the resident surgeon to make the cut using the electrocautery where he guided. Sure, we made the cut. But he showed us where.

Still to this day I use this method of dissection, now showing my assistants where to cut. Some habits never die.

When we rotated on their service, every Sunday morning, after rounds we would spend a couple of hours in a remote corner of the cafeteria for a teaching session with Dr. Lucas. This usually involved a topic that had been brought up on rounds sometime during the week. It was never easy, and he would never let us get away with not knowing an answer to a question, but, nevertheless, we constantly learnt. We were expected to research and present a particular topic. Being up all night and constantly tired was never a reason to be unprepared. It was only an excuse, and excuses were just not tolerated.

Almost 30 years later, I can still vividly recall an emotionally laden Sunday morning presentation that I gave on 'Crush Syndrome'. The fear of failure and ridicule is so etched in my memory that even now I can remember my presentation and the specific citations that I referenced.

Similar resident teaching sessions garnered the spotlight at an annual Detroit Trauma Symposium, where a lighter version, no less intimidating, would take place under the heading, "You're in trouble now."

While most attending staff allowed us a little leeway in the day-to-day management of their patients, this duo did not. With 'L & L' everything had to be done exactly their way. There was no compromise; their way was the only way. They became our 'gold' standard.

They tended to go against the grain of more conservative and established teachings, but they always had scientific research and data to support their approach. Their methods relied on science rather than dogma.

It seemed at the time that they were rough on us, and without a doubt they were, but in the end, everyone was a winner. Our patients received only the very best of surgical care, and we, as their residents, received a superb and unmatched apprenticeship, enough to last us a lifetime of practice. Most importantly we learnt to question everything and to make sure there was data to support everything we did. Our residency supplied us with the solid foundation for our continuing education and maintenance of high technical and ethical standards.

Not every resident in the program had the opportunity to rotate on their service. During my time we had two main surgical services at the trauma hospital that were responsible for all surgical admissions on alternate days. Although I might have felt that I had received the short end of the straw, as those assigned to the opposite service were relieved that they had escaped the wrath of Drs. L&L, really it was both the residents and their future patients who had missed out. Residency was not about having it easy but about learning as much as we could in the short time (it seemed forever at the time) that we had.

However, it was not all so terrible as after rotating on their service, they would take their entire team out to dinner. This would involve a trip across (or then, usually under) the Detroit River to the wonderful French restaurant, La Cuisine, in Windsor, Ontario (this was in the days when you didn't have to hand over your first born to cross the border into Canada, let alone return). It was their way of thanking us for a job well done and to tell us that the 'torture' we endured was not personal. Yet at the time, it was still hard to believe that it wasn't. These were wonderfully evenings, a chance to see the other side of our mentors, the side that liked good company (now that might be a little presumptuous!), good food, and wine. They actually were human, and once the wine began flowing, which it usually did prodigiously, they loosened up and began recounting fascinating stories, most of which involved our predecessors. Besides entertaining, it had the psychological effect of making us feel a little better about many of our own blunders.

Band-Aids and Grinders

FINALLY I was signed over a man who, at first glance, appeared to be resting peacefully. In any other location, one could perhaps envision him taking an afternoon siesta after a particularly satisfying meal. But not here. First, the food was just not that great, and the blood-stained bandage wrapped turban style around his head appeared to signify that he was here for something more than just a nap. Only after removing his bandage could I appreciate the extent of his injury. A large irregular laceration snaked across his forehead from just above his left ear to above the bridge of his nose.

Luckily, Sam, one of the interns from 'nights', graciously volunteered to stay and fix the man's scalp. He was a tremendous help, and it allowed me the time to get properly caught up and not bogged down and even further behind before the day had even begun. Sam's conscientiousness meant the difference between staying ahead or getting uncontrollably behind.

But then Sam was always helpful, always willing to lend a hand. Later I had the pleasure of having him as my junior resident, and he was no different then, always arriving early, getting his work done, and then jumping in to help his fellow residents with theirs. It was just what he did; he was a wonderful all-round team player.

During rounds, it was mentioned that there was one patient who had not yet been seen. We were informed that he had been dumped off at the door without any obvious injury. He was intoxicated and couldn't give a history, but his vitals were fine. We would see to him in due course, or so I thought.

Keith, the night chief was still back in the OR when I first had arrived, finishing up operating on a couple of patients who had decided to have a knife duel with each other and ended up with deep penetrating abdominal wounds, so now they both ended up under the surgeon's knife. He still had the fasciotomy to do. I could understand now why Dr. Ledgerwood was in such a foul mood that morning. She had been up all night, and unlike many Attendings at the time, she scrubbed in on every case. She was rightfully exhausted.

At the far end of the module, I spied Dr. Mitchell gazing ruefully at a patient that the night team had called him to see. The poor fellow had a severe head injury, for which we could do nothing more. Rick Mitchell was tall, slender, and prematurely balding, having only a few wisps of dark hair ineffectually attempting to cover an otherwise barren scalp. Soft spoken, highly intelligent, and knowledgeable, we had the good fortune of having him as our neurosurgical chief resident. He had a habit of responding to questions with an inquisitive lifting of an eyebrow and an almost sinister 'Jack Nicholson' style grin. Yet under this tough facade was a calm, confident, reassuring physician. We loved it when he was on call, as no matter what the case or how busy he was, he always found time to share some of his abundant knowledge with us.

"Hey, Nick, what have you got here?" he asked, half glancing towards me, as he looked at the chart. Instantly up went the inquisitive left eyebrow.

"A real mess, but a good neurosurg consult," I replied. But then was there ever a bad neurosurgery consult? We didn't think so. In general, the more we could get others involved, the more it took the pressure off us.

"Looks like it. What happened?" Rick inquired, as he ambled towards me, never one to complain about extra work.

"He got refused a refund." I continued the banter, knowing how much Rick liked a good story.

"Refund? On what?" inquired Rick, clearly now much more attentive. I relayed to him the story that had been told to me only 20 minutes earlier.

"This guy had bought some crack, but after deciding that it was not any good, he tried to return it to the crack house and get his money back. I guess no one told him that they weren't giving out refunds that day. Instead, he got more crack. This time, right across his head."

The man in question appeared perhaps only in his early 20s, darkly tanned, facial features camouflaged by multiple streaks of dried blood radiating down from his scalp. On closer inspection, he had more of an olive complexion, and under the bandage that covered his head wound, thick curls of black hair snuck out, matching a thick bristly mustache.

A few minutes later, while I was working on another patient, Rick returned and caught my attention. "Want to see his CT scan? It's a beaut."

"Sure, I'll be a few moments," I replied, as I finished up evaluating a man who had been assaulted and was still waiting to have his skull and facial films taken.

Now images can be viewed on our desktop monitors. There's no need to dash off to X-ray. But this advance in clarity and convenience comes at a price. Gone are the days of X-ray rounds and the educational benefit of reviewing films with a radiologist, who themselves have been relegated to a dark, hard to find, dungeon, where sunlight has been replaced by the hypnotizing light of computer screens.

Terminology has also evolved, and X-ray departments have morphed into Medical Imaging Departments (although X-rays are still used to produce the majority of the images evaluated). We can now look at CAT scans at different angles and even in three dimensions. It might only take a few minutes to complete an entire scan, yet frequently it takes significantly longer to decipher what it means and what to do. Technology has not yet replaced the physician. At least not yet.

After leaving my charge in the radiology line, I caught up with Rick, whom I found in the viewing room contemplating the CT scan of the man who had failed to get a refund. Leaning back slightly, slowly massaging his chin, he scrutinized the films. He looked like a Renaissance artist evaluating his recently completed masterpiece.

"Take a look at this," Rick said, as I stood behind him, looking over his shoulder. "It's a real mess. A miracle he's alive at all." He tapped his index finger on the films, highlighting the areas of concern.

I was no expert at reading CAT scans, but then I didn't need to be. The large gaps in the skull made it pretty obvious, even for a novice. There were fractures everywhere, as well as a collection of blood inside the skull. Rick explained that instead of taking to him to the operating room, they were going to watch him, as surgery would likely not help but could easily make things much worse.

My next task was to get him stitched up. After removing the bandage and washing off all the dried blood, I was able to get a better look. The back of his scalp was crisscrossed with dozens of full-thickness lacerations. Before I could fix him, I took a razor and shaved off all the hair in the area. His scalp now looked like the shell of a dropped hard-boiled egg. Just to make it a little extra easy for me, he decided at about that same time that he was not going to stay still anymore, and he attempted to sit up every time I approached him with a needle. When I finally had him all closed up, it had taken me much longer than the half hour I had estimated, as well as a few yards of nylon thread. Even so, after seeing his CT scan, I seriously doubted if he would ever be normal again.

While concentrating on the scalp jigsaw puzzle, my attention was diverted by my nurse who nervously explained to me that she was concerned about the patient two beds down. Although on arrival he seemed fine, she explained, now no matter how hard she tried, she could not rouse him and was having trouble even getting a blood pressure. In almost the same breath, she let me know that a woman who had been waiting for hours to be discharged was now complaining of severe abdominal pain. As I continued stitching the cracked scalp back together, I kept one eye on the nurse getting vitals on the guy in the corner bed.

"What's his blood pressure?" I asked, clearly seeing that she was now becoming more flustered. "Can you get one?"

"I can't really get anything," came the almost expected reply.

"Pulse?"

"Very weak. Rapid."

I was trying to juggle all the information coming in. I had the scalp three quarters sewn up, still trying to figure out how to put the last part together. But what about this other guy? Prioritize, prioritize. Was there something going on with the man in bed one that we had overlooked? Truthfully it was hard to say that we had overlooked anything, as no one had even looked at him.

"How does he look?" I asked.

"Not good," came the simple, rapid reply. Her tone clearly conveyed an unusual amount of concern.

I knew that completing my suturing job would have to wait, as it seemed this other guy couldn't.

"Get him over to resuscitation and call a code. STAT," I told her, realizing her patient must be in trouble. "I'm coming." I temporarily wrapped my patient's head. He would have to wait.

"Code Blue to resuscitation. Now!" came the expected yet still unnerving overhead pronouncement.

When I arrived, the patient was completely unresponsive. Everyone was milling around but no one was taking control. But then it was my module, my patient, my responsibility. It was up to me to take charge. What the hell was going on? Take a deep breath. ABC's, now let's go logically.

"Someone get an airway!" I exclaimed, as I rapidly began going over him, my eyes scanning him from head to toe. He did not move, and his color was a ghastly blue-grey. All we knew, which was not much, was that he had been dumped on our doorstep at around change of shift and subsequently brought into the module.

A neighborly medical resident, who responded to the code, intubated him while I kept on searching—searching him physically and myself mentally as to what was going on. His abdomen was not distended, and there was no blood anywhere that I could see. I racked my brain, trying to think of what could be going on. Luckily, he had an IV in, and we had already given him a big slug of glucose and Narcan (a narcotic reversal) in the unlikely event that this might be a hypoglycemic coma or a narcotic overdose. Fluids were pouring in wide open. His chest was bare except for a lone mid chest Band-aid. I ripped it off, exposing a tiny bloody 3mm hole just to left of his mid sternum. My head was spinning. How could such a tiny hole be the problem? Even a .22 round would leave a bigger hole.

"Still no blood pressure," said the nurse as she looked directly at me, clearly asking "So now what are you going to do, Doctor?" I silently had already asked myself the same question.

"It must be the heart," I thought out loud. What else could it be? Well, of course it could be a lot of things, but really only with an acute heart problem would we have any chance of helping him. And then, let's not forget, there was the hole. The tiny hole. I could feel every muscle of my body tighten. This must be what sphincter tight felt like. The pressure was on. I needed to think, to make a decision. What if I was wrong? A thousand possibilities. It seemed to take forever.

"We need to crack his chest. And now!" I raised my voice a notch or two to add urgency. After all, everyone could hear me fine. They were all staring at me, all waiting for me to make a decision.

I kept going through all the possible scenarios that I could think of. I could not think of anything else. Where was my senior (resident) when I needed him? He should have received the code page. He should have been here by now, I thought, not realizing that it had only been a couple of minutes since we paged him. I couldn't wait, and more importantly, the patient couldn't. If it wasn't his heart, he was 'shit out of luck'. But it had to be. What else could it be? I continued second guessing myself. Should I really open his chest? I was vacillating. But there was no time for that. Decide and go. Soon it would be too late. I was only thirteen months into my training, and I was faced with another life and death decision. Literally.

Where the hell was my chief?

No one was arriving, so it was up to me. I switched into autopilot mode. There was no time to think. I just needed to do. I slopped Betadine all over, and some even hit his chest. As soon as I had made the decision to crack his chest, the nurses had the chest set pulled, unwrapped, and opened. They were lightning fast, amazing, always ready, and at least one step ahead of me.

I grabbed a blade. There was no response as I made my initial deep incision, cutting through his lifeless appearing pale skin and flaying open his chest from under his left breast back up towards his armpit. Swiftly, I sliced through the muscle layers. The dull pink fibers separated easily with less bleeding than a butcher cutting raw meat. Once in the chest, I wiggled the heavy rib spreader then cranked it. There was a nauseating crack as the ribs were forcefully parted. This was no time to go slow. The lung seemed fine, its peppered pink tissue expanding as oxygen was forced in by the resident ventilating him. As soon as I retracted the lung with my left hand, I saw a problem. But was this the problem?

The pericardium was dark, tense, like a tight blue balloon. It must be full of blood, I thought. No wonder he was in trouble. Under the pressure, the heart was struggling to beat and ineffectually at that. This must be severe cardiac tamponade. At least it's what I thought, and right now, what I hoped. Still how could I be sure? What if I was wrong? I was, again, second guessing myself.

Where was my senior? He really should have been here by now. Maybe there was something else going on here. Maybe there was something that in my very limited experience I had not yet seen or thought of. I had never cracked a chest alone before. There was always a more senior resident there, to help me, to guide me and more than anything, to reassure me. Well, I couldn't back out now, the chest was wide open. I needed to continue what I had started. There was still the off chance that I might actually be right.

"Knife," I asked again. I wondered if anyone else could hear the nervous timbre in my voice that I was struggling to suppress. I certainly could. My voice seemed much louder than usual. I could even feel it. I wondered if my hand was shaking as I handled the knife. As soon as I made a little slit in the pericardial sac, blood spurted out. Oh, my God! Did I just cut into the heart? Now what should I do? Did I just kill him?

Blood poured out, but at least it was not pumping out.

My head was being invaded by negative thoughts. I needed to stop listening. I knew the sequence. I needed to open the pericardium wide and let the pressurized blood escape. Without looking up, I turned slightly, fumbling for scissors from the tray open next to me. Were they even the right ones? I had no idea. They would just have to do. I slid them into the small cut I had made and proceeded to slit the pericardium up and down as I had seen and read about. But still, it's different when you are the one who has to make the decision to cut or not to cut. How far should I cut? When should I stop? These were questions that I had never even thought of before. Prior to this, someone else had always told me when to start and where to stop. All I had to do was actually do it. Do it. Now, it was clear that 'doing it' was the easy part.

As I was opening the pericardium, my chief finally showed up.

"What have you got, Nick?" he asked, trying to stay calm as he saw the gaping bloody defect that I had made in the side of the man's chest.

I gave him a quick ten second summary of all that had transpired. I was so caught up with everything that I hardly had time to feel relieved at his arrival. But there was no doubt: I was.

"Great. Let's take a look," he said, as he looked closer over my shoulder.

"I have a pulse," someone said. "And becoming stronger."

Almost at the same instant, as if on cue, the man began to wake and move. There was still a lot of blood coming out from the slit I had made in his pericardium. Clearly the fix was only temporary, but at least for now he was alive. I did not even have time to acknowledge to myself that I might have actually done the right thing.

"Let's get him over to the OR right away," I heard my chief say.

Seconds later, we had him loaded and wheeled him, chest open, rib spreader in place, chest full of blood-soaked sponges, over to the waiting surgical team. He was in pain, grimacing and biting on his endotracheal tube. He would not have to endure it for long; he would be under anesthesia soon enough.

It was some time later, after I was busy back in the module, that we received the 'low down'. He had sustained a small stab to the heart that had been successfully repaired. Despite its tiny size, blood forcefully squirted out like a miniature wayward firehose with every contraction. They deduced that he must have been stabbed with an ice pick. Clearly this was a weapon to be feared and accounted for the apparently innocuous external appearance on his chest, easily covered by a Band-aid.

Another lesson reinforced. Exposure, exposure, exposure. Expose everything. Life-threatening problems can hide behind the smallest of coverings. If you don't know it's there, you can't fix it.

While we were shipping this guy to surgery and I was busy returning my own heart rate to normal, my nurses reminded me of the lady with increased abdominal pain. She had come in overnight, a driver in a seemingly minor car accident who had chosen to forgo the precaution of wearing a seatbelt. Luckily, in all the commotion, she had not yet been discharged, and although reluctant to stay at first, her tune changed as her discomfort increased. When I finally laid hands on her, the examination was markedly different to the report that we had been given. She was 'sick', and not just too-much-booze sick. There was something bad going on in her belly. I went and found my 'elusive' chief who was finishing up the ice-pick case. After performing his own thorough examination, he concurred with my findings, and I prepared her for surgery. On exploration they found that her pancreas had been crushed, but its capsule, luckily, had remained was intact. They knew they should not do too much. Remembering the golden rule—*Don't fuck with the pancreas*—they washed her out and got out. She was discharged a week later. Certainly this was an expensive price for not wearing a seatbelt, but then too many paid a much dearer price.

Not everyone we saw was either an accident or attempted homicide. Many had self-inflicted wounds, some strangely so. One afternoon, I was called to see a man in the medical module with rectal bleeding. His story was that the bleeding occurred because he was leukemic. When I finally got around to him, I was inundated by a barrage of questions from the module's staff about someone whom I had yet to even lay eyes on. Something was up. The patient was extremely hesitant, if not just plainly evasive, when giving me a history and neither he nor his labs appeared to belong to someone with leukemia.

The medical resident who had performed his initial exam took me aside and explained his unusual finding. During the performance of his rectal examination, he was surprised when his fingertip came into contact with a firm flat object. The subsequent X-rays revealed that there was a cylindrical object in his rectum, and that not only did it appear to be made of glass, but there seemed to be a large crack running down one side.

Sadly, foreign bodies in the rectum were a common problem. Neither age nor sex made any difference. Some just had a penchant for sticking things where they didn't belong. If only they would tie a string on the end or had an automatic reverse button installed, it would have made our lives, and theirs, so much easier.

The X-ray findings opened up a whole new set of possibilities and concerns. Was the container already split? Was there a sharp edge? Had it already injured the bowel? Or more likely, would we break it and risk perforating the bowel while trying to remove it? There was no way of finding out before we had tried, and that was not going to happen here.

He needed to be in the operating room, completely anesthetized and fully relaxed (his muscles paralyzed), to give us the best hope of removing it intact, which sounds much easier than it was. This was not a small container. How on earth it got up there was another issue entirely. More to the point was that if it would not come out, then he would have to have his belly opened and have it pushed out or have it removed, and from above. If the latter was necessary, or if he had already perforated his bowel, he would likely require a temporary colostomy, which was certainly never high on any wish list.

Being an inquisitive bunch ('nosy' was more accurate), we were all intrigued as to how this large container (it was a good 7 cm in diameter) got up there in the first place. When we discussed his X-ray findings, he rapidly relented and now miraculously cured of his leukemia, gave us a more plausible story. He explained that he and his girlfriend were in the 'throes of passion' when she stuck the container up his rectum. When I, reluctantly, called Dr. Ledgerwood and told her about my interesting patient, she immediately came down and reviewed the X-rays with us. When she walked in, she was in a great mood, in good humor, even joking a little. When she saw the patient, they clearly recognized each other. She turned to us, and as a slightly crooked grin crept across her face, as she explained to us that this was not his first rectal rodeo. She had an excellent memory, especially for the strange.

He had been here before, or rather down at the old Detroit General, a number of years before, when she had needed to give him a colostomy for a perforated colon. She recalled that things were slow while he was working at one of the local burger joints, so much so that he and a 'friend' began playing around, and somehow the end of a broomstick perforated his rectum. She flippantly remarked that she could not recall if he had received workers' compensation.

I could only imagine how they might have conversed outside of the hospital.

"Oh, hi. You must be Joe, the man who loves to stick things in his rectum."

"Yes, ma'am, that's right, and you must be the doctor who likes to go and get them." Or something weird like that.

This was not a life-threatening emergency, so it did not go back until after 6:30. I hung around after sign out and got to do the case myself. As a second years, we really got the great ones! (But then, truthfully, a case was a case! So we never complained.) Once anesthetized, legs up high in stirrups, I was presented with a huge selection of gleaming stainless instruments, most of which I had never even seen before, let alone used. I was able to slowly dilate up the rectum and visualize the 'prize'. But seeing the dull flat white 'lid' was the easy part. Now then, how to get it out without breaking it? I tried various types of graspers, but none would hold, and all slipped off. We lubricated a red rubber catheter and slipped it up along one side and blew air through it. Surprisingly, this made a huge difference, releasing the vacuum, and with the help of a pair of obstetrical forceps, we were able to deliver a 7 cm by 5.5 cm opaque, white glass jar of mint julep facial scrub. He was lucky and sustained only a few superficial rectal tears, which was most certainly better than a possible colostomy, and he went home the next day. Somehow I doubt that he learnt his lesson, and I was sure that he would be back again, trying to outdo himself.

Daily, we became so overwhelmed with blood and guts, that our patients extracted little sympathy. We cared for them, often inundated by the belligerent and entitled who did little to aid their own disposition. We were not immune to the pain and suffering, but we could not let ourselves become emotionally invested. It was our defense mechanism, our tactic to keep us focused on the bigger picture and not derail our concentration.

One evening while I was making one of my many check-up tours through the module, I approached a young man lying on a gurney with a large bulky bandage wrapped around his right shoulder. He explained calmly that he had been shot a couple of times.

"Oh, yeah. OK, we'll take care of that," I said.

And I meant it, but the message probably sounded more like "Oh, that's no big deal." But it was a big deal. Certainly if that was my shoulder with a couple of slugs in it, I would have wanted immediate attention. But here, one gunshot wound inconspicuously blended into the next. My world was the urban battlefield, and my job was to triage. We were looking for distinguishing features such as the presence of shock, vascular compromise, or some other major organ impairment. He had none. He would have to wait.

Only here could a man with two gunshots not be an outright emergency. Working here had dramatically altered my own system of priorities.

Then there were accidents that forever altered the life of the victim and left a permanent impression (a mental scar) upon us, the medical team, treating them.

It was close to 5:00 that afternoon when our nurse was interrupted by a call from triage. A man was being transported from a nearby meat packing plant following an accident involving an industrial meat grinder. Neither 'industrial', 'meat', nor 'grinder' sounded good in the same sentence as the word 'accident'. I was apprehensive.

I had seen a number of minor grinder injuries before, which usually involved a wayward hand drill. But not this time. No, this was not that kind of grinder. We were notified that his hand was still stuck in the machine itself, and even with all the help at the meat plant, they were unable to remove it. They had to unbolt the entire unit from the floor and were bringing it in still attached to him.

We stood, bathed in the cold bright fluorescent lights of the resuscitation room, waiting nervously. Momentarily we heard the ambulance's siren progressively become louder, and our minds wandered further, each of us undoubtedly envisioning different, but probably equally gruesome, scenarios.

When the sirens finally ceased, they were replaced by a crescendo of blood curdling screams, which rapidly faded to a howl, then a whimper. This brief silence was almost immediately followed by the return of a full-on nightmarish scream. They brought in a young, scrawny kid, who was only 17 and just beginning his second week of working at the plant. He was staggering down the hallway towards us, his left arm draped around the neck of a bulky coworker, who was supporting him. He barely had the strength to keep his head up, his face pale and drenched in clammy perspiration. His right arm was stuck down the funneled opening of a large, heavy, dull grey steel industrial grinder. It was so heavy it required three men to carry it, as they tried keep any excessive (painful) motion to a minimum. Once in the resuscitation room, we lifted the grinder up on the gurney in an attempt to take some pressure off his exhausted arm. He would have to stand for the moment, we could not find a position that would enable him to lie down without increasing the torque on his arm and adding to his suffering. He was continuously being propped up by a couple of nurses, who had their arms around him while uttering reassuring words, trying their hardest not to look at or into the grinder. Fortunately, he could not see their distressed expressions. Even these hardened nurses were having difficulty hiding their own stunned fright. We quickly gave him a good slug of morphine in an attempt to alleviate his pain.

It was an awful sight. His arm had been sucked in, all the way to his elbow, completely occluding the now blood-splattered, well-worn funnel-shaped inlet of the industrial meat grinder. Further down the other end, at the business end, some type of hamburger-looking material had been partially extruded.

Looking at it made me stop in my tracks and retch. It took a concentrated and concerted effort to prevent me from vomiting as I felt my stomach's sour contents well up in the back of my throat. I looked again. Was this material, this ground meat material I saw, part of him? I did not know and truly I did not really want to know. Here again I found myself needing to refocus. I could worry about those things later. For now, he needed my undivided attention.

We still had a major problem. How to get his hand free from the menacingly sharp cutting blades that we were told were tightly packed at the bottom of the funnel. Searching every inch of the grinder, we looked for a way to release the front, where the ground meat usually was extruded. After some time, we had the front plate off, and after pulling out a set of razor-sharp cutting blades, we were met with a gruesome sight which, even though expected, we hoped wouldn't be there. Inside the cylindrical exit area of the grinder was a mass of twisted tissue, a mess of ground, bloody meat, bone, and skin, and yet amongst it there were still two fingers, clearly recognizable as human.

We knew now that the only way to get his arm out would be to reverse the main auger that had pulled his arm down in the first place. There was certainly no way that we could do this with him awake. We contacted anesthesia, who immediately came and performed an axillary block, Anesthetizing the entire arm.

Meanwhile we waited for our hospital maintenance department to bring some heavier duty tools. We had managed so far, with the few tools at our disposal, to separate the front part of the machine, the actual grinder, from its associated large, heavy, electric motor. Now, with a heavy portion of the machinery removed, at least we could lay him down on the stretcher. He was now also starting to lose consciousness, partly due to the relief from the anesthesiologist's block, making him pain free, and partly from the multiple doses of narcotics that no longer had pain to overcome. Up to now, there had been no significant blood loss, just a steady stream of pink 'juice' that dripped from the front of the grinder.

After what seemed like forever, we finally figured out what we needed to do in order to get his arm out. At the back of the grinder, where it had been joined to the motor, there was a huge bolt that appeared to be attached to the auger itself. All we had to do was to turn the bolt in the opposite direction to release what remained of his arm and hand. We were, however, still waiting for the right tools, as we had nothing close to large enough.

In the interim we placed a call to Dr. Sorensen, one of our orthopedic hand specialists, and let him know what we had. Ortho were on call for hand injuries that day, although truly a hand surgeon was not necessary.

There would be no hand. He responded immediately and told us he would be over in about 10 minutes.

By this time, our young patient was not doing so well. He began to vomit and was having serious difficulty breathing. We immediately place an NG tube, sucked out his stomach, and anesthesia intubated him to protect his airway.

Not long after, a couple of the maintenance guys showed up, toting a massive canvas bag with an equally impressive assortment of oversized tools. Searching through their selection, we found the correct socket to fit over the massive bolt. With a long wrench in position, we started to apply pressure on the end of it, yet his hand was stuck tight, and it took an amazing amount of force just to get the auger to budge. Just when we were getting excited about the prospect of releasing his arm, we quickly stopped once we discovered that we were turning it the wrong way. After getting it sorted, we turned it slowly and in the correct direction and were able to extract the remnant of his hand from the grinder.

In reality, we did not remove his hand at all. There was no hand. It was completely gone, ground away. All that was left was the lower part of his forearm with a long, large flap of partially crushed and torn skin on the back of it. Once we had his arm out, we immediately wrapped it in a tight ace bandage to stem the profuse bleeding and readied him for surgery. Once there, Dr. Sorensen and the orthopedic residents took over. We had done all we could; it was now up to them. There was never any real question of reconstruction, as there was nothing to reconstruct. His hand, wrist, and a good part of his forearm were gone. They carefully amputated the nonviable, partially ground tissue and then closed tissue over the bones to make a nice smooth surface at the mid forearm. By all accounts the surgery went extremely well, and we heard a few days later that the long-term plan was to fit him with a myo-electric prosthetic.

NIGHTS

"007"

IN A flash (it seemed) my daytime rotation was over, and I was already a week into my second-year nighttime ER rotation.

Switching from 'days' to 'nights' was not easy, and I was glad that I only had to do it a couple of times during my five years. It took at least a week or so of 'nights' before my internal clock began to readjust, and even then it was hard to shake off the constantly tired feeling, compounded by the forever residency exhaustion.

The adrenaline rushes always helped.

Returning for another night in the ER, it felt, as on 'days', like I had never left. Well, mentally I hadn't. I never really could. That was a luxury none of us could afford. Oh, sure, physically I got away. I dashed home, showered, inhaled some calories, glued my eyes to my old faithful 'CRT'. After a few minutes of Good Morning America, which for me was my Goodnight Detroit, I dove onto my old lumpy, concave, and worn-out mattress. But my brain never left, never shut off. There were always patients to think about, to worry about. There were surgeries to read about, weekly quizzes that we could never prepare for, and the ever looming yearly in-service training examination. To top it off there was the constant fear of being picked on or having to present at the weekly M & M conference. So, no, mentally I could never afford to leave.

Getting to sleep in the midmorning was not easy, and after my first few shifts on 'nights', discovering how useless the blinds on my bedroom windows were, I set about reinforcing them. I repurposed an old blanket with limited success, as sunlight found its way through tiny, and some not so small, defects in my makeshift drape. Despite my tightly closed eyes, narrow shafts of painful brilliance seemed to always find a direct path to my over-tired retina.

Things were so different now that my day and night routines were reversed. We take for granted, to the point of forgetting, how our world (unless you live close to bars, restaurants, or nightclubs) quietens and appears to shut down each evening, just in time for everyone to go to sleep. The daily aural assault of delivery trucks, incessant traffic, honking horns, and jackhammers slowed just in time. But now they were part of my 'night'. On this particular morning, there must have been plumbers working in the apartment next door (or somewhere nearby). They were at least considerate enough to wait for me to enter REM sleep before they let loose on some apparently extra-stubborn plumbing.

Somehow exhaustion always won out, and I managed to get to sleep but often not without a few outbursts of quiet internal, and occasionally not so quiet external, profanities. Their utterance always seemed to make me feel better. Sometimes I needed to stuff my head under a pile of pillows to make sleep possible. Although a chore, I would attempt, perhaps not as hard as I should, to get up by 2:00 or 3:00 in the afternoon. There was always reading waiting to be done. However, on many days and likely more than I wish to remember, I was so utterly spent that I slept in so late that it was about all I could do to make it back to the hospital in time for sign-over rounds.

Then there were the nights of a full moon. These were always exceptionally busy. It was a phenomenon that I had heard about but never believed until I experienced it. Superstitious nonsense, I thought, yet as I discovered, it was absolutely real. Was it because the increased light allowed perpetrators to see better, or was it the effect that the powerful invisible lunar rays had on them? I don't know. But they were always 'nuts'. The use of the word 'loonies' and 'lunatics' is by no means accidental. We were also inundated when there was a big game in town. No matter what the sport, there was always an excuse to celebrate or commiserate, either of which kept the bars full and always resulted in a surge for us.

'Nights' were always far less stressful than 'days'. Although much busier, we always had a lot more help. During my stint on 'nights', besides the three surgical residents, we had a couple of family practice interns, an emergency medicine resident or two, and a varying number of medical students.

If there was a lull in the action, a few of the residents (rarely the surgical ones) tried to get some reading done. The surgical residents tended to use the time more productively (so we would argue), making 'rounds' and attempting to bolster our nonexistent social schedules. Randy (our night chief) was usually off hunting for an elusive free cup of coffee, and it was rare to see him without his Styrofoam sidekick.

Finding a quiet spot, I took out my tattered notebook and, challenging my memory, began jotting down some of the events of both that and previous days.

This night it was a very short break.

The pleasant, almost mesmerizing silence was abruptly interrupted as the PA system sprang into life with its five-minute surgical code warning. We got the message:"Get up off your asses and get ready to work!" Perhaps we should have been concerned about the condition of our impending arrival. But we weren't. We were too busy whining about being interrupted.

One of our new interns who was with us that night is certainly worthy of further comment. Jerry was a young, (but then weren't we all?) tall, pale, almost anemic-complected, emergency room intern with brown curly hair who was on his compulsory emergency surgery rotation. He moved with some discoordination, as if his height had resulted in an insurmountable distance for his firing cerebral neurons to overcome. He was genuinely friendly and fun to chat with, but things were very different when he was taking care of patients. He'd been at the hospital a few months and had already garnered himself a less than stellar reputation. He had even received the nickname '007' by one of our Attendings. This was not because of his suave, dashing good looks, his amazing abilities at the craps table, his penchant for vodka martinis, or his ability conquer multiple adversaries single handedly. Sadly it was because, like his moniker, he also appeared to have a 'license to kill'. Reputations were rapidly established, and especially the negative ones were difficult, if not impossible, to alter.

I had already had the 'pleasure' of working with Jerry and knew him to be somewhat impulsive. He had the dangerous combination of being oblivious to his limitations alongside the erroneous belief that he was much smarter than he really was. He always acted preoccupied, yet accomplished nothing as he beamed with enthusiastic incompetence.

One of the golden rules we learnt was that whenever you had a concern, you called your senior. One of Jerry's main flaws was that, because he never really understood when he was in trouble or beyond his capability (which was almost always), he never asked for help, allowing relatively minor problems to rapidly escalate.

It was a full-time job for us to keep him busy such that he wouldn't really have to really care for a patient, at least not ours! As terrible as it sounded, we knew that sooner or later he would have to take care of someone, but hopefully not any of us or anyone on my watch.

In any profession many are promoted to positions where they are barely competent. In medicine you either take care of patients or you don't. The promotion is graduating from medical school. There is no higher responsibility than being entrusted with the care of someone's health and life. Sadly, the patient rarely knows any better, as they innocently, ignorantly, and naively presume that all doctors are equal.

It brings to mind the old joke:

Q: What do you call the person who graduates bottom of the class in medical school?

A: Doctor.

The word filtered back to us that the code we were waiting for was a man who had been run over while running across a nearby freeway. Even before laying eyes on him, we felt sorry for him. These feelings rapidly evaporated when we discovered that he was actually a dangerous federal fugitive, the target of a nationwide manhunt, who had been 'accidentally' run over by the officers pursuing him.

We all stood patiently poised, prepared, absentmindedly staring along the empty hallway leading towards us. In our inexperience, we thought we were ready for anything that the streets could throw at us. My mind drifted. What was I going to do when I got home tomorrow? I mentally began preparing a shopping list. I needed to call my brother, who was in his last year of undergrad before he started med school at Michigan State. My apartment was a mess. What about the nurse that I met during my rotation at the VA (veterans administration) hospital? Should I call her?

There is always a little bit (actually, quite a lot) of cockiness that goes along with surgical training. To a certain degree it was nurtured. We were expected to be a chimera of both humbleness and swagger. It was no place for the timid, who either rapidly changed or got spat out. When it came to decisions, you could not waffle and remain uncommitted. If there was one thing that we were taught, that was drummed into our apparently thick skulls, it was that we needed to make a decision. We could not decide not to decide. We needed to make a decision based on the information that we had at the moment. It was 'to cut or not to cut', remove or leave, do or don't. We learnt to make decisions rapidly and efficiently and stand behind them (not always pleasant, especially when we were wrong). On our early morning rounds, we saw our patients, wrote orders (made decisions), and that would be it for the day, as we would not get out of the operating room to see them again until the evening, which could easily be 12 or more hours later. It trained us, by necessity, to make rapid (and hopefully correct) decisions. Many were not easy.

As I have learnt to appreciate, speed of decision making does not equate to its ease, but it is synonymous with good training.

Surgical training was a rollercoaster. One moment we felt as if we could handle anything, the next we were humbled, humiliated, and exposed to the sad truth of our ignorance and inexperience. We were constantly reminded of the enormous volume of knowledge we needed to master in order reach our goal of becoming a surgeon. Was it even achievable?

Certainly, many before us had succeeded. Maybe they were smarter and tougher back then, able to study and retain more. This emotional instability spilled over into our limited social lives, where although we might come off as overconfident, secure, and almost cocky, it was just a façade, covering our truly insecure psyche.

This rollercoaster never ends. We just learn to deal with its highs and lows. Still, now just when I feel on top of the world after completing a lengthy, difficult, and perhaps lifesaving surgery, I am rapidly brought back down to earth and humbled by a relatively simple case that ends with an unexpected poor outcome or complication.

The EMS team, flanked by a couple of officers, wheeled our patient down the hallway towards us. They were not rushing. After we got him sorted, it was clear that there was nothing life threatening going on. He was lying face down on the stretcher. His hands were cuffed, and he was shoeless (I never understand how that happens! Is it really faster to run barefoot?), with a ripped button-down shirt and khaki pants. His stay was brief, as we quickly transferred him over to the module. So much for an exciting code.

Later that night, without any of the usual accompaniment of sirens and lights, a sleek, black, 'chromed out', tinted windowed Ford LTD ghosted up to the entrance. There was no squeal of tires, no paramedics jumping exuberantly, batman style, out of their still-running rig, dashing to deliver another critically ill patient. There was not even the usual distorted announcement crackling over the ceiling speakers. No, there was nothing, no warning. Our first inkling that something was up was when we noticed one of our nurses rushing out to the dock, forcefully maneuvering an empty gurney while fighting its wayward, unobliging tendency to stray from her desired course. She scooped up the occupant from the back seat while recruiting help from nearby staff as only an experienced nurse could. Others gawked yet remained as frozen as statues.

There were always people hanging around the dirty, cigarette-butt littered, oil and tire-rubber stained, cracked, concrete driveway that lay beyond the glass double doors of the emergency entrance. It was a favorite hangout for many employees on break, some just sitting on a low half wall, some attempting to satiate their nicotine habit, while others were trying hard just to sample fresh air. Occasionally in the humid summer evenings, a telltale jingle announced the visit from a mobile ice cream purveyor, the once white van adorned with torn and faded, multicolored renditions of his offerings. He always did a brisk business, and his icy treats were a wonderfully welcome, if only brief, respite from the sweat, blood, and stench of the emergency room.

In a matter of seconds, the nurse and her newly deputized assistants were rushing back down the hallway towards us when the overhead speakers, seemingly even even louder and more aggravating than usual, finally announced their arrival.

On first glance the patient did not appear too bad, but closer inspection revealed how dangerously deceiving first impressions can be. His breathing was shallow at best, and the more we looked, the worse he appeared.

He was deteriorating right in front of us.

"Let's get his clothes off," I commanded, a little hesitantly. Within seconds they were history. For a moment I looked ahead, perhaps a little stunned by the rapid response to my request. People actually did what I asked. But then, what did I expect? Wasn't that my job? I pushed the crazy thought aside and continued with the resuscitation, organizing my thoughts and logically formulating a plan.

"What's the blood pressure?" I asked, my voice cracking just a little under the return of a more appropriate anxiousness.

"120 over 60," came the immediate reply, pretty much before I even had all my words out. The nurses all knew what they were doing and had been in the process of taking it long before they ever heard my request.

He was immediately hooked up to the cardiac monitor.

"Sinus tack," exclaimed the resident at the patient's head, who always had one eye on the monitor.

His color was changing right in front of us. The pink had disappeared, replaced by a significantly more bluish hue. This was a sure sign that he was not getting enough oxygen, despite the respiratory therapist bagging him with one hundred percent oxygen. It was not enough. He was immediately intubated and placed on a ventilator. With a couple of large bore IVs in, we forced in saline, utilizing our medical student's ceaseless energy to squeeze the bags. A closer examination revealed the devastating, and likely fatal, nature of his injuries. On his entire left side, the skin was replaced by extensive abrasions. There were long, deep, irregular furrows, imbedded with chunks of gravel and asphalt where he had been dragged along the road. His chest X-ray did not alter our impression, revealing multiple rib fractures with a likely 'flail' segment: a section of rib cage which now moves independently and paradoxically opposite to the rest of the chest.

Sadly, we were missing the big picture as we focused on his immediately visible injuries. We soon noted that both of his pupils were 'blown', that is they were fixed and dilated. He did not even have a corneal reflex, an automatic blinking of the eyes when the touch receptors on the cornea are triggered, and when absent was always a grave sign. Feeling his head,

I could feel a 'step-off' fracture on the edge of his left orbit, and then on the back left side of his skull, under his bloody and matted sandy hair, my fingers delineated the rim of a large, depressed crater.

His head had been bashed in. Our best guess was that he had been whacked with a baseball bat.

We now faced another dilemma, more common in the face of improving resuscitation techniques. What should we do? And who decides? We had already successfully resuscitated him, at least to the point where he had a decent blood pressure and appeared to be oxygenating well, yet we knew he would not last long at all (perhaps no more than a few minutes) without artificial respiratory support.

We knew that to continue was futile. But this was not the way we were programmed. We were not really trained to step back and look at the big picture but rather to deal with each problem as it arose. We were also not trained to stop. Actually, it was the opposite; we were trained to never to give up.

If on arrival it is obvious that further treatment would not be beneficial, a resuscitative effort is not undertaken. That was a relatively easy decision. But what to do if, as in this case, the hopelessness of the situation becomes clear only after resuscitation? There are no easy answers. We often bring patients back from the precipice of death just to watch them slowly spiral over the course of hours to their inevitable outcome. These dilemmas were made somewhat easier if their family members or loved ones were present, who might understand both the wishes of the patient as well as the inevitable non-survivability of the injury. However, more typically, the distraught, shocked, and overwhelmed family, with minimal, if any, medical knowledge (except what they have seen on TV), lacks insight into the patient's wishes and is unable to fully comprehend the irreversibility of their loved one's condition. As a result, we were typically asked (told!) to do everything. But then, we always did everything (that was our programming, our surgical prime directive, if you will). Continuing with the resuscitation often enabled the family time to come to grips with the inevitable outcome. We contacted the neurosurgery resident on call. They would also be invaluable in any discussion with family members.

Although devastating, it was just this type of severe, irreversible, head-injured patient that potentially could breathe life into many other unfortunate patients by their selfless gift of organ donation. Naturally there was still the issue of obtaining consent, but now this was a problem for neurosurgery.

It was always a scary experience for code patients (at least for the conscious ones) when they arrived. They were often confused, frequently disoriented, almost always unsure of where they were and had no idea who it was that was now 'attacking' them. Like a clip from the *Thriller* video, a dozen or so hands simultaneously descended upon them, attempting to perform a multitude of necessary tasks.

If the ongoing physical invasion wasn't enough, in the conscious patient we began an intense oral inquisition, fancifully expecting our answers to be both correct and coherent. It was easy to forget that our patient was a real person, someone who was scared, really scared, scared to death. They believe that they were going to die, and sadly many did.

It wasn't long before the overhead speakers broadcast our next code.

A hoarse and throaty, "Surgical code one, times two, to resuscitation room. ETA two minutes," crackled overhead.

It was shaping up to be another busy night.

The resuscitation room was still a mess with our patient on the ventilator stuck in the middle of it. We quickly transferred him over to module one; we made ready for the code.

Paramedics frequently called ahead with any information they had. It was a useful heads up, allowing us to make the necessary preparations. As the nurses were relaying the information back to us, we could hear the distant wailing of sirens. We heard that it was a couple of motorcyclists hit by a car.

Once again, we took up our positions.

Jerry (007), our hyperactive, 'hypo-cerebral' intern, continued to run around (or at least within the confines of the room) like a child excited to see Santa. He was fidgeting and accomplishing nothing except to elicit, 'what the hell do you think you're doing now' stares from the nurses, who were always stuck cleaning up his messes. The floor was still a shambles, and even though we had tried to clean it up as best we could, we were still stepping through the carnage of the previous code.

"It's about time we had a good chest crack," I heard Jerry say to Randy who had just returned from the OR. Randy looked up at Jerry as a wry half smile, almost smirk slowly spread across his face.

"I doubt you'll get one here," he replied.

"If he doesn't have a chance, can't we just crack him anyway?" asked Jerry indifferently, emphasizing his tendency to talk before thought.

"I haven't seen one," he continued, still dancing around as if he had a nest of bees in his britches. But then this was just Jerry being Jerry. A little crazy, very impetuous, and with no real understanding of what he was asking for, definitely on the ADD spectrum. Randy avoided the urge to reply, knowing that ignoring him was the best option.

We could see the ambulance lights reflecting off the glass and chrome surfaces as they swung up the emergency drive, and in what seemed like only an instant, they were wheeling yet another one towards us.

The first motorcyclist was a very obese male in his late 30s, so heavily tattooed that there was little skin remaining on either of his arms or torso that had not been adorned. He appeared significantly older than his age, likely a reflection of a hard lifestyle, perhaps resulting in a premature aging of both body and mind.

He was bleeding profusely, to put it mildly. Blood was pouring from his nose and right ear, although this latter location we did not come to appreciate until later. Our immediate focus was his shallow, erratic, and labored breathing. He was struggling, and it appeared that at any moment his next breath might be his last. Using suction, I was just able to see well enough to slip an endotracheal tube between his bloody vocal cords. I immediately delegated the med student to 'bag' him until the mechanical ventilator arrived.

Barely a moment later, one of the nurses exclaimed that she had no blood pressure, and we still had no IV. This was a problem. The skin of his upper chest and neck was thick, leathery and covered with 'ink', which along with his size, made finding landmarks near to impossible. As I looked at his chest, I wondered just how much time he must have spent under the tattoo artist's needle. They must be gifted to ply their artistic talents on the uneven canvas of his huge barrel chest. It must have cost a small fortune.

Our nurse again announcing that she did not have a blood pressure brought me back to the present.

We still needed IV access. Valuable seconds were ticking away while he continued to bleed. We eliminated subclavian access, as it would have been a very difficult while were in the process of intubating and bagging him, and for a while everything around the head and neck area was a hectic bloody mess. With a medical student on one arm and a nurse on the other, they had tourniquets up and were attacking his arms with gusto, slapping his skin repeatedly trying to get a vein to 'pop'. This was hard enough to do in hydrated patients, let alone here, in someone bleeding. Neither arm appeared likely to be fruitful, so I moved down to the groin area for a cutdown.

A cutdown is performed in order to obtain venous access when the infusion of large volumes of fluid was necessary. We used the saphenous vein, a large vein that travels close to the skin on the inner aspect of the leg from ankle to groin. When seconds counted, we went for the groin, as here the vein was larger and easier to find and access

I poured golden brown (it looked like thin pancake syrup) antiseptic iodine paint all over the groin, as usual not worrying too much about the mess that I made but feeling better now that the area was stained yellowy-brown. Whether it was important to 'sterilize' the area in such sick individuals, and whether the second or so that we waited killed many surface bacteria is another debate all together. No matter what, when we were making a cut, it always felt better (more surgical perhaps?) if we were cutting through iodine-stained skin. With a quick, yet deft (at least I thought so), wrist flick, I sliced through the skin and right into the pale-yellow subcutaneous fat layer that protruded slightly between the parting skin edges. How the wound looked at the end was never a priority. It was just a matter of getting down to the vein as fast as possible. No one cared what the wound looked like if they survived. If they were around later to complain about the way it looked, then it was an overwhelming success. I cut deeper and was a little surprised when my patient squirmed.

"Next time, how about a little local?" Randy said as he looked over my shoulder. I knew he was just needling me. He knew that the patient was unconscious, and there was no time to putz around putting in 'local'. Anyway, any discomfort he felt would only serve to help increase his blood pressure.

I nodded in acknowledgement and continued concentrating on my task of locating the vein and dissecting it from its fatty surrounds. Not wasting any time, I grasped a scalpel and made a small nick into it, trying not to cut it in half. I needed to go quickly, but it still needed to be done right. This was a time for slickness, not sloppiness. Anyway, I did not want to give Randy any extra ammunition. With a little wiggling, I inserted the cut and beveled end of the 'sterile' plastic IV tubing into the small cut in the vein. Was it really sterile? Was anything here ever really sterile?

We could always deal with the relatively minor sequelae of a wound infection later, again, if the patient survived. This IV tubing instantaneously became a massive intravenous catheter, a pipe through which to dump in fluid in as quickly as gravity and our medical student's crushing hand strength could deliver it. It was a very low-tech method, perhaps, yet still highly effective at getting large volumes of fluid in rapidly. Within a few minutes of incising the skin, the fluids were pouring in. Randy then proceeded, far more rapidly I might add, to perform a cutdown on the opposite groin. It had the effect of, "See, now that's how it's done." I was in awe watching him complete the same procedure that I had done in at least half the time with a finesse and efficiency that I could only hope to achieve one day. Now we had two pipes in with fluids running full bore.

"I have a palpable pressure of 70," our nurse excitedly announced as she looked up from the patient's right side.

"Keep the fluids wide open and hang blood as soon as it's ready," Randy interjected, momentarily raising his head as he completed suturing his catheter in place.

"Check on the blood, please. Find out how long it will be before we have some," he added, not really focusing his comments on any one particular person. Then clearly after a few seconds of contemplation, he continued, "Have them send over some O neg, right away." Blood had been sent to the blood bank as soon as the first IV was in. It was hard to believe that it had only been a few minutes since the blood had been sent. It seemed much longer. It always did.

"He's going into v-fib," the same nurse who was checking his pressure reported, her tone now with an added level of urgency.

Looking over at the EKG monitor, I could see she was right. The rhythm had deteriorated into the irregular, coarse, wavy line characteristic of the most dangerous of cardiac rhythms, indicative of uncoordinated cardiac contractions: ventricular fibrillation.

Looking up at the monitor and confirming that the tracing was indeed this life-threatening rhythm, Randy looked back at the patient as if to confirm that it was real. He again took control.

"OK, let's defibrillate."

He immediately grabbed the twin black plastic handled defibrillator paddles from the top of the EKG monitor, and squeezing out a generous dollop of slightly gritty, electro-conductive gel onto one of the shiny metal electrode surfaces, proceeded to rub the paddles together. After holding the paddles apart for a few more seconds and waiting for the machine to complete its charging cycle, he placed one firmly over the center and the other over the left side of the heavily tattooed chest.

The red ready light on the console flashed at the finale of an accompanying crescendo sound, signaling that the unit was charged.

"OK, standby," Randy said and motioned with his head for everyone to get clear. He watched the monitor.

"Clear!' he said firmly, almost with a shout as he pressed the red button on one paddle handle. The patient jolted, his muscles contracting as a sudden surge of electrical current coursed through his body.

There were a few moments of uncomfortable silence as everyone's eyes were glued to the screen.

"Nothing." The nurse stated the obvious as we could see the unchanged, irregular oscilloscope tracing.

"Resume CPR," Randy said, his eyes also focused on the rhythmless tracing. "Give two more amps of bicarb and one epi (epinephrine)."

We pushed the meds, injecting the contents of the predosed plastic syringes directly into a side port of the IV tubing closest to the patient. We resumed CPR. A few moments passed.

"Hold CPR!" Randy ordered, then after a few seconds he added, "Anything?"

"Still in fib," came the expected reply.

"Let's shock him again," Randy said, and he started the process of preparing for another round of defibrillation. It did not take long.

"Clear," he again commanded.

The patient jolted again, announcing the almost instantaneous repeated rush of electrons dashing through his body, triggering muscles to contract.

We waited. Seconds passed. We looked up at the tracing and waited. Time ticked on. It seemed like we were watching the screen forever. Then the familiar regular, rhythmic beeping sound of the monitor returned.

This auditory signal was almost more reassuring than the visual tracing. Interestingly, we all seemed to hear the response before we clearly saw the return of a normal tracing.

"We have sinus!' said our nurse, who, with the panache of a 17th-century town crier, announced the return of a normal rhythm.

"'Pulse?" Randy inquired.

"There's a faint one here," an intern replied, his right index and middle fingers pressed against the patient's neck as he felt his carotid artery. "It's a good one," he added after a few seconds, sounding as surprised as everyone felt.

We had been pumping in 'tons' of fluid, six liters at least, by the time we started transfusing blood. Somewhere he was bleeding 'like stink'. But where? We needed to find out and quickly. The only place where we could see bleeding was his head, but it did not seem to be enough to account for his low blood pressure. His belly seemed fine, soft and not getting any bigger, so it was an unlikely source. His lungs sounded fine, although we were still waiting for the chest X-ray 'shot' just after he was intubated.

There was a deep, irregular laceration extending from under his right eye down the side of his nose to just above his lip, and I could clearly feel the jagged, bony edges of a fracture. Now that his blood pressure was back up, blood was pouring out of the side of his mouth, over the side of the cart, forming a sizable puddle on the floor. I needed to pry open his jaw to look in his mouth. Working around the endotracheal tube, I pulled his tongue with a 4x4 gauze and used a sucker to clear the blood from the back of his mouth. No sooner had I finished sucking it out than it returned, as if with a purposeful vengeance. The blood continued to pour from the back of his throat. But from where exactly? It did not seem to be his lungs. He was intubated, and there was no blood in the tube. So then where was it all coming from?

I checked his belly again. It remained soft; the NG tube was sucking out bile, not blood. Yet blood just kept pouring from the back of his mouth. It was not slowing, and if anything appeared to be even more brisk. Using a strong flashlight, I looked further up towards the roof of the mouth. There I could see a large disruption of his hard palate. The blood appeared to be coming out from the posterior pharynx, way in the back of his mouth in the area hidden by his soft palate, the fleshy extension at the back of the roof of the mouth. Like a wide-open faucet, the Kool-Aid consistency blood poured out. We had to find a way to stop it, or at least to slow it down, or this man was going to bleed to death.

We decided to try a foley catheter, normally usually used to drain the bladder, but here we were counting on the inflated balloon to apply pressure behind the nose. Removing the NG tube, we slipped the catheter in easily, inflated the balloon, and applied traction. However, there was little if any improvement. Blood still poured out as if we had done nothing. Truly we had done nothing, at least nothing that helped. Moreover, we continued having difficulty maintaining his blood pressure.

We seemed to be sucking out blood as fast as we could put it in. In short order we had transfused six units of blood. We tried, in vain, to pass a catheter through the opposite nostril but were met with an impenetrable resistance. He must have a considerable fracture there, which was likely contributing to the torrential bleeding. We were running out of options. There was not enough time to go to surgery or to the angiography suite. He would not last long at this rate.

We just did not have the time. We needed to find a way to stabilize him. We packed the back of his pharynx. Everybody pitched in with ideas. We tried everything we could think of. But no matter what we did or how hard we tried, nothing helped. He just continued to bleed.

Then we noticed bleeding from his right ear. We thought it was blood that had made its way there from the mouth. It was difficult to know where it was coming from. There was blood everywhere. On closer inspection, blood was coming from deep within the ear canal itself. Trying to use the otoscope was pointless as there was too much blood pouring out, blocking any hope of seeing anything.

We were losing the battle. Despite doing all we could, it was not enough. Every bit of blood we poured in, poured right back out, and perhaps even more quickly. We had been working on him for close to half an hour at this point and were losing ground. We thought that he likely had sustained a massive skull fracture. He had not really been neurologically responsive in any meaningful way (except when I made the cut in his groin) since coming in, and the bleeding showed no sign of letting up.

No matter what we did his blood pressure kept dropping.

We continued our frantic efforts. Pushing blood, pushing fluids, applying pressure. Nothing worked.

Soon Randy interrupted.

"OK, I'm going to call it," he said, looking up at the clock, and announcing the time. "Stop all the IVs. Disconnect the monitor. Stop bagging." His last words trailed off. He had made the always-very-difficult decision to stop the resuscitation. He was, as we all were, dejected and frustrated that we could not save this man lying in front of us, blood still pouring from his mouth, ear, and nose.

This was the opposite of our previous code. But the result would be the same. There the body was alive and able to sustain life, but his brain was dead. Here, notwithstanding that he probably also had a severe cerebral insult, his body could just not sustain life.

As we all stepped back, we looked at the monitor and then back at him. A lifeless bloody mess. His heart tracing was already agonal. He had no spontaneous respirations. In reality he had been gone for a while.

The man's biking partner, who was brought while we were all busy, had sustained only relatively minor injuries.

I sat at the front desk and filled out the notice of death form and notified the coroner's office. Many times we had to guess at answers to questions, like the time of death, the cause, and the proximate cause. We just wanted to write down that the cause was the huge hole in the chest (often true), and that the proximate cause was the poor judgement in sleeping with the gun-toter's wife (frequently also true).

The head nurse on duty that night came over to me.

"Dr. Maxwell. Have you spoken to Mr. Robinson's family?" she asked.

"Mr. Robinson?" I replied, having absolutely no idea who she was talking about.

"The man in the code, the DOA," she explained.

We rarely knew the names of the patients who arrived as codes.

"He has a name now?" I asked, somewhat flippantly.

"Yes. The police were able to ID them and notified the families. They are all here, now," she replied, then, after seeing my questioning look added "And they know nothing."

"All?" I wondered why she phrased it that way.

"Oh, yes, there's a whole crowd there," came the dreaded reply.

Up until this point, he was known to us only as John Doe 220. It was much easier to deal with the critically injured, the dying, and even the dead when they were anonymous. It seemed less real and did not bother us as much as when a lifeless body had a name.

"Well, actually, no. I haven't. Has anyone?" I replied, hoping that she would tell me that the families had already been spoken to and had gone home. Her look of incredulity at my naivete was enough to tell me that I was not to going to get away without dealing with it myself.

"Where are they?' I inquired apprehensively, still hoping someone would intervene to tell me that everything had been dealt with. I hated talking to families of those that had died. I felt powerless, useless, so ill-equipped to deal with their questions. I was sad for their loss and always somewhat surprised that they frequently had little idea of what their loved one was involved in. I often felt (insecurity again!) that they looked at me as if we should have done more. Should we have? But what more could we have done? I felt guilty, like I was responsible, in some strange way. Of course, I wasn't, but still it was the feeling that surfaced when trying to explain someone's loss to a crowd of questioning, probing, answer-seeking, and often surprised family members.

"In the meditation room," she replied, much to my chagrin.

The meditation room, a poor euphemism for the 'bad news delivery room', was a small room situated along the long corridor between the emergency room entrance and the resuscitation room. The blank walled room had a single couch and an easy chair. Here the families of critical patients waited. It afforded us a little privacy.

"Are the relatives of both patients there?" I asked.

"Yes, and there must be at least a dozen people packed in there." Things were not looking up. I thought for a few seconds. I knew I needed help.

"Can you get a hold of the chaplain?" I suggested. I knew it would be helpful, but I was also happy to stall a little.

"OK. I'll also see if I can get the patient advocate to go along too," she added, as I watched her pick up the phone, hopefully to page them.

"Sounds good. I'll go and speak to them as soon as they're here." It always seemed easier to talk to families if there was more than one of 'us'. It seemed to diffuse the situation and perhaps redirect the family's anger, making it harder for them to assign blame to any one particular individual.

Before I went to talk to them, I had the unenviable task of informing the second motorcyclist that his friend did not make it. He was in the X-ray line, and although shaken up, he did not appear to have any major injuries. There was an intense odor of rancid alcohol on his breath as he explained that he had been heading home on the back of his friend's bike when they had been hit by a car. He had been thrown clear, whereas his friend had sustained the brunt of the collision.

Being the bearer of bad news, telling a family that their loved one has died or was likely to die, was one of the most difficult responsibilities that we had. It was also one of the most important. Here, on the trauma service, it was sadly a very frequent event. Unfortunately, it was a task usually assigned to a junior resident. These were not patients with long-standing or terminal illnesses but generally healthy individuals who had their life cut short by malice or accident. The families certainly had not had time to prepare for the news of loss, it being often the first peice of real information they received when arriving at the hospital.

It is a sign of changing times (and a good one) that the delivery of such important and delicate news is no longer relegated to the junior house-staff. This task is now carried out by more senior physicians in conjunction with other members of the trauma team, including nurses, social workers, and chaplains.

Walking into the room, I felt slightly relieved as I was reinforced by our patient advocate arriving almost simultaneously. Inside there were at least a dozen people, some sitting, others standing, but all looking right at me with penetrating, searching, pleading eyes that were all asking for the same information: Tell me that my son, my relative, my friend is alive. For some, the news that I was to deliver would be a huge relief. For others it would be tragic and a moment that they would never forget. I stood there for a few seconds, more than anything just trying to gather my wits, as I looked around the room trying to decide how to begin. I was overwhelmed by all the eyes staring at me, still not quite sure how I was going to deliver my sickening news, yet I knew the delivery was critical.

The best way to relay bad news, is always to deliver it straight. Relay the facts yet do it with empathy for those who are on the receiving end. We should not sugarcoat or lessen the severity of the news just because it makes it easier for us. The task of giving unpleasant news is a duty that many physicians are reluctant to perform and therefore do it poorly. No one likes to do it, but the manner in which it is received has all to do with the way it is delivered.

After introducing myself, I went ahead.

"Are you the relatives of Mr. James Robinson and Mr. Lloyd Williams?" I asked, as I carefully searched the room for any cues.

There was no clear-cut response, just some grunts, a nodding of heads and sad, piercing, searching eyes, still trying to penetrate and read my mind. Before I even spoke, I found myself fighting very strong feelings of guilt, of inadequacy, of failure.

Failure is especially difficult for surgeons. It was one thing that we were trained not to accept, and for surgical residents, a word that was not allowed in our vocabulary. From medical school through residency, failure was just never an option. We were trained not to let it enter our mind. But life does not work that way. Diseases occur, as do bad outcomes, but that does not mean that we have failed. (Now tell that to your Attending and see what happens. No thanks!). So it was difficult when we came face to face with 'failure', especially when it involved the loss of a life. But was it really our failure? Certainly, we had failed to save the patient, but then sometimes it was just not possible.

"Mrs. Robinson?" My eyes scanned the room and were met by a dozen or so intense, silent stares. I finally focused in on a rather elderly but well-dressed lady who appeared visually to respond the most to my question. I waited for her to nod her head.

"I'm very sorry to have to tell you this, but your son was so severely injured in the accident that he did not make it." I stopped for a moment and waited. Had it registered? I looked at the crowd as my message started to sink in. Some remained frozen, mouths wide open, others' faces slowly contorted as the news registered. "We could not stop the bleeding. There was nothing we could do. I am so sorry."

I felt empty, deflated, and knew that my words were totally inadequate.

I just wanted to disappear. Leaning forward on the couch, she buried her face in her hands. But then she dropped her hands, stood up, and began wailing. I really could not understand what she was saying. The lady with her, or at least the one next to her, put her arm around her and tried her best to console her.

"What about Lloyd? Is my baby all right?" came a voice from the other side of the room. The ambient noise had now exponentially metamorphosed from whispers into an eruption of random questions directed towards me. This was all occurring against the backdrop of the deceased mother's inconsolable wailing.

"Tell me that my baby's OK," came the voice from the corner, at first indiscernible above the increasing background noise.

I took a step over towards the woman who was talking, presuming it to be the survivor's mother.

"Yes, Mrs. Williams, your son is alive, but he was involved in a very serious accident and will need to stay in the hospital," I said, hoping, but not really sure, that I had the right person. Short of checking IDs, how could I know?

As I spoke, one of the men sitting near me got up and ran out of the room shouting angrily but incomprehensibly. His words may not have been clear, but his tone certainly was. He looked as if he was on a mission. He ran straight out of the emergency room, and despite sending one of the security guards after him, they were too late. He was gone.

I quickly decided that I had said enough. Hopefully not too much. I let the families know how contact us and left them with the patient advocate and newly arrived chaplain. I left deflated. I felt so uneasy with the whole thing. But why? Maybe it was just too close to home, seeing young men dead who we all knew were alive only a few hours earlier. Or was it just that I felt bad for doing such a shitty job (of informing them)? I knew that I had not approached it in the best way. But then, what was that way? It was clear to me that I had no idea.

Talking to a family and giving them bad news is not something that we were ever taught. I doubt it is in any surgery program. By observing others, we picked up ideas of how to do it and more importantly how not to.

The recent emphasis on palliative care has helped greatly. As physicians we could all benefit from more education and guidance when dealing with end-of-life issues. Now, in surgical practice, I have the benefit of working closely with a trained palliative-care team who excel at explaining difficult news to patients and their families. I can't but wonder sometimes if, with this, we have just shifted the responsibility of delivering it to someone else.

A Laparotomy

ALONG WITH the very sick, we dealt with many, much milder ailments. There was always a potpourri of accidents and altercations, stabs and slashes, (lead) slugs and (bar) scrapes. When we weren't dealing with the life threatened, we still had to sort through the bloody, smelly, pussy, alcohol-stinking, vomit-ridden, vile, 'module-one' breath patients. It was our night's work. At the very least, it was never dull.

Then there were the times when we might actually get to help someone. Now that made everything worthwhile.

Back in the first bed was our man from the first code of the evening. He was hooked up to a ventilator, multiple fluids hanging all around, a maze reaching down from above like roots drooping from the limbs of a banyan tree. Above the chatter, we could hear the rhythmic soft mechanical 'woosh' of the ventilator's bellows as it forced air into his lungs, accompanied by the faster, higher pitched staccato sound of the cardiac monitor. Neurosurgery was on the case, and his CAT scan revealed massive intracranial swelling but no bleed. They 'pushed' another slug of mannitol to help decrease the swelling. Even a slight decrease in swelling would result in less vascular resistance, reslulting in increasing blood flow and its essential supply of nutrients and oxygen.

Neurosurgery had decided to proceed aggressively (Overly? Perhaps.)

and take him to the operating room to place an intracranial pressure monitoring bolt. This small device was screwed into a hole drilled into the skull, enabling measurement of the pressure within its non-expandable bony confines. It allowed for therapeutic interventions to be monitored and adjusted accordingly.

When I rechecked his belly, I noticed a significant change from earlier. His previously soft and benign abdominal exam was now much more distended and firmer. This was a big change and potentially an even bigger problem. What was causing this change? Was his abdomen filling up with blood? Was there an injury to his gut, his liver, his pancreas? There were a million possibilities. None were good.

Due to his head injury, he could not tell us if he had pain, let alone if it hurt when we pushed on his belly. But we needed to know what was going on. We needed to know if there was bleeding or perhaps a bowel injury. As 'neurosurg' was planning to take him to surgery and put a bolt in, then we would tag along and perform a diagnostic peritoneal lavage (DPL). Basically this meant washing out the belly and looking at the fluid that came out. If we found a problem, then we would need to explore his abdomen (a laparotomy). A more recent chest X-ray showed that he had collapse of his left lung, so he also needed a chest tube. As was typical of trauma patients, nothing ever remained static, and with time other problems, some even life-threatening ones, arose. We checked and rechecked and expected the unexpected.

With advances in imaging technology, DPLs are now rarely performed, having been replaced with the far more rapid, less invasive, and in fact, more informative CT scans. These can accurately determine the location and extent of injuries. This capability is supplemented by the bedside, ultrasound, FAST exam (Focused Assessment with Sonography for Trauma) that can determine if there is free fluid (blood) in the belly.

Once in surgery, I proceeded to 'staff' one of my interns in placing a chest tube. Now I, a mere second year, was the teacher, and it was my job to instruct my intern how to place the tube. It was all part of the efficient, if sometimes intimidating, residency education method. It was my chance to pass on knowledge (that I hardly recognized I had) to my juniors. More than anything, educating others consolidated our own knowledge and allowed us to gain further elusive fragments of confidence. As surgical residents, we took for granted such procedures. It was something we performed, often many times in an evening. It was only when we taught others that we realized the importance of breaking them down into their component steps, each of which had its own recipe for trouble if not correctly performed. But then that is true of all of surgery, and why proper training is so key.

With the chest tube was in, I then 'staffed' my intern for the DPL. This was definitely a notch up from a chest tube insertion, and even though it was usually not performed in the operating room, this was certainly the best environment to learn. The DPL allowed us to determine if there was BPS (Blood, Pus, or Shit) in his belly. As I looked over my intern's shoulder, I resisted the urge to tell him how to do every step. He knew the sequence. After making a small longitudinal incision in the skin just above the umbilicus and following a couple of nervous pokes with a hemostat to separate the fat, he tentatively advanced (with 'gentle' encouragement) the plastic catheter-covered metal trocar through the single layer of tough, muscle-connecting fascia and into the belly.

Even such a relatively minor procedure as this can be problematic. Push too far and you might pierce the bowel, stab a vessel, or even strike the aorta. Not far enough and the catheter does not even make it into the abdominal cavity. There is a definite pop that is felt as the catheter pierces the thin peritoneum, and it is the recognition of this feel that we are trying to teach. Connecting the catheter to a syringe, he aspirated. BPS? Most often the immediate return shows nothing. Next we irrigated (lavage) with saline and sent it to the lab to evaluate it for red blood cells, white blood cells, and bacteria.

But as soon as he pulled back the plunger on the syringe, there was blood. I was confident that we had a good 'tap' with minimal trauma, so this one was indeed truly positive.

Now what?

The real-time nightmare for our patient was going from bad to worse, just as it seemed impossible for it to get any worse. He already had a bad head injury, and now we had a positive peritoneal lavage, so that at a minimum he would require a laparotomy (abdominal exploration) to locate and repair the cause.

But should we do anything? That was the real million-dollar question.

The family were still too overwhelmed and stunned; it was just too much bad news too quickly. They had not even had enough time to process one piece of bad news before they were hit again with the next. The neurosurgeons and social workers had spent a great deal of time going over with them the grave prognosis and options around organ donation. But they were not ready to make such a decision. The only thing that we heard was, "Please do everything you can." It was impossible for them (as it would be for most of us) to grasp the irreversibility of his injury and that nothing would bring his brain back. They just wanted us to keep up a full court press and were not interested in any discussion of organ donation. Like so many families, they thought that agreeing was tantamount to telling us to 'pull the plug'. They were not willing to give up. But then, none of us ever were.

The plan is that we would go ahead and explore his belly once neuro-surgery had completed the placement of the ICP 'bolt'. For novices this was an unsettling procedure, as drilling a hole through someone's skull tends to be. Although drilling a hole in the head (trephining) harkens back to ancient times, where it allowed the escape of 'evil humors', to watch a hole being drilled into the 'brain' was still disconcerting. Sure, it wasn't really the brain, just the bone of the skull, but still, that was frequently stomach curdling enough.

After the neurosurgeons ('neurons') had the dull cream-colored bone of the cranium exposed, a specialized electric drill was used to bore through. Clearly, this was the tricky part. It needed to go through bone and only bone. Millimeters were as good as inches. Too little and there was still bone to go through, too much and you were in the brain (never a good thing!). Like the pancreas (remember: *don't fuck with the pancreas*), there was never any leeway for error here. With the bolt screwed in, the intracranial pressure could now be measured.

The 'neurons' left the room, and the team prepared for the laparotomy. Randy, who had been quietly observing and intermittently interjecting instructions, came over to me.

"This is your case, your Lap, if you want," he said.

He didn't have to ask twice. Of course I wanted it! This would be a real case, not just a chest tube or drainage of an abscess, but a laparotomy—a laparotomy for trauma, no less. It was rare enough for any of us to do any case during the ER rotation, let alone a real one like this.

Once again, I had left the module in the capable hands of the first year, who was on his own 'high' after placing the chest tube and performing the peritoneal lavage. I knew my own high could be halted at any moment by the next arrival. I was very aware of the emotional roller coaster; the higher you went, the better you felt, but the further you had to fall.

Sure, I knew that the real reason I was being given the case was because this patient's outcome was already pretty much sealed and that we were just trying to buy time in the event the family agreed to organ donation. Still, I was really excited to do a real case and with my chief, no less, which was so much less stressful than doing it with the Attending.

I prepped the abdomen 'high and wide—from the neck to the pubic bone. Another axiom of trauma surgery was that you could never prep too much. You never knew what to you might find, and although we might start in the abdomen, not infrequently we needed to extend our exploration up into the chest.

I gowned and gloved, trying to act like an old pro, not letting any-one see me concentrating intently on getting my hands into my gloves properly, all the fingers in their rightful spot. I did not want to make the rookie error of putting two fingers in one glove finger, resulting in the tell-tale dangling empty finger of latex. I pretended that this was just another routine case for me as I bellied up to the table. Randy stood opposite. Just another day at the office. I'm sure he and the nurses knew otherwise.

I took the scalpel from the scrub nurse, and after a quick glance at Randy, made a long midline incision, certainly the longest incision I'd ever made. I was not really sure how long to make it, but I knew that longer was better, so I continued until I thought it was long enough. Surely Randy would stop me if I went too far. It had been drilled into our heads that small incisions had absolutely no place in trauma surgery. It was critical to be able to see everything. You can't fix what you can't see.

Yielding under the pressure of sharp steel, the skin separated, exposing golden yellow fat, which pushed up slightly and then bled. Wow, it was a big cut and now appeared to be bleeding a lot. Too much, it seemed at first, and for a moment I wondered if I could get it stopped. But I had only just begun; I was not even in the belly. I took hold of the skin and fat on one side, Randy did the same opposite me (actually, he always got there first), and with a gentle opposing pull, the fat yielded, down to the tough whitish midline fascia, the gateway to the abdomen.

As soon as I had made a small opening through the fascia and into the abdomen, I was met with a torrent of blood. It poured out, and I rapidly sucked it up, popping the sucker through the small defect I had created before lengthening it. This fluid was a very dark red, and after the initial unsettling gush, it rapidly slowed. Making the cut longer, I packed multiple 'lap sponges' (each the size of a facecloth) into each of the four abdominal quadrants. This was done to control bleeding and allow us time to perform an organized exploration. Inserting my hand almost to the elbow, I began feeling around. This was another first. It was the first time that I had really felt the inside of the abdomen since my anatomy refresher (Anatomy for Surgeons) during my last year of medical school, but that person wasn't alive! So it was the first time that I was 'up to my elbows' in a 'live' belly. Strange disjointed but fleeting thoughts bounced aground in my head: "Boy, it's warm in here (not the cold lifelessness of a cadavers' innards). The bowel is so slippery. I have my hand inside a living person. I wonder what my buddies from med school are doing right now. There is no formalin smell. I'm glad I have gloves on. This feels quite nice actually. I bet none of them are doing anything this cool." The random thoughts continued.

The soft, smooth, almost silky, loops of small intestine slipped between my bloody latex-covered fingers as I started feeling around. They were very hard to grab a hold of. "Wow," I thought again, "this is going to be my job, having my hands in people's bellies and touching their intestine." I guess I was just going to have to get used to it.

I had a mile wide grin hidden under my mask. This was so damn cool. There was a part of me that still could not believe I was actually doing it. I needed to pinch myself, but then I was too busy delving deep into this man's belly.

I methodically worked my way back around each of the four abdominal quadrants, carefully withdrawing the blood-soaked sponges as I tried to locate the source of bleeding. Once again, I was learning to use my fingers to 'see'. While the third-year medical student held the 'sticks' (retractors), Randy staffed me. He essentially gave me free rein as he showed me the sequence of an organized examination of the abdomen for trauma. Palpating (feeling) the upper abdomen, I could clearly feel (see?) cracks in the usually silky smooth liver and then, with the medical student really hauling on the retractor under the right rib cage, I could truly see them. Extending up from the edge of the liver about four inches were three irregular, parallel cracks; appearing as they had been torn by an animal's (*velociraptor comes to mind now*) claw. Surprisingly, none of them were actually bleeding. Searching to his left, I found the stomach—a partly deflated thickened bag within which I could easily feel the long, pencil thin NG tube. Behind it, high under the left rib cage, was the spleen. I very gingerly (I was reminded, at least a couple of times) slid my fingertips over it. Its surface, a little reminiscent of the liver, felt normal to me. Randy checked my every move! There were no cracks here. This spleen was intact.

After washing the old blood and clots with bucket (actually, large stainless pitchers) loads of warm saline, I looked around again for any other injuries. I 'ran the bowel', using both hands to slide along its soft, silky, slippery surface, turning it over and back again, a foot or so at a time, checking both sides for possible injuries. A number of areas showed bruising but luckily no evidence of any active bleeding or bowel injury. Randy showed me how to check the duodenum and pancreas (areas notorious for hiding potentially lethal injuries). They also appeared normal.

This, as it turned out, was the perfect beginner case for me. The patient had remained stable, and although we did not waste time, there was also no real rush. The source of the bleeding, the liver lacerations, had likely self-sealed following his temporary drop in blood pressure. Once we were sure there were no other serious injuries or, for that matter, anything that needed attention, it was time to be done and get out.

One of the most underrated parts of surgical decision-making, especially when it comes to abdominal explorations, is knowing when to be done, to know when all the bleeding has been taken care of, to know when spending further time (dinking around) would just place the patient at increased and unnecessary risk. As with most things in surgery, this generally overlooked skill also comes down to experience.

Soon I began closing up the long incision, taking large deliberate bites with a heavy suture, fighting the upward pressure of uncooperative bowel, which was constantly trying to force its way out. Anesthesia was not really helping the issue, as they had already decided it was high time for the case to be over and that I was taking far too long. Consequently, I was now struggling against the contracting abdominal muscles pushing the intestines out and into the wound.

Nevertheless, it was still a great case. I really felt like I had made a huge step, albeit, in reality, a small one, towards my goal of becoming a surgeon. Residency always seemed to be a process of two steps forward and one back, and sometimes even, two or three back. This, for a change, felt like a giant stride forward. We were in and out in under an hour. I left the operating room feeling about seven feet tall. I had finally lost my laparotomy virginity. I felt as if I had a neon sign floating above my head, saying, "I just did a laparotomy!" It was not a difficult case in any sense, yet it was still a milestone.

The operating room is at first a very confusing and intimidating place (this is by no means an accident). We were usually dumped in without explanation, introduction, or instruction. We were on the lowest rung on the medical ladder, the extras on a busy movie set who appeared to be there without direction. It seemed total mayhem—a chaos of a thousand seemingly random actions all taking place simultaneously.

My first time in an operating room was as a first-year medical student watching a coronary artery bypass at the Royal Victoria Hospital in Montreal. I backed up against the wall, trying to be inconspicuous as my green scrubs stuck out like a sore thumb against the stainless cabinets and white tiled wall. I received glances of disapproval from the more seasoned nurses, apparently guilty of a crime I had yet to commit. Slowly with time (and multiple further, still awkward, visits), a certain order precipitated out of the confusion. This appeared to occur by osmosis (i.e., experience), as no one ever stopped to explain the roles of the various personnel, what was going on, who was who, and who was doing what and why. We knew nothing of operating room etiquette, the complexities of sterile technique, or the intricate hierarchy of the staff therein. For a long time, it all remained a big mystery.

At the 'head' of the operating table was the anesthesiologist, the conductor orchestrating care as he sat, half hidden, behind the blue perpendicular drapes that separated him from the operating field: the ether screen. This name persists even though 'ether' has not been used for at least 50 years. In most elective cases, they ran the show from their comfortable swivel chair, giving medication and adjusting the proportions of anesthetic gases. It was only in an emergency, when the 'shit was really trying to hit the fan', that they would stand up (it took a lot for that to happen!). Anesthesia has been described as hours of boredom interspersed with seconds of sheer terror. It was for those latter moments that we were appreciative of their skill, knowledge, and calmness under fire. There were also a multitude of nurses in the room, and waiting by a back table in the invisible, unmarked sterile area was the perpetually stern, somewhat aloof, yet always experienced scrub nurse. Here they patiently waited to take care of their charge, the surgeon, who backed into the room, scrubbed hands held shoulder high.

This was their domain, and it was no wonder that they used to call it an operating theatre, for that is precisely what it was: a theatre. Here the surgeon was on stage and in front of all present, they performed. Just as an actor revels in the admiration of his audience after a stellar performance, so does the surgeon; and never more so than after a difficult or technically demanding case. There may not be the shouts of adoration or roses thrown from the observers, but all were aware when they had performed well.

There are still a few hospitals, especially in older European cities, that have the true surgical theaters. Small, cramped, dark-oak-paneled semicircular amphitheaters so steep that everyone in the audience, all of whom were by necessity standing, had an excellent view of the proceedings on the theater floor almost directly below them. It was here where surgical and anatomical teaching went on until the 1950s. This has now been replaced by closed circuit video monitoring for observers in the next room or half a world away. The audio is supplied directly by the 'miked-up' surgeon, who returning full circle is now back center stage, performing.

And then there are the tools, the surgical instruments. There are just so many shapes and sizes. And who came up with all the crazy names anyway? Many of them do not make any sense. There are, 'right angles' where the angle is only sixty degrees. There are peanuts and peons, and clamps galore: curved, bent, straight, long, short and of every conceivable length and shape in between, skinny ones, fat ones, some with teeth and some partly or completely edentulous. Then there is a similar assortment of retractors. Many instruments—Allises and Adsons, Kochers and De-bakeys, Javids and Castroviejo's—bear the names of famous surgeons who designed them (or at least are given the credit). However, just to add to the confusion, many instruments have different names in different institutions and even by different surgeons in the same one.

Confusing? You bet. But it did get better slowly—very, very slowly.

In my early days in the operating room, I always tried to keep it simple. I would just ask for a clamp. Not any specific type of clamp. Just a clamp. This was mainly because I did not or could not remember their correct names. Sometimes I just wasn't really sure which one I needed, and so I would wait and see which one the (far more experienced) scrub nurse would hand me. They always knew the one I needed for a particular portion of the case. They had seen it all before. This technique of less is more helped me tremendously with the procedures, but it didn't help educate me as to their names. That was truly information osmosis in action as slowly I assimilated the knowledge over time. Figuring out the sutures and all their combinations of needle types, sizes, and material was yet another hurdle not quickly overcome. It appeared (and still does) that the designations are completely random. Luckily, the needle packages have a facsimile of their contents on them.

*Even now, I find myself asking for a particular suture on a BFN (Big F%#*ing Needle) as at least then my staff knows exactly what I want.*

It was 5:00 in the morning, only an hour and a half until the day resident returned to relieve us. I sat for a while in recovery writing orders, thinking I was 'hot stuff'. Although tired, I was still on a post laparotomy 'high'. But I knew it would be short-lived. Soon I would be brought back down, made to feel inadequate, incompetent, and ignorant. I refocused, got on the phone, and dictated the case I had just completed. With adrenaline waning, I took my time making sure the patient was stable and the recovery room nurses had the orders they needed before ambling back to the module.

Just dictating the operative report was stressful enough. What should I say? It needed to sound professional. Once again, there was no direction. No one explained what needed to be included. We learnt by trial and error, and there was a lot of error. We learnt by reading other operative notes, likely also dictated without direction, and tried to make ours appear similar. Most likely, we were just perpetuating the errors of our predecessors.

With just over an hour to go until this night was over, I could already hear my bed calling. But I needed to stay awake. I still had to complete the sign-out then drive home and find food. These last couple of hours were always the hardest. This was when the fatigue really started to set in, which was far worse if the pace had slowed, our adrenaline output proportionally decreasing.

On rare days when we did get out on time, we might head over to

Butchers, our favorite breakfast spot. Situated on a quiet sidestreet on the northeastern edge of Eastern market (a Detroit landmark for over a century), it was definitely worth getting out on time for. Usually the entire night crew (if no one was operating) and many of the nursing staff would head over to this little hideaway gem, which was about half a dozen blocks away. It had a well-deserved reputation for hearty breakfasts and generous mimosas. This was no time for caffeine for we had neither the need nor the desire to stay awake. When breakfast was over, it was get home and crash. This was our time to unwind, the only real social time we had during the entire rotation.

But even here, work was impossible to avoid. Having experienced both the exhilarating and the depressing, conversation naturally gravitated towards work.

It was great camaraderie. Before too long, we were sitting, satiated, catatonically staring at our empty plates, intermittently sipping at any remaining beverage and not wanting to expend the energy to leave.

We were exhausted, a feeling not improved by our newly carbohydrate-full bellies. I just wanted to find a corner to curl up in and sleep until it was time to go back for my next shift that evening. But no, I knew I needed to get home to bed, then wake up that afternoon and try to get some reading done. There again was old my nemesis, reading, always on the forefront. There was always reading to be done, and it was the same old battle, sleep vs. reading, but no matter how much I tried, the sand man always won.

Two days later, the man on whom I had performed my first trauma laparotomy died. We knew that even optimistically his chances were slim. So although not a surprise, it was still depressing to have my first laparotomy end up in the morgue.

So why do anything?

No matter how slim the odds, we always needed to give our patients a chance. These were previously healthy individuals who had sustained sudden, life-threatening injuries and occasionally 'miracles' did happen.

Some did survive. If anyone had a chance, it was usually in this very resilient population. We also needed to learn. Learn by doing and not just watching. This was an opportunity for the patient to teach us, to help us, even if it appeared that there was little we could do that would help them. Unlike in an acute gunshot victim, here seconds were not as vital, and an experienced, fast, efficient surgeon would make little difference. But the experience that this unfortunate gentleman gave me was priceless.

In this and many similar cases, one of the main reasons for keeping such severely head injured patients alive was the possibility of organ donation. There is always the possibility that despite such tragedies, they might give life to, or improve the life of, others.

Lead, Drugs, and Alcohol

WORK, EAT, sleep, repeat. This was my daily routine. Occasionally, if time permitted, I downed a meal at one of the hospital cafeterias, renowned for their economical prices and matching quality. I woke up at 2:30, a little earlier than normal, for 'nights', hoping to manage a few hours of reading before heading back. That, at least, was my intention. But with so much to read, where did I start? The textbooks were mammoth, and the stack of articles I needed to review was piled high on the floor. It was all a bit overwhelming. I would attempt my attack in stages, usually picking a chapter, trying to get through perhaps a dozen or so pages at a sitting. As for the articles, the pile just got bigger.

I picked up a small, easy-to-read abdominal trauma book by the celebrated trauma surgeon Donald Trunkey. This made a whole lot more sense, as it was anatomically descriptive, and I could specifically relate it to what I was experiencing every night. Even so, it was not long before I was jerking myself awake, my head firmly flattened against the old worn top of my desk. Its top, despite its hardness, easily managed double duty as a pillow.

The only guarantee when I returned that evening was that I had no idea what would be waiting for me. There was no such thing as a typical night.

Turning the corner into the module at precisely 6:30, it was already packed. Behind each curtain was a surprise and even perhaps the next surgical disaster. As always, so many of the injuries were either alcohol- or stupidity-related. A large proportion were a combination of the two.

Much of training was teaching us the ability to recognize the really sick and sieve them out from the rest—the search for the weak signal against the noisy background. Although a difficult skill to teach, this is the essence of all clinical medicine. Medicine, like good detective work, is an art that is honed with time but always requires a solid foundation.

After sign-over, I deployed my 'troops', delegating residents and students to various tasks, so that we could begin to mop up the mess that had accumulated during the latter part of 'days'. So many patients had, in their own words, "done fell out" (DFOs). Many were so intoxicated that they had serious injuries caused by falling, some even knocking themselves unconscious. They would usually arrive with associated bruises, lacerations, or broken bones, all as a souvenir of a time that would forever remain a blur.

The blood alcohol level of many of our patients would be greater than 300 (0.3%); some might reach the 'elite' liver and brain cell destroying heights of 400 (0.4%) or greater, gaining entry into the '400 club'. For most, a blood alcohol of 20 to 40 (0.02 to 0.04%) results in feeling relaxed, as they begin to be impaired with the warm, fuzzy feeling that we get (although for some it takes a lot more) after a couple of drinks. The majority of us realize when it's time to slow down or even stop, but some don't and continue, some joining the 'brainless' elite, flirting with death from alcohol poisoning as they enter the '400' club. This BAC of 400 means that 0.4% of the bloodstream is alcohol. Now at that level, even vampires become intoxicated.

Almost daily we saw patients presenting with the combination of just having had a seizure and reeking of alcohol (the majority of our patients).

Sure enough, when we asked them if they took seizure medication, they might admit to being on phenobarbital and Dilantin but said that they had not taken them. Their excuse: they were following their physician's instructions not to take their anti-seizure meds with alcohol. So rather than abstain from alcohol, it was the medications that were skipped. Logical perhaps, idiotic definitely, as most of the seizure disorders were related to over alcohol indulgence in the first place.

Many such patients sported evidence of recent hospital visits, their wrists adorned by assorted hospital identification bracelets, worn proudly like combat ribbons. The great majority of these patients were 'frequent fliers', and there was one particular gentleman who I had the pleasure of treating at least a half a dozen times during my rotations. Mr. Sydd was tall, thin, and malnourished, his deeply tanned, wrinkled face topped with prematurely greying hair flowing out from beneath his favorite brown-stained once-yellow Dekalb seed cap. He was such a regular that everybody, from the administrative staff to the nurses and residents, knew him by his first name, and all knew his history and meds. He was always belligerent and stinking drunk (both stinking and drunk) on arrival but was always pleasant and thankful the following day when he was sober (but still smelly) and being discharged. The last time I saw him, he had somebody else's footprint clearly embedded on his forehead as he stood in front of the nursing desk with his right hand raised in a feigned salute. We all knew that he would be back.

I have often wondered what happened to the patients that we so frequently took care of and Mr. Sydd in particular. Where did he go after he was discharged? Did he go home? Where was his home? Did he even have a home? Perhaps he was picked up by family, his friends? It is more than likely he spent his days roaming the streets and his nights in some kind of shelter (If he was lucky). So often he was just beaten up and left languishing in a secluded alleyway.

Before too long, the police brought in our first code of the evening, a young woman in her early 30s who was screaming at the top of her lungs.

We very rapidly reached the limit of our patience and wanted to tell her, "Shut the hell up!" We, of course, bit our tongues as we did with so many of our vocal visitors. She was unable to stay still, writhing around like a trapped python. Her clothes were blood-soaked, and a fresh pool was rapidly developing on the sheets beneath her. We knew that as long as she was able to scream with such forceful bravado, she could not be too badly off. It was the quiet ones that we learnt to be wary of. They were always the most severely injured, and the ones that needed our immediate attention. Although still clearly injured, she displayed a marked hysterical component, most likely chemically enhanced.

The nurses completed the not insignificant ordeal of removing her clothes, a golden jacket with matching shorts (quite gutsy for the Michigan fall), and insesrted a couple of large bore IVs. This did little to calm her down. As we progressed with our initial survey, she continued her combative and potentially self-injurious behavior, resulting in her being placed in restraints. Our assessment, which had begun the moment we heard her screams, made it clear that she was very much awake, somewhat alert, and had likely not sustained any significant thoracic injuries. Her lungs, even from a way off (the next building even), sounded in fine fetter. This assessment did not change once we examined her up close. She would not stop moving, making it doubtful that she had any fractures or even significant intra-abdominal injuries.

She had a huge, deep gash on her left flank, so deep it was as if someone had tried to slice her in two but stopped short of entering her belly. She remained thoroughly uncooperative, unable to tell us in any intelligible manner what had transpired. The wound was a little longer than a foot and appeared to have been made with almost surgical precision, the fat and muscle layers of her flank superbly delineated as if mimicking a page from an anatomical atlas. Examining her more closely, or at least as close as she would allow, I didn't think that the peritoneal cavity had been violated. But then this was only a cursory examination, and the combination of her squirming and the amount of blood and clot in the wound made this hypothesis impossible to substantiate. I did not want to dislodge any clots right then, at least not until I was prepared to deal with the inevitable bleeding.

In short order, she was 'shipped' over to the module but remained highly agitated, certainly far out of proportion to the apparent extent of her injuries. As a result, she remained in 'leathers' for the time being, and we gave her something for pain. The size of a wound does not necessarily correlate with its severity. A 3mm stab that penetrates the heart is clearly far more serious compared to a very large laceration such as here.

The meds we gave her appeared at first to have had little effect, and her thrashing around just made the bleeding worse and certainly did not endear us towards her. It was clear that I was going to have to try to 'lay down the law' if I was to going to get anywhere and have even a remote chance of sewing her up. Many of our patients appeared not to comprehend reasonable and rational requests such as, "Please be still so that I can sew you up." Certainly this lack of comprehension was sometimes due to head injury (they usually stayed very still) but more commonly from self-administered chemicals (in which case, unless an overdose, they were never still).

I knew from previous experience that I would have to attempt a different tack. This usually meant wording things in the form of a veiled threat: "If you don't stop moving, I won't be able to sew you up, and you'll bleed to death." For those who had trouble with that, we would have to take it up a notch, attempting to make it much clearer and be far blunter: "If you move, you might die." In the end, we used any tactic that would help us get the job done. Frequent stories we used were to say that we were either close to the heart or, in males, to say that we were close to the testicles. Even the most inebriated male seemed to understand the latter comment and usually froze. It may have been a fabrication, but it had the desired effect.

Nothing I tried worked. She was too high, apparently still orbiting another planet. Our impression was corroborated by the results of her drug screen, revealing that she had taken a concoction of narcotics, alcohol, and cocaine. Being stable, we would just have to wait for her safe return to earth before contemplating any sort of repair.

Sometimes, even when too intoxicated to cooperate, patients with head lacerations might still need to be repaired expeditiously, if only because we just did not have time to wait. One evening, having neither the time nor inclination to wait, we used a technique taught to us by our seniors that involved suturing the man's earlobes to the mattress. Although cruel sounding, it caused minimal discomfort unless he moved his head, which he now, sensibly, was reluctant to do. It was then a simple task to get him sewn up and on his way, no worse for wear.

When she finally became a little more cooperative, I was able to take a better look at her wound. But even that was only possible after numbing up its edges with gobs of 'local'. She did not take kindly to that either and made no attempt to hide her displeasure. However, once the anesthetic took effect, she completely inverted her disposition. Her pain, likely augmented by her medley of illegal medications, soon vanished. With the pain essentially eliminated she had taken a 180 degree turn and now lay on her bed with a satisfied yet 'narcotized' wide, toothy grin. She was never able to give an explanation of how the injury had occurred, although judging by the precision, it was likely not accidental. Rather, it was performed with the intent of inflicting significant harm.

I flushed the wound aggressively with saline, which afforded me a better glimpse into its depths. While inspecting it and organizing my instruments in preparation for closure, I was personally reminded of the importance of eye protection in healthcare and especially for surgeons. While looking into its depths, I was struck in the face, point blank, by an over-zealous and wayward arterial bleeder. The accuracy was of marksman quality, but fortunately my glasses came to my rescue.

Proper protective goggles wrap around the side to prevent a possible side assault. Before such protection, we were always advised to never look away from a bleeder.

Looking through my blood-stained glasses, everything took on a pinkish hue. The floor, the walls, my instruments, all were just a little pink. Unfortunately, I had to put up with it at least until I was finished and had the chance to clean them. I immediately ligated the problem bleeders that appeared hell-bent on hosing me down and returned to evaluating the extent of the gaping cavity in front of me. It was deeper than I had estimated. She was so thin that my first thought was that even though her belly felt fine, the wound must have entered or at least come very close to penetrating the abdominal cavity. I needed to extend the incision a couple of inches at each end to better evaluate where it was undermined. After I explored the area, I sat (a luxury I allowed myself for lengthy repairs) and closed the wound in layers, bringing together the muscle layers first and then the fat layer with dissolvable sutures, finally re-opposing the skin with nylon.

Many surgeons would have taken her to the operating room to explore and close her wound. But not here and certainly not this night. The ORs were far too busy, and it was my chief's decision to care for it right here in the module. So that was exactly what I did. It helped having absolute confidence in him. Just shy of half an hour later, the wound was closed. I stood back to briefly admire my handiwork. The black nylon skin sutures were evenly spaced. I was happy.

Despite the time it had taken me to get her wound closed, her incision remained numb, and she almost reasonable as I sent her off to get some belly 'films'. They were fine, and so it was off to the OCU to spend more quality time sobering up, and 'we' would reevaluate her prior to discharge in the morning.

Once that was done, it was time to see what new 'insults' had come in, as that was the responsibility of the second year on 'nights'. But as if on cue, as soon as I had finished writing her up her note, contemplating seeing my next patient, the overheads crackled into life again announcing the promise of no rest with another code's imminent arrival.

Although we might complain about them, that was exactly why we were here. We (the surgical residents) lived for the codes, and the bloodier the better! It's what kept us going, kept the adrenaline pumping late at night and through the early morning hours, a time when routinely we were all struggling. So we did not want it to stay quiet; the busier the better. It kept it more interesting, if not just plain fun, and it was the crazy busy nights that would fly by. Just the overhead notification of a code hit us like a cold shower and brought our sluggish, sleepy senses back to full alert (or at least, as close as was possible).

We were informed it was a GSW (Gunshot wound) to the right neck.

Within minutes the ambulance was pulling up.

As they came down the hallway towards us, one of our students remarked.

"At least no one's doing CPR."

While waiting, the team was busy in subdued conversation, reminiscent of a busy coffeehouse. Soon the noise level of inconsequential chatter rose exponentially.

"Maybe it's too late. It's probably just another DOA." The comment was distinct from the background babble. It was so loud now that I could hardly hear myself think.

"Hey, come on, guys. Let's focus," I interjected, trying to stay calm and in control. I was always on a knife edge before a code arrived, never really knowing what to expect. It was always a crapshoot and certainly not the time for idle banter. It was not conducive to concentrating and more than anything, I needed to concentrate. When the code arrived, I needed all my ducks in a row, to be organized physically and mentally. My chief was busy, so this code was mine.

It wasn't too late. We lifted her onto our clean, white, crisply sheeted gurney. We all could see what appeared to be a gunshot entrance wound on her right neck, a small hole surrounded by dried blood. There was barely any bleeding. We found no other obvious injury. We immediately placed her neck in a 'Philly' collar and dove into our trauma routine.

She was young, perhaps only in her early 20s, thin, dark-complected but with much thicker, wrinkled facial skin, announcing to all that she had begun her not insignificant smoking habit at a young age. She looked up at us, her eyes wide open, dark, and penetrating, deeply searching ours. Her chin and lips quivering ever so slightly under her shortly cropped, dark brown hair. She was probing us for good news. But she knew. They always did. We had none. She was frightened, petrified, scared to death. Scared of death.

She kept looking straight up at us, blinking rapidly.

At first she remained calm, but her demeanor soon changed, and she became agitated, her tone aggressive, almost hostile, remaining adamant that she had been shot twice. But what we saw and what she told us did not correlate. We were trained to trust what we saw, so we remained skeptical. She never wavered from her story, that she had both felt and heard two shots. She had been in a bar, and while trying to break up a fight involving her boyfriend, was shot at close range.

Her blood pressure on arrival was barely 70, and we immediately began to tank her up with fluids while attempting to sort things out. There was not an obvious source of blood loss to account for such a low blood pressure. This was worrisome, but then she also did not act like someone who had lost that much blood, either; her skin remained warm and pink. Could she really have lost that much from her neck? Of course, it was possible, but not very likely, and anyway the wound was not even bleeding.

I continued with my evaluation, which quickly revealed far more distressing findings. She could neither move her legs nor feel anything below her upper chest. She could move her shoulder a little but could not wiggle her fingers. I checked it all a second time, hoping I was mistaken. Sadly, I wasn't, and there was no change. Shit! Things were definitely going from bad to worse. I had a bad feeling about this one. Everything pointed towards the same conclusion. She must have a high spinal cord injury. If this was true, she would end up paraplegic.

When we log-rolled her, we found another wound just below her shoulder. The second entrance site? It looked as if she actually had been shot twice. Because she had no sensation, she had been unable to guide us to its location.

Even after five liters of fluid, her blood pressure had not budged. Still, we had no obvious source to account for her low blood pressure. The picture was becoming frighteningly clear, and it was not a good one. The only thing that made sense was 'spinal shock'. Usually when someone came in with low blood pressure and a gunshot wound, the projectile had penetrated a major vessel and caused massive bleeding. This, strangely enough, would probably have been far better for her but it also did not correlate with the rest of what we were seeing. She had normal breath sounds. One glance up at the view box revealed a crystal-clear chest X-ray. There was definitely no blood hiding there.

We kept her in the resuscitation room to keep a close watch on her, and when we reviewed her neck films, things were not any clearer. Two bullets were fired, and there were two holes, so there should be two bullets. Seems logical. We looked at her films, then at each other. Back and forth we exchanged befuddled stares. Our tired neurons firing slowly. There were no bullets that we could see. So where were they? They were not on her cervical or chest films. Inspecting the holes closer, perhaps one was the entrance and the other the exit. Both bullets (if indeed there were two) must have taken the identical path. Two bullets following the exact same trajectory. Rare indeed. But then the number of bullets was not important, only the result.

We removed the c-collar that had been placed on arrival as soon as the radiology resident notified us that he could not see any evidence of an unstable cervical spine injury. There was a tremendous amount of swelling in the neck around the wound that we presumed was the entrance site. Now with her blood pressure was perking up, and after we removed the brace, her neck began to 'bleed like stink', but at least her breathing was easier.

Pressing on the side of her neck just above the 'entrance', I immediately managed to stem the flow. It must be an injury to the internal jugular vein, I surmised, quite impressed with my anatomical deduction.

Right about this time, Dr. Ledgerwood, the staff surgeon on call, happened to come by to see how things were going.

As she walked in, I nervously caught her attention.

"Dr. Ledgerwood, we've got a 26-year-old woman shot in the left neck. I think the bullet hit the internal jugular on the left." I waited for the inevitable dry response.

"Well, now, isn't that exciting," she replied, slowly, measured but with her typical sarcastic overtone, not even breaking stride as she headed over to see the X-rays. A couple of minutes later she returned.

Of course, as soon as she was away reviewing the X-ray films, the patient seemed to dramatically deteriorate. Murphy's Law in action? She became much shorter of breath and even a little stridorous. I was worried that bleeding in her neck might be compressing her trachea (windpipe). In the back of my mind, I thought she might need to be intubated.

One of the golden rules of surgery, of which we were frequently reminded, was that the time to act was when the action is first considered. If one procrastinated until there was no doubt, then the opportunity for successful intervention had frequently long passed.

Even in my inexperience, I knew that this was no ordinary situation. I had a woman with a gunshot to the neck in front of me who appeared to be rapidly deteriorating, and my Attending (whom I was always trying to impress and apparently failing) had just walked out. I knew she would return any second, but still I needed to do something. I did not want to be like a deer frozen in headlights. I was certainly not going to wait until the patient stopped breathing to do something.

"Let's have a tube and laryngoscope ready, please," I asked the nurse standing a couple of feet away, over by the crash cart.

"Are you going to tube her?" she asked with nervous excitement, hurriedly preparing the instruments that I had requested. What about Dr. Ledgerwood?

That of course was the million-dollar question. What about Dr. Ledgerwood? I did not want to wait, appearing indecisive, but then I did not want to make a rash decision and do the wrong thing. So, what to do?

"If I have to, I will," I said, purposefully not answering the second half of her question. "I just want everything ready. Just in case."

Right at that moment, as if on cue, Dr. Ledgerwood returned from the X-ray department and immediately noticed the commotion that I had managed to stir up in her short absence.

"Now what's going on?" she asked in a condescending tone. I took it as, "Can't I even leave you for a few minutes without you causing trouble?"

I swallowed hard, took a deep breath, and immediately went on the defensive. It's what we all did. A knot tightened in my stomach as I prepared my reply. We were told it got better when we became senior residents. But we had to get there first.

"She became suddenly very short of breath, and I think that she might need to be intubated," I replied, a little hesitantly, yet still trying to appear confident and with authority, my left hand still holding pressure above the entrance site as I tried to stem the increasing bleeding. But more than anything else, I was just nervous. I knew that Dr. Ledgerwood was watching everything and likely much more than I knew. I didn't want to screw up. Was she testing me? Sure, she was. She always was. She was watching how I responded under pressure. This was my chance to impress her and show that I knew what I was doing.

But did I? That was the real question. The answer: perhaps not so much.

It was her way of educating us. Preparing us for the real world where we would have to make life-and-death decisions under the gun with no one around to ask for help. But at the time we couldn't see the big picture. We were in survival mode.

"Get your hand off her neck and let the blood out," she said, or rather barked. My hands flew off, as if suddenly shocked. Blood and clot immediately squirted and then oozed out of the wound, but her breathing improved almost instantaneously. Better out than in, I guess, otherwise it would just build up in the tissues and that truly would compromise the airway.

Another important lesson.

So many lessons. So little time.

Seeing that all was under control, she added, "Get her ready for the OR. Now." Then she abruptly stopped, about faced and left. Everyone was left a little stunned, but then again, that was exactly the effect she wanted. When she was around, all of our fight or flight mechanisms were so heightened that we really hardly knew what was going on until after the fact. It was education by intimidation at its very best. But it worked. We learnt, and we rarely ever made the same error twice.

Rapidly we had her over to the operating room for a neck exploration. Later we heard that the bullet had pierced the left internal jugular vein but luckily had missed the carotid artery. But that was essentially the only good news. On its destructive journey, the bullet had completely severed her spinal cord. She had no sensation below her neck, would never again be able to move her legs, and she would have very limited arm function.

It would take a couple days until she was out of neurogenic (spinal) shock and the swelling around the injured spine had begun to subside before anyone could evaluate the true extent of the neurological damage. However, at the time of surgery, they could see the devastating extent of the anatomical damage, and it was clear that there would be little hope of much improvement.

Only a few days later we heard that despite all the heroic efforts, the battle to save her had been lost.

At only about 11:00 pm, the night was still young, and we already had a couple of good cases to make Randy, our night chief, happy. His role on 'nights' was mainly as 'cutter'. Sure, he was also responsible for overseeing the smooth running of the surgical module, but he would rather just stay in the OR, so the more cases we lined up for him, the better. It was always best to keep our chiefs operating. Just as a chef likes to be cooking, so a surgeon likes to be operating. If it kept him happy, we were, too.

Around midnight EMS brought in a lone driver. According to the officer accompanying her, she had been heading along the freeway, suddenly veered off, bounced off the median strip, and the vehicle came to rest on its side in the fast lane. The extricated patient was an attractive middle-aged woman, impeccably dressed in a dark sage green business suit. She had no external signs of trauma. She had been well 'belted' in. She would not, or rather could not, answer any questions. Although completely inappropriate, she did not appear to have been drinking. We could not smell alcohol, a skill that our highly trained and finely tuned surgical noses had become very adept at. No, something else was going on. The actions did not match the picture. What was it? Drugs?

Immediately the nurses went about starting an IV, which was an ordeal in itself, and it took four of us just to hold her down, while she assaulted us with a barrage of confused, yet almost polite, curses. Although this was nothing new, it was still out of place coming from the lips of someone so well dressed. Once we had a 'line' in, fluids running, and labs sent off, we gave her two amps of D50 (concentrated sugar solution) while the nurses ran a Dextrostix (a one-minute test for blood sugar). Donning a pair of blue disposable gloves, the nurse designated as 'searcher' for the night began going through and cataloging her belongings. In her purse, she found an insulin prescription with her name on it. She was a diabetic, and not surprisingly, her Dextrostix returned as zero.

Very quickly, within seconds, really, of pushing the second 'amp' of

'D50' into her IV, she began responding. She was suddenly both comprehensible and rational. Now, she began asking the questions. Where was she? How did she get here? Why was she restrained? They were all very reasonable and appropriate queries yet still a bit of a surprise from someone who had been so inappropriate just minutes before. Now that we had an idea of the problem, we were not surprised to see her blood sugar return at only 21. Twenty-one for anyone was crazy low. Dangerously low.

Our protocol for patients with altered consciousness was to immediately give them intravenous glucose (in case of an insulin overdose) and a narcotic antagonist (for the drug ODs). The D50 IV candy bar was enough to jump-start them out of a hypoglycemic (low blood sugar) coma. We never waited for a blood test result, as every second of hypoglycemia can bring the patient closer to irreversible brain damage. Our bodies may be able to last some time without a meal, but our brains cannot survive long without glucose or oxygen.

Now fully awake, she was pleasant, rational, and methodical as she pieced together the events of earlier. By her own admission, she was a brittle diabetic who, due to her hectic work schedule, had not taken her routine morning insulin but had waited until around noon. Exacerbating matters further, she had hardly eaten the entire day, heading home around midnight after a prolonged meeting. This was when the glucose lowering effects of the insulin were peaking. Her blood sugar fell precipitously, causing her to rapidly lose consciousness while behind the wheel. Fortunately, we found little else wrong with her, and after observing her for a few hours, she was released.

I had a number of insults (consults) I needed to see that were taped to the side wall of the nursing desk. Amongst this collection of 'goodies' was a man with a large abscess above his right eye, a consequence of a strike he had received earlier in the week during yet another alcohol-fueled brawl. Now, after a few days of maturing, it was more than ripe, and I was pleasantly surprised (this was going to be fun!) that it had not already ruptured. It was red, tense, shiny, and just begging to be drained. And, boy, did it drain! When I sliced it open, it erupted its grey-beige, foul smelling contents all over the drapes. Unlike on other occasions, this time I was out of the line of fire.

No doubt it was gross, but then sometimes the more disgusting the problem, the more satisfying the solution. As interns, these were our surgeries, our chance to cut and cure and see how it made us feel.

We always heard that one of the signs that you will make it a surgeon is the ability to really enjoy draining pus, and the fouler and smellier, the better. When you are getting that stuff out, you know you are making your patient better. How could you not? If you are smiling, making jokes, and the rest of the team is gagging, then you have made the grade. You might just have what it takes.

Following that short, yet brilliantly stinky, adventure, I admitted a GI bleeder for further workup. An elderly man who, as like the majority of our GI bleeders, was a heavy drinker and came in because he had vomited blood a couple times. Sure enough, he told us he'd had a day and a half of some 'pretty intense drinking'. It's hard to believe how much booze these guys could consume. A fifth every evening was par for some, and even that wouldn't be enough to get them here. When we put a tube down and irrigated his stomach, there was no evidence of any active bleeding, just a bunch of old clots. We parked him in the OCU for the night and stuck him on the list to be 'scoped' in the morning. The booze had probably pickled his stomach, and sadly, this pickling was never just confined to that organ.

The only way to find out was to take a look—down into his stomach that is. We were very fortunate to have the services of one of the foremost surgical endoscopists in the country; a diminutive, bald, brilliantly skilled Japanese surgeon, Dr. Sugawa. We were always looking for any excuse to work with him.

Having taken care of the paperwork and making sure that the 'scope' was scheduled, I hoped again for just a little respite before the next onslaught of patients, who appeared to be constantly arriving as if falling from a conveyor. Sitting, I began to feel a slight wave of relaxation wash over me. The module nurse brought me back, waving a pink consult slip in my face. "Don't get too comfortable. You've got another consult." I did not take the bait and tell her what I really thought. As if reading my mind, she continued.

"It's only for a breast mass. In module three."

I soon located the right bed in module three where a thirty-something-year-old lady was lying on a flowery 'brought from home' pillow. She explained how the lump in her breast had been getting bigger for a week or so, but she finally came in when the pain prevented her from sleeping. On exam there was a hard red mass under her left nipple. It must be pus, I thought. I checked with my senior who agreed.

After putting a lot of local anesthetic in her breast, I made a cut over the mass and, extending it deeper, struck the mother lode. There was a forceful gush as the cavity erupted its foul-smelling, putrid contents.

Later, our good friend, Charlie Sydd, was back, only this time in the medical module where we had been asked to see him. He said it was because his feet did not feel right. He was spot on: his feet were not right, or more exactly his toes weren't. They were black, not dirty black, but a shriveled-up, dead, gangrenous black with the foul, fetid odor that accompanied decaying flesh.

Charlie was a true frequent flyer; almost all his issues were alcohol-related. We knew him well. When he was sober, he was easy, and tonight was no exception. His life appeared to be a series of unfortunate circumstances, crappy really, living from one soup kitchen to the next, staying anywhere he could locate a little warmth during the harsh Michigan winters. Usually, the only heat that he felt he found came from a bottle.

It did not take an advanced rocketry degree to figure out that he needed to be admitted. What was not clear, however, was if his dead toes were the result of poor blood supply or had they frozen because it was so damn cold. When I examined his feet, all the toes of his right foot were black, hard, and shriveled. Clearly his condition was not a recent one. They appeared to be long dead, so mummified that they could easily have belonged to Tutankhamen or one of his long-deceased relatives.

It was clear that Charlie needed surgery, as for starters his toes had to go. From my brief evaluation, it appeared that the culprit was the severe Midwest cold, especially as he had been living outside with only minimal protection against the frigid nights. Consequently, he undoubtably would not be leaving with anywhere near as many toes as he had arrived with.

He never appeared bothered by all the attention. If anything, it was the opposite. He was exceptionally calm, content, apparently happy to be in our well-heated hospital where he now had people to take care of him and even some that came to chat. He knew he would be getting three squares a day and a nice warm bed with clean sheets. Did it get much better? Sadly, for Charlie, it didn't. Losing a few toes, in the grand scheme of things, may have seemed like a good deal.

"Please, take your time. I'm in no rush," I'm sure was his thought. I immediately began getting him admitted, rapidly delegating him to a medical student who would continue his work-up and get him up to the floor. There, they would get Charlie fixed up, which meant amputate his dead toes. Sure, Charlie's feet would be fixed, but nothing else would change, and before too long he would be back to see us again. We might have treated his current problem but certainly not even touched on its cause. It was difficult for me to come to grips with the fact that we could only bite off small pieces at a time (no pun intended), fixing what we could fix, yet never really fixing the underlying problem: his disastrous social situation. This, of course, was the issue in so many of our patients, but at least I could take some consolation that we were at least fixing something.

During the rest of the morning, the hour and a half of it that was left, we managed to get the module cleared out, such that there were no 'real' patients left by 6.30 sign out. It almost made it seem like it had been an easy night. Once again, appearances were so deceiving.

During our training, we learned to categorize everything, and, it seemed, even more so when it came to trauma. We had a grading system for every type of injury. This pigeonholing system allowed us to compare one patient with another, supposedly to help us with treatment. This was one of the times when I realized that the university world of publishing papers and number crunching was not for me.

But that did not mean that we could not have a little fun with the idea, especially on 'nights' when we all too often saw patients with similar excuses:

"I was minding my own business and, well, Doc, I just done fell off the porch." This became so commonplace that we made up our own grading scale: the Porch Injury Severity Scale (PISS scale). We were not only making fun of grading systems, but even more so of the, often preposterous, excuses that our patients came up with for their injuries. As you might guess, the majority of these injuries involved the excessive intake of alcohol or some other substance abuse.

* 'PISS1': Falling off the lower step of their stoop and involved only minor cuts and bruises.

* 'PISS2': Involved some type of foot or hand injury, often just a sprain.

* 'PISS3': More serious injuries, falling from a little higher, often with a much higher level of alcohol intoxication and frequently resulting in a broken bone or two.

* 'PISS4': These were more serious still, often an injury acquired not so much after falling off the porch but often, from falling from a height, the equivalent to the second floor. These patients would have multiple fractures, potential internal injuries, and would all require hospitalization. Although explained as an accident, they also occurred secondarily to alcohol excess, and these people were frequently assisted on their journey by an intentional shove from their significant other.

* 'PISS5': This was the most serious and would always involve outside help to cause the injury. Whereas 'PISS4' may have had a little push, this next level of ineptitude would involve not only a fall from a greater height but more often the victim sustaining a gunshot as they were fleeing. They were never too worried about the height from which they were falling as they were too preoccupied by the lead projectiles chasing them.

My First Appy

DAY 14 —There were some days when I didn't really feel like going in, and this day, a Sunday, was one of them. This was not typical, so I put it down to having exited on the wrong side of the bed or perhaps any of a dozen other equally invalid reasons. Another 12-hour stint in 'the pits' was just not that appealing. Maybe I was sick. But then surgical residents couldn't be sick. Nothing short of death or emergency surgery was ever an excuse.

I was tired. Tired of working 12-hour days that always ended up being 14. Tired of never having any down time, no respite, no break, no time to recharge. I was exhausted, and even a number of days after I flipped from days to 'nights', I was still not acclimatised. My internal clock had not yet switched. This residency stuff was hard work, really hard, and none of us had any idea of how hard it was or how hard it would test us, both physically and emotionally. We just hoped that the end justified the means.

I needed to read . . . read . . . read . . . read. There again, was that omnipresent, haunting, four-letter word. There was so much to learn, and I was already so far behind and only at the start of my second year. Reading was always at the forefront of my 'need to do' list but never my 'want to do' list. That was sleep! Just as I always had done as an undergraduate and in medical school, I would sit down to read, look at the page, stare at it, and then slowly stare right through it. Before too long I would be out cold. I had a long way to go to finish my five years. This was the easy part, as we were constantly reminded by our seniors, who tried and succeeded to intimidate us.

Although in these first two years we did not do a lot of cases, they were definitely the hardest, the most intense, and the most stressful for us. In comparison it made medical school look like a cakewalk.

Many surgical programs graduated fewer residents than started. This was the feared pyramid program, where every year a few residents were weeded out until you arrived at the chief year, by which time everyone tended to be much more cordial as they no longer had to compete with their 'fellow' residents for a place the following year. This system did little for collegiality or to encourage cooperation among residents. Although ours was not such a program, if you failed to make the grade, one way or another, you were still out.

We always needed to be on our game. We knew it would be a battle to get to the top (and, at the time, we thought that was our chief year!). We were young and, as we all thought, invincible. After all, we were the ones saving the lives, bringing people back from the brink. It was an adrenaline rush, for sure, with the added dangerous ingredients of immaturity, ignorance, cockiness, and machismo thrown in. Surgical residents had a reputation of burning the candle at both ends, and we were not going to let anybody down in that regard.

Slowly, we began to become accustomed to the chronic sleep deprivation, many days spent in a tired haze with one melding into the next. Day and night were inexorably entwined. When I finally did get out, sometimes after a number of days of being on-call, I remember standing motionless, exhausted, inhaling the strange fresh air, squinting skyward with my sullen, unshaved face as my sleepless, dark-ringed eyes looked with childlike wonder upon simple clouds floating by.

The nurses constantly came to our rescue. After all, they were the ones who really took care of the sick, the ones attending to their needs, listening to their stories, bathing them, changing their dressings. Sure, we might think we care for the sick, and we do, but it is the nurses who truly administer the healing touch. When we were sick, we felt their compassion, which was frequently accompanied by a well-deserved dressing down along with a lecture highlighting our patent stupidity (usually involving a combination of too much alcohol and too little sleep). They would come to our rescue, popping in an IV and pouring in a liter or two of fluid overnight into our inebriated, dehydrated carcasses. We would rapidly feel resurrected, and there would be no 'dragging ass' the next day. A couple of times I even left a capped IV in for the day, just in case I might need a top up later. We would camp out in an empty ICU bed, where we cared for our sickest patients and had some of the best nurses to care for us!

Entering the hospital, I was immediately immersed in a different world, almost a different dimension to what existed outside. We immediately needed to get straight to business.

We needed to arrive ready.

In one corner was a motorcycle victim, his left leg surrounded by an array of ropes, pulleys, and weights. He was in traction for a femur fracture. Someone had fun with that one, I thought.

Placing a patient in traction was a procedure that we learnt during our orthopedic rotation as a first year. It was pretty much a daily occurrence. At the time (1986) it was the preferential procedure for the treatment of femur fractures. Although not complicated, it still was quite a shock to me the first time I had to do it.

We needed a bed decked out with an overhead gantry, to which were attached numerous pulleys and a 'cats cradle' maze of ropes. When put together, it appeared reminiscent of a medieval torture device. But then, was there actually much difference?

Most patients benefited from a little sedation (I think we could have, too) to help them relax, as it was still an uncomfortable and nerve-racking procedure for them (and us). The goal was to keep the lower portion of the broken femur under enough tension to prevent the edges from overlapping and cutting down on any movement (newsflash: broken bones rubbing together doesn't feel good!), keeping them aligned as the healing process began.

A stainless-steel pin was placed through the bone (tibia) just below the knee. Strong nylon cord wound and looped its way through the complex arrangement of pulleys, connecting the pin to a set of weights sufficient to overcome the intrinsic muscular forces attempting to pull the bones out of alignment. Placing this pin was achieved mainly by brute force (which pretty much sums up orthopedics!) and a little finesse, very little actually, with help from an old-fashioned hand-powered drill. Although bones vary in strength, I recall that it took a lot of pushing and shoving while I tried to keep the sweat from dripping. It was one of my first introductions to orthopedics and confirmed my decision not to consider it as a specialty.

This procedure has now been pretty much relegated to history, as such fractures are now treated by surgical rodding or plating. Far superior to traction, this allows for almost immediate ambulation, a shorter hospital stay, more rapid recovery, and a concomitant dramatic reduction in complications.

Opposite the module, at an L-shaped desk was the nurse coordinator, our 'flight controller', guiding the movement of patients to and from their appropriate module. Nearby, amongst a mess of papers, I found Dave, the third year in the module this day, looking far too relaxed, apparently engrossed in *The Detroit Evening News*.

"Another day's vacation, huh?" I asked, flippantly.

At first, he did not bother to reply but looked up with an 'I'm way too good to be talking to you' expression.

Dave was new to our program, having recently joined us from an East Coast program from which he had transferred so that he could finish earlier and begin his subspecialty training. That was his story, although we all thought that most likely he had been cut from a pyramid program, a theory reinforced by his 'holier than thou' arrogance. He was not happy that he was only given a spot in our third year, having already completed three. Today, Sunday, he was working the module giving the second year on 'days' the day off. He made it abundantly clear, with a liberal smattering of East Coast snobbery, that the rotation was beneath him.

Apparently immersed in the sports section, he looked up, and as if suddenly remembering something, added nonchalantly, but with a typical condescending attitude,

"Oh yeah, there might be an appy in four." Not waiting for a response, his eyes returned immediately back to what appeared to be far more important.

"An appy in module four," I repeated silently. "Sounds great," I thought but acted as if I barely cared. Two could play this game. Maybe I would get a case, is what I really thought. The news instantly brought both my ARAS (ascending reticular activating system) and my ASS (a little lower down at the base of the spine) online, bringing me immediately more awake.

After sign-over rounds, I rapidly headed over to module four to locate the prospective surgical candidate. I sure as hell wasn't going to let anyone else get there first and steal 'my' case. After looking behind a number of curtains and receiving an equal number of clueless looks, I finally found her: A young Hispanic woman, with long dark hair and olive skin who appeared barely out of her teens. Even on first glance, she looked unwell. I pulled the green curtains closed behind me and began questioning her. The more she replied, the more she sounded like a 'textbook' history for appendicitis. Her constant grimacing reinforced that she was in a great deal of pain. I wondered why Dave had not called someone earlier. Was the sports section that exciting?

I had assisted on a number of 'appys' before but had never actually done one myself, let alone seen someone with such a classic history. Usually I was just another pair of hands helping retract so that a second year could do the case. But now, I was the second year.

I began daydreaming, fantasizing about doing the case. I knew the steps. I must have read them dozens of times. First the incision. Find McBurney's point, one third of the way from the iliac crest to the umbilicus, then make the cut. But which way should I make it? Then what? Put in the retractors. But which ones? What were they called? I began feeling a little confused, perhaps even overwhelmed. Stop overthinking, I chastised myself. That's why we had our seniors.

I really wanted this to be appendicitis, not because I wanted her to be in pain. No, of course not, but I really wanted to do an appendectomy. My mind was going a mile a minute, as I tried to think ahead to what I needed to do to get her ready. But hold on a minute. First things first; how about doing an exam? I selfishly hoped I would not be disappointed with my findings.

I began palpating her abdomen, making sure that I followed the careful and logical sequence that had been drilled into me since physical diagnosis class during med school. Always examine the abdomen from standing on the same side and in exactly the same manner, every time, starting at an area the furthest away from where the problem was suspected to be. This not only is more pleasant for the patient, but it enables them to relax their abdomen a little before we get to the area that hurts. So I started gently pressing on her left side, carefully watching her face. As I pushed, it appeared to hurt her a little, but more than anything she complained that it caused her pain on the opposite, right, side. Seemingly strange, this was a classic sign for appendicitis (Rovsing's sign; everything in medicine has someone's name stuck to it). Finally, when I finally gently pushed in her right lower abdomen, she went through the roof. As part of my thorough exam, I performed a digital rectal exam, which also elicited some similar pain.

*This has changed dramatically over the years. No one with pre-
sumed appendicitis gets a rectal exam, as now it appears that when
they present to the ER, the first stop is the CT scanner.*

Initially, this girl's family would not permit us to do a pelvic examination, which is (was?) essential (although perhaps now also superseded by
the CT) in women to be sure that we were not missing a tubal infection
or another gynecologic cause for her pain.

The mother contacted their priest and with his blessing, the gynecology resident went ahead and confirmed our impression that it was most
likely appendicitis. I started to get her prepared for surgery.

But hold on, did I forget who was really in charge? I needed to let my
chief know. With that in mind, I went off in search of him. I soon found
Randy in the laceration room, slumped in a chair, his blue bootie-covered
loafers resting up on a gurney. He appeared engrossed in the glossy pages
of a 'throwaway' surgery journal.

This laceration room was never used as its name suggested but had
found renewed life as a hangout for the chiefs, or storage for extra carts,
and occasionally even for patients waiting their turn for X-rays. As I got a
little closer, I could see that his eyelids were tightly shut; he was 'crashed'.

"Randy, I think I've found a case," I said a little quietly, almost whis-
pering, but once I knew that I was not getting through, I increased my
volume a couple of notches, repeating myself. After the third time, he
responded.

"I heard you. What you got?" he asked, clearly with awakening grog-
giness as he tried hard to cover up the fact that he had been out cold.

"A hot 'appy' in a 21-year-old woman," I began, as I moved around in
front of him so I could speak more directly.

"A guy?" Clearly he was still waking up.

"No, a girl."

"You sure?"

"Yes. A girl for sure," I replied.

"No, are you sure it's appendicitis?"

"Pretty sure," I answered, not wanting to sound too cocky. "She began having right lower quadrant pain yesterday morning. Some nausea and vomiting and is extremely tender on exam." I regurgitated a presentation that I had rehearsed on my way over. I was hoping like hell that I had the right diagnosis and had not missed some other obvious problem. I did not want him to make me look like a fool. I thought about the diagnosis I had made. Was I sure I was right, and this really was appendicitis? I began doubting myself. I could feel it eating at me. God, I hoped I was right.

Randy always had a habit of asking something obvious, to which we didn't have an answer, or showing us a finding that we had overlooked. It was never malicious. It was just his way. It was the way he taught us. He was a great chief, someone for whom I had great respect. I did not want him to catch me out.

"Fever?" He continued his interrogation.

"Only 99.8 degrees."

"White count?" he countered.

"Sixteen-four," I replied, hoping that's really what it was, and that I had not mixed it up with someone else's. Well, at least I remembered that it was elevated.

"OK, let's go take a look," he finally capitulated.

Walking rapidly, we went over to module three to find 'my appy'. I carefully watched his hand rapidly push, prod, and elicit the same un-comfortable response. Agreeing with my findings, he called the OR and set up a time for surgery.

I wondered how many times my patient had been examined to make this diagnosis. Did she also wonder how many it took to make the diag-nosis? It would have been at least the fourth time, not including medical students, that she been questioned, poked, and prodded.

But this was the university way, and the way of all good training programs. There was no CAT scan to help. We had to trust our clinical judgement. But the findings of a mere junior resident were not enough, and all findings needed to be corroborated by the senior. Although safe and a great educational tool, it did little to enhance efficiency.

It was now about 10:00 pm, and we were 'boarded' (scheduled) for midnight, which gave me ample time to get her ready. I spoke to her mother, explaining the suspected diagnosis and plan. She listened carefully, understanding the necessity for surgery. I had to believe that this conversation was much easier than her previous discussion over the pelvic examination.

Between sorties to check up on my 'appendicitis lady' and see other consults, I continued to pop in and out of the module, helping my interns and med students with any problems or questions that arose. As always, we were simultaneously the trainer and the trainee, teaching our juniors while being taught by our seniors. This paradigm never ends until the day we stop practicing. We remain a pupil to each and every one of our patients. We never stop learning and passing on the sometimes hard learnt lessons.

We were constantly inundated with consultation requests from the medical modules. The busier we were, the more we appeared to receive. We gained great finesse at reading between the lines of these requests. Many labeled; 'rule out acute abdomen' would turn out to be nothing of the sort. Then there were those that became synonymous with, "I don't have any idea what's really going on; please would you come and take over care." Of course we always acted as if we were more than glad to oblige. This was, of course, far from the truth, but it was the impression our Attendings wanted to give. So we complied, even if somewhat reluctantly.

Then there was the forever nebulous 'rule out bowel obstruction' note stuck on the module wall. Nine times out of ten, this had nothing to do with an obstruction but could run the gamut from absolutely nothing to an elderly patient on boatloads of colon-slowing medications, brought in from a nursing home plugged up with a fecal impaction. Thus 'rule out obstruction' might easily be synonymous with, "Please come and dis-impact this patient for us." This was precisely as exciting as it sounded. However, it allowed me to exercise my rapidly evolving delegation skills and pass on this unpleasant, yet important and educational, task to the intern or medical student who had the misfortune of working with us that night. We had all spent some memorable (not necessarily enjoyable) 'quality' time cleaning out patients on the medical services, praying that the thin latex gloves covering our fingers would remain intact. Lube, lots of lube; now that's the ticket.

I never could decide if the referring docs thought that the job was beneath them, or if they just hated us that much. I think it was a bit of both. But not one to let an opportunity slip by, here was the chance for our juniors to show off their plumbing prowess. Still, we detested those consults almost as much as we despised the laziness of those requesting them.

Occasionally it appeared that no one could make up their minds as to what was going on. We would be asked to come by and 'check it out'. "It's probably nothing," we were informed, "but we'd just like to have your opinion." It was all very patronizing and served to get us all pissed off. We wanted to blow them off. However, it was always these seemingly innocuous, aggravating requests that hid the sickest and yet the most interesting of patients. It was frequently these 'nothings' that ended up in the operating room. As much as we hated it, we constantly bit our tongue, swallowing another slice of 'humble pie'. Very occasionally we even admitted (not really!) that they were right. Of course, that is not to say that we were happy about it, for the majority, were 'dumps', but we saw them anyway.

We learnt to be stealthy, to 'fly under the radar', and sneak in and out of the medical modules as if navigating a mine field. If detected, we were soon sucked in to see others. It was imperative to stay out of sight and so out of mind.

At about 12:30, surgery finally called for 'my appy'. As the nurse's completed their preoperative check list, I checked in with Johann, my 'first-year' (resident) that month. We went over all the patients, and I felt confident in leaving him for a short time alone (not really alone, as he still had a bunch of students and still other residents with him). He already had a month up on the wards with 'L&L' under his belt, so I knew that he was well prepared. I headed over to the OR, where the anesthesiologist was talking to the patient. When they were done, the OR nurses took over with their own, but thankfully brief, inquisition. It was all necessary for the best care of the patient. It was check and double check. Nevertheless, I was impatient. I wanted to get going. It would just be my luck if a code came in right then, and I would have to give the case up. So, yes, I wanted everyone to hurry up. Although we might complain about the speed (or lack thereof) of our anesthesia colleagues, they were all outstanding. After all, they were the ones who kept the patient alive while we were 'dinking around', learning how to, and attempting to, fix injuries, while often losing way too much blood in the process. Occasionally (luckily, very rarely), following the command of our chief or even Attending, we took the patient directly through to the room and transferred them on to the operating table ourselves. This invariably got us into hot water with everyone from the nurse in the room up to the OR supervisor.

As Randy and the third-year medical student helped the nurses get the patient situated, I went ahead and began my scrub. Standing outside the room at the oversized stainless sink, which was almost big enough to bathe in, I began the 'scrub'. We started by using a small plastic nail file to clean under our fingernails. Then we scrubbed our forearms from the elbow down, utilizing various types of newfangled bacteria-destroying soap. This tended to occur in silence. I for one was too busy going over in my head each step of the case. This 'scrub' not only cleanses the hands but also helped cleanse the mind. It is a ritual, an almost Zen-like sequence that helps get us into the correct frame of mind before we enter the operating room. Does it really sterilize the arms? Of course not.

This reality is diametrically opposed to the view portrayed on medical drama shows, where the well-coiffed surgeons, having just stepped out of the glossy pages of GQ magazine, are scrubbing their hands while chatting with a colleague, their masks crisply hanging below their necks, so we can clearly see their perfect Hollywood smiles. Soon they are huddled around the patient, masks magically tied on. In reality our faces are covered (no TV cameras here) while we scrub, and there is little, if any, conversation as we prepare ourselves physically and mentally for the upcoming case. Usually the more complicated the case, the quieter the scrub.

I was nervous, excited, apprehensive, scared. A multitude of seemingly conflicting emotions were sprinting through my head. Any positive thoughts I had were immediately replaced by negative ones. I was back on the surgical emotional roller coaster. This was going to be 'my' case. I had seen the patient, I had made the diagnosis, I had done the work up, and now I was going to take out her appendix. I had done everything. God! I hoped it was not a normal one. But then we were expected to remove some normal ones, ten percent actually. Even so, normal was not what I wanted here. If it was normal, it would still count as a complication, an error, and I would have to present it at the next M & M conference. It did not matter in the least that it was expected for ten percent to be normal. I would still get raked over the coals. Ninety percent accuracy was not good enough. I really hoped I was right.

Now, with the ubiquitous use of CT scanning, we are surer of the diagnosis ahead of time. The use of scanning rather than clinical assessment is now so pervasive that today if I take a patient for an appendectomy based purely on clinical grounds, invariably I'll be asked by someone if I should get a CT first. Luckily and appropriately, there are still some ER physicians who will make the diagnosis and call me on just their clinical findings. A real doctor.

I had scrubbed many times before, but this time it felt different. I was going to perform an operation, where it was my decision that she needed a cut on her pristine abdomen. The pressure was definitely on, and I felt it. As I entered the room, I could feel everyone watching me. I needed to act properly, like a surgeon. Whatever that meant.

I walked over to the scrub nurse, my arms held up and out. She helped me put on my gown and gloves. I purposefully tried not to make eye contact. I did not want her to see my uneasiness, my uncertainty, as I slid each hand into the outstretched gloves. Ah, yes, the gloves. The guaranteed way to weed out the greenhorns. How hard can it be? The nurse even helps you. So did my fingers go into the gloves properly? No. No such luck, not even close. As I feared, two fingers slid into one glove finger. I was busted. By now I was sweating a little and praying that no one could see it. I walked briskly over to the semi exposed patient, rapidly fixing my glove en route.

She was now anesthetized, lying naked, vulnerable, waiting. Randy and I carefully positioned the sterile drapes over her freshly painted abdomen, unfolding a large blue drape, we lined up the precut hole over her lower abdomen. Her skin was now an even deeper shade of golden brown where it had been antiseptically painted by the medical student. The three of us—Randy, the medical student, and I—would be the only ones 'scrubbing in'. Once again, I felt a touch of relief knowing that my 'staff' (the attending) was not going to scrub in. That was at least one thing that I didn't have to worry about. But there was still the scrub nurse, circulating nurse, and anesthesiologist there to observe. Plenty to spread the word if I screwed up.

I 'bellied' up to the table. Randy took up his position opposite me.

I turned towards the anesthesiologist. "OK?" I asked, wanting to be sure he was ready for me to start. I wanted to be polite. There was nothing worse than starting before they were ready. That I would surely hear about.

Once given the nod, I turned to the scrub nurse.

"Knife, please," I said, trying to speak with authority, not arrogance, but then, on the other hand, not timidly either. It was a fine line. I sheepishly avoided eye contact.

She handed me the knife, or rather slapped the handle of the scalpel into my outstretched palm. I moved it around, settling on what I thought was the most 'surgeon-like' grip. It was not the first time that I had held a scalpel, but I think I made it feel as if it was. Carefully, keeping the skin taut between my left thumb and index finger, I slowly pressed the blade down and pulled it towards me. I had made the incision. It still took two or three tries before I got all the way through the skin. I was surprised that it did not bleed more. I'd had paper cuts bled more. I exchanged the knife for the electrocautery, 'Bovie', or 'buzzer' (due to the sound it makes) as I called it, carefully coagulating a few wayward bleeding vessels as I progressed deeper.

A small white plume, the byproduct of the electrically cut tissue, rose up from the tip of the cautery. More challenging at first was the accompanying smell of cooked flesh. Very rapidly we all become accustomed to it as just another of the many sensory triggers present in an operating room. Some residents would jokingly exclaim that the smell made them hungry. I can say for sure that, right then, I smelt nothing, at least not consciously. I was far too focused, concentrating to the point of exclusion of all else. My world at that moment was an eight-by-eight-inch square of golden-brown skin, bordered by four green cloth drapes, in the center of which I had made my incision. I worked my way through the fat, and luckily there was not too much of it, down to the fascial layer, which I subsequently also incised, opening it up and exposing the next layer. "Was this the right way?" I thought. Randy made no comment, so I guessed that it must have been OK. Randy was holding the tissue apart with a pair of antique appearing stainless retractors and would chime in with the occasional, "Yup and Good" or a "That's right" and "Perfect," all to make me feel more at ease, which it invariably did. He was always a tremendous confidence booster, and it did wonders for me. He carefully moved the retractors in a subtle but precise way, showing me where to make the next cut. He was a sublimely slick teacher.

I kept going deeper, gently separating each muscle layer to get to the next. Randy intervened, slipping the retractors under the muscles and giving them a good stretch.

"There you go," he said after a good tug, and holding them in position, passed them off to our obliging student.

Wow, what a difference that little stretch made. All of a sudden, I had an opening twice as big to work in. Surgery is all about exposure, and this was one of my first, of many, lessons in what a huge difference good exposure made.

After opening the final, tough fascial layer, the glistening one-cell-thick layer of peritoneum was revealed. This was the final layer before entering the abdomen. This was the holy grail, the 'Holy of Holies'. I could almost hear the choir singing.

I was just about there. I asked for a couple of hemostats and carefully clamped the peritoneum with small bites, tenting it up slightly. After a snip from a pair of Metzenbaum scissors, I was in. Enlarging the defect, I was immediately met by fat and bowel forcing their way up into the wound. Shit. Now I couldn't see anything (at least anything that I wanted to see!), just shiny moist fat and intestine everywhere. I felt a little wave of panic creep over me. How on earth was I going to find the appendix in all that? All I could see was fat and guts. Even in this thin gal, there seemed to be so much fat.

Exposure was all part of surgical training; the appendix does not just pop up and sit there waiting for us with a nice pretty flag on it saying, "Here I am! Come and get me." In most surgery the hardest part is proper exposure, and it was these techniques that I also needed to learn. In comparison removing it was relatively straightforward. As I had seen done before, I rolled up some small, saline-moistened gauze sponges, slipped them down into the wound, and used the stiff blade of the retractors to hold them in place. As I saw the sponges disappear into the abdominal abyss, it became clear why the sponge count at the end of every case was so important. The sponges helped keep the bowel out of the way and offered a (slightly) better view of the deeper abdominal structures visible through the small incision. But it was all too easy for a bloody sponge to disappear. The fluid in the abdomen was a cloudy yellowish grey, certainly not normal, and a sure sign that there was something not right in there.

My first task was to find the caecum, the beginning of the colon, where the small bowel entered the large. This was also where the appendix (literally) 'hung out'. I used a couple of stick sponges (a small wad of gauze at the end of a long ring-tipped clamp) to move the bowel around and tried to find something I could recognize. No luck. Now I was feeling a little stupid, ignorant really. I could not even find the caecum. If I couldn't even find that, what hope was there for me? I had failed before I had hardly even started. I was convinced that everyone in the room was watching me, exasperated, wondering who the hell was this guy who could not even find the appendix. Some were probably hoping that I would let my chief take over the case. But then, they clearly did not know me. I was not going to give up that easily. I didn't make it through four years of medical school and my first year of training just to give up.

I kept at it. There was bowel slipping around everywhere, despite my increasing efforts at retracting. Looking up, my eyes met Randy's. He gave me a reassuring nod, and I doubled my efforts on my caecal search. It seemed like forever, as these things always did at the time. Seconds seemed like minutes. Time stood still. Then, 'voila!' There it was! I had found the caecum. For a second I felt like Stanley finding Livingstone.

"Mr. caecum, I presume?" I felt pretty chuffed.

"Take it easy," I continued talking to myself. "You can still screw up." I still had not found the appendix, but it can't be too far off now. It has to be down there somewhere.

After some gentle hinting and persuasion from Randy, I resorted to using my finger as a probe. I knew that he was willing me on, guiding me with his lean but helpful comments and a few specifically directed eye and finger movements. I had seen the 'finger probe' trick done a few times but never really knew what it was they were feeling. It all seemed like magic: insert index finger, deep into the wound, rummage around and then, hey-presto, up pops the appendix. This was usually followed by some Neanderthal grunting and chest excursion with an unmistakable eyebrow raising and non-verbal facial expression of 'Look how good I am'.

Now it was my turn to attempt this finger exploration. I put my index finger in, but all I could feel were the moist loops of small intestine slipping and sliding all over as I swirled my finger around with a motion similar to slowly stirring a cup of coffee. What was I feeling for? Would I even know it if I found it? I kept searching, a little more half-heartedly perhaps, with my index finger, convinced that at any moment I might have to capitulate and let Randy take over. No, I was not going to let that happen. I needed to take my time. Anyway, what was the rush? There was none. I continued with my slow, swirling, fingertip search. A moment later, as if my fingertip was reading the textbook, I finally felt something. I was not sure what it was. I kept quiet and kept checking, probing with the tip of my index finger. Yup, this felt different all right, very different, perhaps even abnormal. But then what did I know? This was my first time doing this. What my fingertip felt was not soft like the intestine that had been trying so hard to thwart my search. Now I had to try and visualize what my fingertip was feeling. Was this a normal anatomical structure? If so, what was it? It felt firm, hard even. There was nothing in there that should feel like this, I thought, as I attempted to recall all of my minimal surgical experience up to that time. In my mind I was rapidly searching pictures from 'Clemente', my med school anatomical textbook. Whatever it was that I was feeling, it was really stuck. I was getting a little excited. Was this it? Had I found her apparently elusive appendix? With some more finger dissection the structure became a little more mobile, and now I could even begin to get a sense of its outline, its shape. This must be an inflamed appendix, I thought, even though my fingers had never really 'seen' one before.

One of the less obvious skills of a surgeon is the ability to utilize our fingers as extensions of our eyes. We learn to delineate how tissues 'look', solely by their feel. This is not easy. It is a painfully slow process, dependent on first learning the feel of normal tissue. With time we are able to differentiate not only normal from abnormal but frequently, benign from malignant based purely on feel.

So, now, what should I do? I used my finger to continually work the possible appendix free from where it was adhered to the surrounding tissues. I needed to get it unstuck. Easy does it! If I get too carried away, and if this really is the inflamed appendix, I might rupture it or make it bleed. Either way I would be causing more harm (remember: '*Primum non nocere*'—first do no harm). Yet if I'm too gentle, I'll never get it out of there. There is always compromise.

I hoped I had not ruptured it. Moving the retractors around, I could now finally see my quarry. At the bottom of the stainless-steel-retracted, sponge-buttressed pit was the three-inch-long worm-like structure of her inflamed appendix attached to the caecum. The tip of it, for about two inches, was swollen, stiff, angry pink with a purulent, grayish-white exudate adhered to it. This was the disease all right; this was appendicitis. It was not ruptured. I rode back up the emotional roller coaster as I realized that I had indeed made the correct diagnosis. Now I needed to get the damn thing out of there. My mind froze. I drew a blank as I tried to recall the next step. A moment later my mind cleared, and an orderly sequence returned.

"Babcock, please," I asked the scrub nurse. She handed me a clamp with which I could grasp the caecum without hurting it. I placed it on the bowel and gently rocked this portion of the colon into the wound. Now her pink swollen finger of an appendix was sticking out of the incision, flopping right in front of me, giving me 'the bird'.

Not only is the appendix attached to the colon, but there is a single blood vessel encased in fat that fans out into multiple tributaries to supply it. This appendiceal blood supply needed to be dealt with first.

"3-0 vicryl ties," I asked, suddenly with a fraction more authority and anyway, it sounded right. If I was wrong, I hoped someone would speak up. It remained quiet. I cut the tissue between the clamps as I slowly tied off each one. As I stretched out my hand, palm up, the needle driver with needle was slapped into it. It was a pretty hard slap. Nothing personal, I hoped, but firm enough so that I knew the instrument was there. I slowly began placing a purse-string suture circumferentially about a centimeter away from the base of the appendix. Amputating the appendix between two small straight clamps, I carefully handed off the offending 'beast' to the scrub nurse. I sutured the stump closed, and Randy pushed it in, while I snugged down my previously placed purse-string at its base.

Drum roll, please. The appendix was out. I had done it. My first appendectomy.

A moment later I derided myself, "Let's not get too excited. There is still a bloody great hole you need to close up." But first things first. We needed to wash any and all the muck out.

"Irrigation, please," I asked.

I was passed a small stainless jug of saline, which looked identical to the ones used by baristas to froth milk. With everything well irrigated and making sure the sponge count was correct, I began closing up each layer in the reverse order with which I had cut through on my way in.

I was ecstatic. This was the first appendicitis that I had evaluated, diagnosed (correctly!), and then also fixed. It probably still looked like a struggle to those watching, but we were in and out in just under an hour. This case, especially just finding the appendix, was another small yet significant step in the long serpentine road of surgical education.

While I was putting in a few skin staples, Randy went out and spoke to the patient's family. After a couple of days, she was home with just a little scar on her right side as a souvenir of her ordeal.

With the advent of laparoscopy, even a relatively simple operation, such as an appendectomy, has become quicker, safer, and less painful, with smaller incisions and a more rapid return to full activity. It not only allows patients to be discharged within a few hours of surgery with minimal discomfort but the procedure gives an unparalleled visualization of intra-abdominal structures. During my training, even this would have seemed to be science fiction.

One evening, with Randy off interviewing (for a real job), Dr. Horace, another fifth year, was pulled from his elective surgical rotation to cover 'nights' in his absence. Now Dr. Horace had a reputation throughout the medical center of being a very aggressive chief and like Randy, a good one. It appeared that his reputation had spread far beyond our concrete confines, as many EMS drivers also appeared well aware of his penchant to crack a chest (ER thoracotomy) at the drop of a hat. It certainly seemed to us that they adjusted their plans so as to end up here if they knew that he was 'on', often transporting patients who were already pretty much dead.

"Let's take him downtown. Horace is on tonight; he's bound to crack the chest," we thought the conversation in their rig might have gone.

They were usually right; he'd crack the chest of anyone entering the resuscitation room without vitals, who at a stretch and often a very long stretch at that, had even the faintest flicker of vitals at the scene. But then that was our job: to give patients a chance, no matter how slim. Certainly doing nothing would never help.

Another evening, during Dr. Horace's stint as interim night chief one of our e. med residents was ranting to him that he had not yet had a chance to crack a chest, explaining how important it was for him to learn how to do it. Dr. Horace kept a straight poker face hiding his amusement, as he listened to the spewing flawed logic. Following a dramatic pause, giving the appearance of overwhelming reluctance, he conceded to allow the resident to crack the chest of the next one that was brought in. His own philosophy, mirrored by most if not all of the surgical chiefs, was such procedures were, and should remain, the sole domain of surgeons. He knew that the minimal knowledge gained by attempting one ER thoracotomy could be far more hazardous than none at all.

Sure enough, later that evening, EMS delivered yet another 'corpse'. This man had been shot in his left chest, and the driver explained to us that they were on the scene quickly and that he was still moving as they put him in their rig. Although this appeared highly unlikely, they knew what to say. After they had brought the victim in and laid him on the gurney, they retreated against the wall, jostling each other for the best spot from which to observe the ensuing show. They knew this one would be a 'crack'. Dr. Horace did not disappoint, and as soon as he had assessed the situation and decided there was no hope for the patient, he started in on the e. med resident. He was meanwhile dancing around nervously impatient. Shades of '007'?

"What are you waiting for man? Let's get that chest open," Horace let loose on him

Acting surprised, dazed, and bewildered, the resident looked up at Dr. Horace who was trying to hide his developing grin. He knew what was coming, and like a master chess player, his every step had already been carefully planned.

"You want me to crack the chest?"

"No. I want you to stand there like a fool and watch him die," he responded, even more sarcastically than usual. "Let's see what you can do," Horace continued, clearly knowing how things were unfolding but still trying to contain himself and maintain his steely deadpan expression.

"Let's go. He's not going to get better by waiting," he continued.

The resident continued fumbling around, finally managing to open the thoracotomy tray, stainless instruments going everywhere. The nurses, knowing full well what was going on (they had seen this movie before!), poured betadine all over the victim's chest. Taking the knife, he gently laid it on the patient's skin and looked up at Dr. Horace.

"Is this about right?"

"Yes, go go go, the patient's dying man. Get into that damn chest! What are you waiting for? This is what you wanted. Do something. Save him," he replied, keeping the pressure up. Of course, the patient was, pretty much, already dead. There was only minimal remnant electrical activity on the EKG monitor. Rigor mortis may not have set in, but it certainly wasn't far away.

With his first attempt, the cut barely nicked the skin.

Dr. Horace expected this, and as if on cue, continued, "It'll take all year to get in that chest if you keep going like that. Cut man! Cut! Cut!"

This time the resident got through the skin, and after a few more insults were hurled at him, he finally got into the chest cavity. There was old, dark blood everywhere, and it was hard to see what was going on. Once he finally had slowed down his shaking, wiggled the rib spreader into position, and cracked open the chest, we could see that in his eagerness to get into the chest, he had sliced deep into the left lung.

"If the bullet doesn't kill him, you just might." Dr. Horace did not let up for a moment. He was delivering a message. This was not a procedure that he or any other e. med resident should ever be attempting, as the outcome would be the same. This patient never stood a chance from the moment the bullet had struck. With or without the 'crack', he was dead before they started. But he hoped a valuable lesson had been learnt.

Dead or Alive

DAY 15 —Precisely every 12 hours, like the changing of the guard at Buckingham palace (an English thing) or the exchanging of crews in a ballistic missile silo (an American thing), the surgical resident shift change took place in the trauma module.

Tonight, we were, as was our habit, all congregating around the nurses' desk waiting for Mike, one of my classmates and the day surgical resident that month, to give us his sign-out. The module clock registered 6:30pm.

I was struck by brightness. More than usual, the room seemed brighter, a dazzling brightness. Harsh light reflected everywhere, from the white painted walls, the steel bed frames, even the floors. It was fluorescence at its eye paining brilliant best. My eyes squinted as I longed for dimmer, more pastel surroundings.

I made my way to the front of the assembled group, where I could more clearly hear the sign-out, looking through my eyes now closed to slits. I hoped that no one noticed, as I fought the urge to rid myself of a light induced headache by closing them completely. I became increasingly aware of the steady, rhythmical groan of a mechanical ventilator. Forcing oxygen in with precise regularity, it was easily audible above the commotion of the ongoing shift change. This was always a sure sign of a busy shift and a pile of 'clean up' work to be done.

Being the second year, just like on 'days', it was still my module, my responsibility, so I needed to hear about every patient. Sure, I now had many other members on my team and the not insignificant security of knowing that my chief was never too far away.

"This is a 48-year-old man, who was struck by a hit-and-run driver while crossing the road this afternoon." Mike began his sign-out, pointing over his shoulder to the man on the ventilator, speaking in a flat, humdrum, monotone, a far cry from his usual jovial self. He looked beat, his face glistening with grimy perspiration as he did little to hide the fact that he just wanted to get home. Like a burnt-out preacher delivering another uninteresting and boring sermon, Mike continued his summary.

"On arrival here he was hypotensive and then had a respiratory arrest in the resuscitation room," he continued, as we all swarmed around the bed, surrounding it on three sides.

"He was 'tubed' and resuscitated with three liters of 'Ringers'. He has not been responsive at all since coming in, and a neurosurg consult has been obtained. Well, at least the consult has been placed." Then Mike added, with an unusually tired, sarcastic overtone, "They haven't shown up yet."

In all fairness, it always took a while for the neurosurgical residents to show. Incredibly knowledgeable, having already completed a full five or six years of a general surgery residency, they were usually tied up in the operating room, perhaps not even in our hospital. We all knew that for most patients, it was a waiting game, and there was nothing anyone would recommend above what we were already doing. But we needed their official consultation, and more importantly, we wanted the patient admitted to their service, getting them out of 'our' module and decreasing our load and responsibility.

Randy asked Mike a few pertinent questions while carefully looking over the patient, investigating the ventilator settings, and performing his own brief examination. He nodded with approval as Mike answered to his satisfaction. The patient, intubated, paralyzed, and on the 'blower' (ventilator), was completely encased in a web of wires and tubes of various shapes, sizes, and colors, some delivering while others withdrawing.

The entire picture was surreal, confusing even to those not accustomed (which was me only 12 months earlier). His care was wholly consistent with another important axiom in the care of the multiply injured: a finger or tube needed to be placed in every orifice. Certainly Mike had excelled on that account. However, the corollary was that survivability was inversely proportional to the number of tubes inserted. In this case, therefore, this poor fellow's chances were slim.

Once Randy was satisfied that he had all the information he needed, then and only then did we all move on. Like a swarm of bees, we surrounded the next patient. In the second bed, as Mike elucidated with his typically bone-dry humor, was just another routine malodorous, alcoholically intoxicated man who had fallen off his porch. Dripping into his IV was the fluorescent yellow, all-curing banana bag elixir. However, due to his inability to cooperate, he needed to be secured (not too well, as it turns out) to the frame of his gurney by a set of our deluxe leather restraints. No matter how much the staff tried to settle him down, he continued to thrash around. Nothing seemed to help. Although fully conscious, he was certainly not in any way truly 'with it' and not in the least coherent. He constantly attempted to reach a urinal hooked to the side of his cart. Every time a nurse came and gave it to him, he responded with a volley of asinine, nonsensical obscenities while flinging the fortuitously empty plastic container across the room. Soon the nurses gave up playing 'fetch'. With all the IV fluids running in, combined with his self-induced alcohol diuresis, he was likely feeling quite uncomfortable. With his obnoxious behavior doing little to endear him to anyone, he was pretty much ignored. He did not seem to have any significant injuries, just a couple of lacerations on his scalp that had already been dealt with. We should have learnt by now not to turn our backs on such individuals.

We were three patients further down the line when we had our first inkling that something wasn't right. Mike was in mid-sentence, presenting another patient, when we heard the shrill shriek of the ventilator alarm. Maybe only a second or so later it was punctuated by an, "Oh, my God" expletive from one of the nurses behind us, with a tone suggesting more surprise than concern. By the time anyone had figured out what was going on, it was too late.

The ventilator-dependent patient in the first bed, encased in tubing going every which way, lay defenseless yet adjacent to our intoxicated man. Certainly in hindsight, this may have been poor planning, but patients were placed in whatever space was available without attempting to predict their future actions. Our intoxicated, full-bladdered, Houdini impersonator had managed to wriggle his hand out from his (not so) secure leather restraints, and reaching over towards the patient next to him, disconnected the one-and-a-half-inch diameter, opaque, ribbed-plastic ventilator tubing that took the waste gases away. He then proceeded to use the open end of the tubing as his personal urinal, into which he promptly relieved the entire contents of his bladder. This, which he was able to do without spraying the floor, was in itself quite a feat of dexterity and contortion. By the time we had any idea what he was up to, he was lying back, relaxed with a grin of satisfied, empty-bladder contentment, clearly announcing to all: mission accomplished.

Despite still being intoxicated, he serendipitously had the courtesy (dumb luck) to urinate into the tubing that was exiting the patient. It was only the alarm that notified us that something was amiss. It gave us important seconds to intervene before anything could escalate. No harm was done, the tubing was replaced, and our more comfortable, empty-bladdered patient was moved a little further away.

Mike completed his sign-out and rapidly disappeared.

We did not have to wait long before we received our the first of our evening visitors to resuscitation. A petite Black woman had been shot in her left upper abdomen. We heard her arrival long before we saw her. Rather, we could hear the prolonged hiss of compressed air being released from an awkward appearing mechanical device, precariously balanced over her chest. This device, a 'thumper', was performing automated cardiac compressions. She had no vital signs, there was no pulse, no blood pressure. But when hooked up to the monitor, there was still a cardiac tracing chasing a small green dot across the screen's dark background. Her heart was alive, or at least it had some electrical activity. It was clearly not dead. We soon had 'O neg' blood hanging, and getting the nod from Randy, I grabbed the 'Bat phone' and called the OR to tell them that we had someone we needed to bring 'right back'. There was nothing more that we could do here. Her only hope, and it was a dim one at that, was to get her opened and the bleeding stopped. She had been here only minutes when we wheeled her out of the room. Like the waving flagella around a giant bacterium, the team surrounded her cart as it was pushed down the hallway, each preoccupied with our varying responsibilities. Not slowing to put on hats or masks, we stopped only once we were alongside the OR bed. She was still fully clothed. This did not last long. While anesthesia was sorting out the IV lines, the nurses had her stripped naked. The bright surgical lights shone down on her bare torso with its scar-free distended abdomen adulterated by a single bloody hole on its left side.

As a large bottle of brown antiseptic was unceremoniously dumped, then painted over her chest and abdomen, Randy explained how he would enter the chest first. The goal, he explained, was to clamp the aorta to prevent any further bleeding, then enter the abdomen. We knew, as did Randy, that it was her only chance.

We quickly gowned (there was no time to scrub) and gloved as the drapes were unfolded. Unfolding in front of me was the nightly, crazy, but carefully-choreographed life-fighting ballet. It had taken less than five minutes from her arrival to the incision. The scrub nurse had loads of white surgical 'lap' sponges piled on her back table. Although this might have been one of my first rodeos, it was clearly not hers.

The scrub nurse passed Randy the scalpel, and then in one swift, precise motion, and with an experienced finesse, he made a curved slice through the skin of her left chest. In only seconds he was wiggling the stainless rib spreader into position. Turning the ratchet, we again, heard the unmistakable cracking of ribs breaking. With the chest open, I arched my wrists over the steel to hold the lungs out of the way. I fought hard to hold back the lungs, as air was being forced into them by the ventilator, so that Randy could see. I could see his hands diving into the wound, and then he asked for a clamp. Although I could not see anything from my vantage point, I knew that he had the aorta identified and was compressing it with a large Statinsky clamp.

Hopefully the clamp would help stem the bleeding. While Randy looked away, I stole a peek into the chest. From my very uncomfortable and inverted viewpoint, I could see that there was no bleeding. The heart was still beating faintly, a testament to youthful myocardium.

Continuing with vigorous open cardiac massage, Randy proceeded to open the belly. As he began making a long incision, Dr. Bouwman, the Attending on call, entered the room. Randy exchanged a few quiet words and gave him a précis of what had taken place up to that point. Now fully appraised, Dr. Bouwman spoke purposefully loudly so that all could hear.

"Looks like you have things under control." he asserted. He knew the score, and after years of treating scores of similarly injured, he also knew that nothing would alter the inevitable outcome.

With the abdomen having been rapidly opened wide, I was now holding the retractors there, too. They began taking inventory of the injuries. There were holes through and through the small bowel and colon. Those were not immediately life threatening, but something was. Something was killing her. Searching deeper, they found a hole in the duodenum, but it was what they found deeper that was the real problem. Here, Randy explained that he could feel a massive hole in the aorta. It had been almost completely transected, its ragged edge and missing chunk testifying to the bullet's destructive force.

As Randy began placing clamps on the aorta, the anesthesiologist informed us that her heart was fibrillating. We all knew what this meant: the battle was over, and we had lost. Even when Randy first entered the belly, we knew things were bad. Not only because of the injuries and that the bowel was grey and not pink, but there was also an unmistakably dreadful odor that rapidly permeated the room. It was the smell of death. Clearly she had been 'down' much longer than anyone had realized. Her fate was sealed when the hunk of lead tore through her aorta.

Randy knew there was nothing anyone could do. Looking up at the clock, he 'called it', announcing the time of death.

It had only been 45 minutes since her arrival.

Later we learnt that she had been at home with her mother. Investigating a commotion, they discovered two people trying (and succeeding) to steal her two-year-old brown Pontiac Bonneville. Standing on their well-lit porch, they were both shot, her mother receiving only a glancing strike to her shoulder.

As we headed out of the OR, we were notified of an attempted hanging. My mind was still contemplating the awful fate of our last patient, who had been fine just an hour before. We were told that our new arrival had been 'dangling' for at least 20 minutes at the end of two leather belts suspended in his garage from a ceiling joist. His wife, who sadly had discovered him, surmised that he must have climbed onto the hood of his car, strung himself up, and jumped.

He was immediately placed on a ventilator. His face was grotesquely swollen, his eyes bulging and bloody, his skin a blotchy mottled blue with deeply indented furrows on either side of the neck where the belt had cut in. We gave him Decadron and Mannitol, which was the protocol for suspected spine injuries, even though we were all pretty sure it would make little difference. Surprisingly his C-spine films came back completely negative. There was no fracture yet he was completely 'decorticate', an ominous posture whereby the patient is rigid, his arms bent with fists clenched, representing a severe central neurologic dysfunction, which, when present, is generally never survivable.

With the help of neurology, we broke the news to his family. This was a slow, deliberate, and difficult conversation in which, luckily, I was, for a change, just an observer. I kept putting myself in the position of the family members, trying to understand what they must be feeling. How could they possibly deal with such devastating news? Only a few hours earlier he had been chatting with them around the family dinner table. Life was so tenuous. It was just another constant reminder.

With time, the family came to the difficult conclusion that 'cerebrally' he was gone, and they gave permission for organ donation. We didn't waste any time contacting the organ procurement team. He was kept on life support until they arrived to harvest his organs and hopefully give life to a number of other, once less but now more fortunate, individuals.

That same evening, a man from an MVA was brought in under police custody with one hand securely cuffed to his stretcher. We heard that he had a penchant for driving after snorting some of his favorite white powder. However, somewhat foolishly, we failed to transfer him to a sturdier cart, leaving him cuffed to the much lighter weight, foldable one on which he had arrived. His neck was immobilized in a 'Philly' collar to protect his cervical spine until the appropriate films had been obtained. At first it appeared that he might actually cooperate, despite his loud outbursts. Perhaps thinking of himself as a professional orator, he made it quite clear that his lungs were not in any way impaired. Sadly, he did not quiet down or even stay put for long.

Soon the incessant screaming that we had attempted to ignore changed in nature and was interrupted by an intermittent staccato, exertional howl. He had managed to twist himself around and soon was standing up in the middle of the module, scantily clad in his torn white pants. His cuffed left wrist was now extending over his shoulder, still secured to the stretcher, which rested upon his back like an oversized backpack. The lightness of the gurney, which was its major advantage to the ambulance crews, had now became a major disadvantage as he began wielding it in circles above his head like a medieval mace. Did he believe he was the reincarnation of a long passed Olympian hammer thrower? He certainly had the strength. Alone, in the middle of the room, he swung the cart, at first waist high, then above his head. The long sweeping arcs smashed everything within range. We thought that after a few minutes, he would tire and stop. Yet it was quite the opposite. He appeared to become more energized, more frenzied, more manic with every swing. The 'coke' appeared to have taken full effect. He was completely out of control. What were we to do? The police who brought him in were not interested in being flattened. Most of the other patients nearby and who were not frightened (and therefore probably under some influence themselves) joined in the cacophony. With their own howls, jeers, and cheers, they appeared like Roman spectators encouraging their favorite gladiator into combat.

This man had not been brought in alone. His 'significant other' had also arrived in the company of the police and had been placed in a module across the hallway, although clearly not far enough away. This was an area reserved for those who did not have any really serious injuries or as an overflow for patients awaiting discharge. However, following a loud exchange of 'pleasantries', our cart wielding 'crazy' made it abundantly clear that he was planning to do significant harm to his 'friend' across the way once got there. He now appeared to be making significant progress towards his goal. According to him, she had already opened her 'big mouth' too much. He rapidly had become beyond our control. If we went near him, we would undoubtably be flattened.

He was a veritable one-man wrecking crew as he weaved through the ER, dispatching all in his path. He completely destroyed our nursing station and then the nearby triage desk, leaving in his wake splintered desks and demolished computer terminals. Papers were strewn everywhere like confetti.

Although everyone was watching (from a safe distance), no one wanted to get too close. No one, that is, except Tony. Tony was one of our emergency medicine residents, who not only claimed a strong Sicilian heritage but also regarded himself as a solo peacekeeping force. The real Italian Stallion, as he advertised himself. He was always the first to volunteer in confronting belligerent patients, never hiding the fact that he enjoyed using his, not insignificant, strength to help subdue them. Perhaps he had missed his calling as a professional wrestler or a nightclub bouncer?

After deciding that he had seen enough, Tony ignored the advice of the observing police officers and, as was his style, took matters into his own hands. Flinging himself at the man's legs, rugby tackle style, they crashed to the floor to the accompaniment of raucous applause from the ever-increasing crowd of spectators. He loved the attention and was only too happy to perform.

Once grounded the two officers, who had been carefully watching the proceedings, took advantage of the downed man to intervene. The first officer grabbed his Philly-collar-protected neck and put him into a tight headlock, and with such a sudden twist that if his neck was not broken before, there was a good chance it might be now. At any rate, if he still had neurologic function (although one could easily make the argument that he didn't have much to start with), chances are he had nothing seriously wrong with his neck in the first place. Certainly, it was not our recommended way of assessing the C-spine.

This time he was placed in four-corner leather restraints on a much heavier and more robust gurney. We did not want a repeat. Our ears received a well-deserved rest as he was taken for X-rays, where, much to the relief of the 'headlock' officer, his neck films were normal. We all received an even bigger break when we were able to hand him off to the police such that he could enjoy further quality time under their care.

The Visiting Professor

DAY 16 —Every Saturday evening, the 'night' crew had the opportunity to work with the Visiting Professor. This designation sounded exotic, exciting, and perhaps even a little mysterious. To some what came to mind was a smart, dark polo-neck attired surgical maestro with a neatly trimmed five o'clock shadow over a chiseled face. To top it off, he would be expounding technical pearls in broken English with an almost incomprehensible, unplaceable, yet alluring, accent.

Sadly, it was not that exciting. The Visiting Professor was our nickname for the fifth-year chief resident who worked the Saturday night ER trauma shift. The 'professor' took the place of the regular 'night chief' so they could have one night a week off. With a total of eight chiefs, it left seven to split up the duty of covering the ER on Saturday nights. (Of course, this number would be less if one of them had the audacity to take vacation.) For us, mere novices, it was our chance to see another of our chiefs at work. They were to us, at the time, the Gods of our surgical world, the pinnacle to which we all aspired, and let's be honest, being the Visiting Professor also sounded damn cool. For some perhaps the term 'professor' elevated them to a degree not always warranted. But as with all surgeons, there was huge variability even amongst our chiefs who were all trained at the same program. Yet, as a first or second year resident, we could only dream that someday we might reach their lofty heights.

Here, they seemed to operate without the nervousness and trepidation rampant amongst us juniors. Would it ever change? And when? We knew that it was still many hard years and untold sleepless nights away. It was difficult, if not impossible, to contemplate that far ahead, as we were far more worried about surviving today, tomorrow, and the upcoming Saturday morning M & M conference.

Saturday nights were always busy, and it was not unusual for the chief to be 'scrubbed in' doing consecutive cases for the majority, if not the entire, night. This was a double-edged sword. They relished the opportunity to operate all night and especially not having to worry about the post-operative care (that responsibility would fall to the regular in-house team when they assumed care the following morning), but it still came at an exhausting cost. With our ignorance, wholly born from inexperience, we viewed it as 'All play and no work'. It was not uncommon for them to be still operating at noon or even later the next day as they cleared through the backlog of the Saturday night cases. Their duty of covering the ER on Saturday nights invariably destroyed any chance of a normal weekend, but then surgical residency had already done that.

It was the chief's first priority to take care of the patients on their service, and Saturdays were no exception. Their day began, as it did for all of us, around 6:00 with rounds that involved seeing all their patients and dealing with any problems that may have developed overnight. Then it was time to get the team (occasionally an intern needed to stay behind to deal with pressing problems) downtown to Harper Hospital for the Saturday morning teaching conference and the weekly 'M & M'.

When we were rotating at the (now demolished) VA Hospital in Allen Park, Saturday mornings were always a rush. After disposing with rounds, we hopped back onto on to I-94, weaving in and out of the sedate Saturday morning traffic in our not-so-trusty-rusty vehicle; frequently speeding to be there by 8:00. We would invariably be late as we raced the clock and each other in our attempt to arrive on time. Sneaking into the rear of the huge Kresge auditorium, we hoped that we would remain anonymous, as we attempted to silently locate a seat in the dim light of the already begun presentation.

The first half of these Saturday conferences was a didactic presentation given by one of our fellow residents, usually a third year. It allowed for a quick nap before the main event: the always dreaded M & M. The presenting residents stood apprehensively in front of the assembled surgical Attendings, fellow residents, medical students, and anyone else who wanted to come and watch us try not to make a fool of ourselves. In the front row, along with many of the faculty, sat our chairman, the world-renowned South African surgeon Dr. Alex Walt. Here was a man, a surgeon, who expected nothing less than perfection. His philosophy was that surgeons should be well-rounded physicians besides being knowledgeable technicians. This expectation only escalated our level of intimidation as we gazed down, in the dim light, upon his menacing, Hitchcock-esque silhouette. Without looking, he had a knack for picking out the resident, by name, who had just entered REM sleep to ask an unanswerable (his only type) question. We all learnt the art of napping with one eye and one ear open. He would frequently use this time to pull the 'chiefs' back a peg, as only he could, and to remind us all that we could not allow ourselves to become complacent just because we were close to the end of our training.

We all hoped that we would not be called upon to answer any question posed by our chairman. Those of us not in the 'hot seat' would always try to hide out in the back of the auditorium where the 'premier' spots were often already occupied. You needed to get there early to get a good napping spot, and we were rarely able to do that.

Presenting in front of so many was daunting and formidable, especially for those of us with an inherent ineptitude for public speaking. I recall arching over the wooden lectern, fidgeting clumsily with papers as my eyes longingly sought out the red exit signs in the distance. Fighting off waves of nausea, I would become acutely aware of the erect hairs on the nape of my neck, my hands tingling, sweating as I swallowed hard, readying my throat to speak. I had spent many weeks preparing and rehearsing the presentation in the hope that I might receive a favorable review from our chairman, although sadly this was rarely the case.

If we were lucky enough to pull off a great presentation (good was never enough) and successfully navigate the ensuing minefield of interrogation, it might put us in our chairman's good graces. Of course, as some discovered, the opposite was equally true. During my intern year, a presenting senior resident was severely reprimanded when he had placed one of his slides (Yes, we still used slides. Kodachrome was king) in the carousel backward. A simple mistake for sure, but one that he was never allowed to forget. The message was clear. A surgeon needed to be a perfectionist; there was no room for error and certainly none for excuses.

One of our Attendings would always remind us when we attempted an excuse, "Excuses are like assholes. Everyone has one, but no one wants to hear from them."

The M & M that followed was the weekly forum in which we hung out our 'dirty laundry' for all (the other surgeons) to see. We would present our complications and discuss them openly. All the while, the front row critics second guessed our every decision, and with the benefit of hindsight told us in no uncertain terms how we had screwed up. Sounds like fun, right? It was the job of the chief to stand up in front of his or her educators (critics) and peers and present the week's complications from his or her service. He or she would frequently be humiliated for decisions in which they had absolutely no say. But no matter whose decision, the real goal was to prevent us from making a similar error. If only it was that easy. If the chief was unavailable, the duty of presenting fell to the second year or even the intern. I must admit to never having had the dubious honor of presenting as an intern, although I more than made up for it in subsequent years.

It was an extreme and overbearing environment, but nevertheless we learnt (although still forgot a lot!). One of the greatest lessons learnt was humility. Our chairman wanted us to admit our errors (in front of everyone) and explain how best to avoid them. This was difficult when we thought there was no real error but just a bad outcome. So just as we thought we might get off the hook, our chairman would step in and find some seemingly innocuous point to scrutinize and 'beat' into us. It was a harsh educational experience (now, we might even term it abusive), but then surgical complications are harsh (on the patient), and we all learnt the importance of keeping them to a minimum.

> *At the time, it was hard to realize just how important these M & M conferences were. We were all too busy just trying to survive them, yet we all benefited greatly from the frank and open discussion of everyone's errors. Of course, these conferences are a far cry from the milder more gentlemanly ones that occur in private hospitals, where we still need to hold each other accountable, but there is not the verbal berating and humiliation that we experienced during training. The goal is still the same: to improve, by critical analysis the decision-making, delivery, and outcome of care for our patients. Sometimes the hardest part of any review is to admit that we could have done things differently.*

For those of us who did not have to get up and present, it was a wonderfully exhilarating feeling to have escaped the wrath of the inquisitor (our chairman) for at least another week. Perhaps it was not personal, but when it was your turn to be grilled in front of 'everyone', it certainly felt like it.

After the M & M, if there were no outstanding problems, the Visiting Professor could dash home (or to their spartan call room) and get a few hours of well needed shut-eye before starting their evening 'professorship'. The next morning or, if they were really 'having fun' (operating), then by the afternoon they would head back to their base hospital to make rounds with their team. If they had a good team, most of the work would have already been completed. Then it was home, a quick chat with the spouse or partner, and straight into the sack to rest for the week ahead. It made for a busy, exhausting, yet often exhilarating weekend.

On that Saturday our Visiting Professor was Dr. Dan Henry. Now Dan, or 'Dandy Dan' as he was better known, had in his few short years in the program, managed to acquire a significant reputation. This was aided by those residents who had experienced the unenviable pleasure that came from working with him. As with many surgical nicknames, his was not meant to be complimentary, but then neither was the notoriety he had acquired from his habit of stealing cases from his junior residents. Instead of passing down the simple and easier cases to his juniors (which was the norm), he would do them himself. Sadly, he was not the most gifted of surgeons, and there was no doubt that he needed all the practice he could get. However, it was still not reasonable for this to occur at the expense of diluting the cases available for his juniors. It was the simplest cases, the abscesses and appys that he would do himself instead of supervising ('staffing') his juniors in performing them.

Even during my first few months, it became clear that there was a definite unwritten hierarchy of cases. There were those that were 're-served' for the interns and those for the more senior residents, with the complexity of cases commensurate with their years of experience. Always the major cases remained the sole domain of the chief. However, as long as there were juniors around, the chief was expected to delegate as much as possible to them.

As I came to understand later, when I entered the ranks of a more seasoned (senior) resident, it was in fact much more self-instructive and took a far greater depth of knowledge to teach someone how to perform an operation than to do it oneself.

I had just finished a two-month rotation with Dan at the VA (Veterans Administration). It was for the most part a tremendous rotation as even junior residents were allowed significant autonomy (read: there were no Attendings around). We got along fine, once I had become used to his way of running things, which was slow—very slow, sloth slow, so slow you-just-wanted-to-scream slow. He would take a couple hours every evening to round on only about a dozen or so patients, which would have taken less than half the time with any other chief. I think if we had gone any slower, the patients would have gotten better (or worse) and discharged themselves home (or to the morgue) before we got around to seeing them. It was not that he was lackadaisical, no, it was more of a measured plodding, a procrastinating slowness, that if anything highlighted his own insecurity and lack of confidence. That might have been okay and even expected for us (interns) but not for a fifth-year chief who was in his final months preparing to enter the unforgiving, hectic real-world of private practice.

These were not really teaching rounds per se. They were just very prolonged evening rounds where the only educating going on was teaching us how not to make decisions (which, I guess in itself had some value). Dan took forever to discuss any plan that we might come up with and would, out loud, go through all the possible diagnostic and therapeutic permutations as if broadcasting his inner thoughts. He then looked to us for affirmation of his decision. We never left until very late, returning early the next morning for more of the same.

On 'nights' in the ER with Dan, he would always feel it necessary to come by and interrogate patients after we had already seen, fully evaluated, and painstakingly presented them to him. Usually we would call the chief as a courtesy, to update them and to let them know what was going on. It was never a call for help, for those we made unmistakably clear. Most of the chiefs we worked with would either agree or infrequently alter our plan over the telephone, giving us some freedom and responsibility. But not Dan. That was just not his way. He would wander down, then very slowly (for that was always his way) and painfully start from scratch. This micromanaging would cause us to pray for a busy night such that he would be stuck in the OR and then be forced to make decisions over the phone. His indecisiveness seemed to evaporate when under pressure in front of the other staff and nurses in the room. He was far better when he did not have time to doubt himself.

He would walk up to the patients, and after a prolonged pregnant pause born of intense insecurity, he would begin with his usual stunning array of complex questions.

"What brought you to the hospital, sir?" he asked with the intensity of student asking for an explanation of General Relativity.

The patients would look back to him with a dumbfounded look that clearly expressed, "Is this guy for real?" They would then reply, "I came by bus," or "the ambulance brought me," or some other reply that was equally as plausible and just as equally useless.

Not quite getting the answer he was seeking, it might take him a further 15 minutes (not kidding!) to extract the information we had already shared with him by phone as he continued with his inanely slow line of questioning. By the end of my rotation with him, I must admit to not having the greatest respect for his capabilities as either a physician or surgeon. Now that may seem harsh and a terrible thing to say about someone who was our senior and supposed to be our mentor. But he was far too slow and intensely indecisive. This was such a waste of time for all of us.

As surgeons it is imperative to be decisive. Taking too long to decide what to do is never a viable option. It is one of the reasons that surgical residency is so intense. We are taught to make decisions quickly, under pressure and hopefully correctly. It is too late to put a piece of bowel back one once we have removed it, to put vessels back together once cut, but we also can't stop and procrastinate over every choice, every possibility. We are trained to think ahead, many steps ahead, and plan for every scenario that we can possibly think of. Then we can proceed, knowing what option we will take if and when the time for decision arises. Yet like everyone, we still make mistakes. We are only human (although many of our medical colleagues would vehemently argue that point), but our training must enable us to keep errors to a minimum, limiting them to the ones of least impact to the patient.

Jimmy Spithill, the world class sailor, America's Cup winning helmsman and amateur boxer, is well versed with performing under stress. To paraphrase, he once said that in sailing, like boxing, you have to make decisions when you are totally exhausted, and decision making is the first thing that goes when you are tired. This is exactly the same with surgery, and one of the crucial functions of a good training program is to teach discipline and how to make vital decisions (hopefully correct ones) under pressure and when exhausted.

Our night with Dan started out perfectly. We all received our silent wish as he disappeared to the OR with Jeff, one of our interns. Jeff was a hard worker, yet at the same time laid back and easy going. He and Dan had taken a young man with a peri-rectal abscess to surgery who had been worked up on 'days'. Jeff was hoping that he would get to do the case. The module was in pretty good shape, especially for a Saturday. We all knew this apparent order was deceiving and would never last too long. The crazy, busy, bloody, noisy, alcohol-fueled Saturday night was just around the corner.

Things continued at a steady pace. As yet, we had not really seen any real 'Saturday night specials'. It may seem a little strange, but that's really what we were all waiting for. That's why we were doing our surgical residency here. We were waiting, not only for the gunshots or the stabbing, but also the crazy stories that inevitably accompanied them.

EMS brought in a young man who, according to them, had attempted to commit suicide. He was a short, stocky kid who appeared to be in his late teens, wearing a baggy, ripped, dark-blue Detroit Pistons shirt with matching filthy shorts. He would not say anything to us, not a word, not even his age. With pudgy, rosy cheeks, he might have even been considered cute if it were not for the angry, indifferent, almost contemptuous expression plastered across his acne-scarred face. Whether this was in part because he had not been successful in his attempt or that he was embarrassed at having been found out, we could not decipher. More likely it was all part of the game he was playing, whatever that might have been.

When EMS responded to the 911 call, they found him alone in a small olive green, 60s-style kitchenette, littered with an assortment of paper and Styrofoam take-out containers. The majority, still half full, were carpeted with fuzzy green mold growth. He was sitting at the table, busily working a knife into his forearm. The place appeared not to have the recipient of any type of household cleanser for a very long time. However, it all still begged the question, who actually made the 911 call?

Leaving the knife in place for fear of starting torrential bleeding if dislodged, the EMS crew wrapped his right arm and delivered him to us. His wound and knife were hidden deep beneath a blood-stained, coral pink crepe bandage.

When questioned, he offered no reply. He gave no indication as to his thought process. He just stared vacantly through us. His face had a creepy blank look usually reserved for campy horror movies. He smelled awful, a combination of rank body odor and stale urine. Besides the smell, his unclean, disheveled appearance validated our opinion that he cared as little about his personal hygiene as he did about his dwelling. Removing the bloody crepe dressing, the knife was still jammed deep into his arm with only the hilt of its worn wooden handle visible. It did not appear to be causing him any significant discomfort, nor did it appear to be interfering with any arm motion. The pulses in his wrist were bounding, his hand, warm and pink. On closer inspection the entire area around the entrance site was surrounded by thick, irregular scars that fanned out from the knife's entry site. This guy was definitely not a novice and had appeared to have stabbed himself in almost the exact same spot on multiple previous occasions. Palpating his arm, I could feel the entire length of the knife blade just beneath the skin. Clearly with the intent of limiting any real damage, he had forced the knife in at an angle parallel to the skin. I removed it easily. This would have been an altogether different proposition had he plunged the knife perpendicular to the surface, in which case he would have required surgical exploration to remove the knife safely and repair damage.

It was an ordinary kitchen utility knife with a four-inch blade (which was probably as clean as everything else on his kitchen table!). Because of the scarring, his arm did not bleed much, and we sent him off to X-ray to make sure there were no unseen injuries.

Talking to him was an exercise in futility. It appeared that he just did not want to communicate or at least not with us. He continued to stare dead ahead, catatonically, into thin air.

What was this boy thinking? I wondered. What was his game, his goal? What was he expecting? Attention seeking, pain medication—I didn't have a clue. It was at times like this that I wished (only for a moment) that I had spent more time paying attention during my med school psych rotation. On the other hand, I knew that psych was not really my cup of tea.

Because of the risk of infection, we did not attempt to suture the wound but washed it out and left it open, packing it with gauze. We were pretty certain that it had not been placed under sterile or even clean conditions. Once he had been medically cleared, we shipped him off to the crisis center, where others could try their luck at making contact with him. He was a frequent flyer, and they all knew him. No matter how much help he received, we knew that sooner or later he would be back again. There were some things that we could just not fix (Maybe that was the reason psych was not for me).

Back at 'base', I was about to learn another important lesson. Occasionally your gut tells you that something is wrong, but you are not sure just what its message is. You have a sick feeling in the pit of the stomach that something is wrong, but you just can't put your finger on it.

As a resident, even a junior one, part of our responsibility was to pass on our hard-earned knowledge to those making their way up the convoluted path of medical education behind us. This involved teaching our junior residents, med students, and students of other medical disciplines. For the most part they really enjoyed their stint here. For some (perhaps future surgeons?) they would boast that it was the highlight of their surgery rotation. For most it was their first experience seeing acutely injured patients. Here they were in the front lines, putting their hard-earned book knowledge to practical use.

As each new group of students rotated through, we attempted, when things were not too crazy, to orient them as well as explaining not only what they should expect from us but also what our expectations were of them. We showed them where the laceration sets and sutures were kept and told them what type of suture to use and when (a relatively simple topic that so many had never been taught). Then, far much dearer to our hearts, we explained to them how to fill out the various ER forms (we loved to have them do as much of the paperwork as possible), including the all-important X-ray requisition slips. If time permitted, we would explain but rarely have time to show them, exactly how to sew lacerations. It was a truly 'see one, do one, teach one' philosophy, where occasionally the 'see one' part was omitted. We sometimes just assumed they knew!

No matter how much previous suturing experience they had, we found ourselves correcting bad habits, showing them how to do it the right way, our way (our surgical ego in training!), the surgery way. Luckily, there was always a seemingly endless supply of lacerations. It was sewing heaven for students. We would start them out with simple cuts, often on a patient's extremity or back, and with time let them graduate to more complex wounds, some requiring a layered closure.

Later that evening, I was roaming the module overseeing our students who were busy suturing a potpourri of lacerations. One of the students was working on a young man with a five-to-six-inch clean gash on his left shoulder. It was deeper than it first appeared, yet it hardly bled. "This will keep him busy for a while," I thought. As he made preparations, I chatted with the patient about how it had occurred. He was in his kitchen having a discussion (as he describes it) with his now ex-girlfriend, who was somewhat irate and struck him with a large meat cleaver. As she initiated her swing, he turned, such that when the cleaver came down, it struck him squarely on the shoulder. Luckily this was a relatively innocuous location and made for an ideal area for a student to work on. After listening to his emotionally charged version of the event, I returned attention to my student.

He was arched over his patient, totally preoccupied with his task, to the exclusion of all else. I was immediately struck that something was wrong, out of place, but I just could not put my finger on it. When he shifted slightly, I glimpsed the circular opening in the blue paper drape and the yellow-brown iodine-stained skin around the gaping bloody wound where he was working. Everything appeared to be in perfect order. The sterile field was neatly arranged as he continued with his slow, methodical, and meticulous suturing of the laceration. He was doing a really superb job, and I was duly impressed. So then, what was it that was bothering me?

It suddenly hit me, and I could not believe that I had not noticed sooner. My excuse: he had his back to me. Everything was all so well organized, draped, and being done under sterile conditions. Everything except his hands. They were naked. He did not have any sterile gloves on. In fact, no gloves on at all. I chuckled to myself and could hardly believe what I was seeing. And he was doing such a superb job. The sutures were all placed perfectly and all bare handed!

How could this be? Had we forgot to mention this, when we were showing him the suturing kit and how to use it? Had we just presumed, that everyone knew that they needed to put on sterile gloves? This was as much a lesson for me as it was for him. Never assume. Assumptions can be dangerous.

It would be of no use to tell him anything then, certainly not in front of the patient. He was almost finished, and it looked great, gloves or not. Hopefully it would be fine, and there would be no infection. After all, in years past, sterile gloves did not even exist and pretty much all wounds would heal up just fine using clean as opposed to sterile technique. When he was finished and the opportunity arose, we discussed the importance of sterile gloves. Speechless, his face rapidly turned various shades of red. I knew he would never forget to suture without sterile gloves and I never to assume.

"Don't Move"

WHILE MY slightly misguided medical student was busy taking care of his cleaver victim, sans gloves, we received a young lady who had been in a car accident with three of her friends. Surprisingly her friends were fine, but despite believing she would be safe in the back seat without being belted, she had not been so lucky, sustaining serious injuries as the car lost control, slid across the median, and was subsequently broadsided by an oncoming van.

The car was 'totaled', and the rescue team had to use their favorite hydraulic 'jaws of life' to extricate them. The wreckage, from the 'Polaroids' that the EMS crew showed us, was a hardly recognizable mangled mess of twisted steel and shattered glass. We were hard pressed to even tell that it had once been a car.

The Polaroids, besides their shock value, were useful as an adjunct to assist us in understanding the severity of impact and perhaps as yet other undiagnosed injuries. I was always surprised and duly impressed that, from out of some of the wrecks we were shown, anyone survived.

They brought her in strapped on a wooden spine board, her left leg elevated slightly in a splint. When I examined her, she did not appear to have an obvious femur fracture, yet she continually complained of severe pain in her hip area. Her pain, I thought, could be due to the lengthy cut on the outside of her thigh, which was sliced wide open, exposing the various layers of muscles. But it was still not enough, and I was sure there must be something more serious going on. We wrapped her leg up in thick gauze bandages until we had had the opportunity to evaluate her in more detail. Our first priority was always to address any potentially life-threatening injuries. Her entire pelvis was exquisitely tender, and while we were very careful transferring her onto the X-ray table, she again let out a gut-wrenching scream. A few minutes later our suspicions were confirmed, as the films revealed that she had sustained a severe 'straddle' fracture of her pelvis. It was now time to get the 'ortho boys' involved to help take care of this. This was never just a simple break and needed to be addressed ASAP.

At around the same time, we received word that an emergent transfer from an outlying hospital was in route. Nicknamed 'Elsewhere General', this smaller suburban hospital, would frequently send us business. Sometimes we would be lucky and be transferred an 'appy', but more often it was nothing so easy or even so clear-cut.

We received little information: a man had sustained a close-range shotgun blast to the chest. That was all. He was reported to be 'stable,' but we knew enough to be skeptical. What we were told usually had minimal correlation to what we received. Consequently, we often wondered if we were even receiving the correct patient. We frequently found ourselves asking simple questions to the referring hospital. Do you have an IV? Is the patient intubated? What is the blood pressure? We spent some of the waiting time preparing the resuscitation room. After all, it could really be anything. On at least one occasion we had experienced the advertised straight-forword cut turn out to be a life-threatening stab.

At around midnight, the transfer was wheeled through the front doors. We did not waste any time, placing our usual two large bore (red devil) trauma IVs and sending off the requisite 'bloods'. Looking at him, he really did not appear have any other significant injuries but then having a good part of the chest blown away was surely enough. Under his slick, slightly curly, jet black, shoulder length hair was a 30-something male, his complexion perhaps Hispanic, his skin pale and shiny from frightened perspiration. His brown eyes were penetrating, dark, and sunken, yet remained wide open, searching, straight into ours and indeed perhaps right through us. Intermittently darting from side to side, they never really settled on anyone in particular as he recounted his near-death encounter, one that by now he must have been tired of rehashing. He spoke rapidly, stuttering, then quietly repeated himself, his lips trembling ever so slightly as he went over the fateful, almost fatal, events of earlier that evening.

As the owner of small, down-river, corner convenience store, he had been working the evening shift in place of a sick employee. While sorting cigarettes with his back to the entrance, two men with sawn-off shotguns entered. The first sign of anything amiss was when the barrel of a shotgun was thrust into his chest as he turned around. It was accompanied by an order not to move.

For whatever reason, and exactly why he could not recollect, he flinched. Maybe it was just nerves. After all, he had the business end of a shot-gun pushed up against his chest, which was certainly not conducive to staying calm. In the microseconds that followed, his assailant made good on his threat. The resulting blast sent our patient hurtling backward, slamming him against the rear counter and then the floor. There he remained, still, lying in an ever-increasing pool of his own blood until the police discovered him.

He regained consciousness in the emergency room of the 'Other Hospital' as he called it.

When we received him, it had been a couple of hours since he had been shot. Physically he appeared to be doing surprising well; but mentally, knowing how close he had come to getting 'blown away' and still unsure of what was still in store for him, he was expectedly an emotional wreck.

He was so lucky, so unbelievably lucky. But then we only saw the lucky. The unlucky ones were pronounced dead at the scene. Gingerly, I removed a huge wad of gauze laying on his upper chest, apprehensive as to what I was going to find. It can't be that bad, I told myself. He is still wide awake and rock stable. In his left upper chest, there was a 15cm in diameter, maroon, clot-filled, irregular round crater, its macerated borders randomly adorned with pieces of his red and black plaid shirt, some fragments of which would be destined to stay with him forever. Although still bleeding, more of an ooze really, it was under control, most of the vessels apparently having been cauterized by the blast.

The fact that he was alive at all was nothing short of a miracle. The shot had apparently missed everything vital, if only by inches. Could he really be that lucky? His X-rays were equally impressive. The entire area of his left upper chest was covered with a fine spray of small metal fragments. This was birdshot. It was everywhere. There were piles of the stuff, some just lying in the wound with more on his chest, his clothes, and even in his hair. Clearly, he was not on the grim reaper's list that day, yet had his assailants' weapon been loaded with buckshot he would have been.

He was cold, clammy, and shaking all over. As I went over my findings with my senior, he stuttered, asking nervously, "You guys sure you know what you're doing?"

"Yes. You couldn't be in better hands," came the immediate interjection from one of our nurses, rapidly coming to my rescue. I was glad that she responded so swiftly as I, for one, was still trying to think up a suitable reply besides just a simple "yes" or the more truthful "I think so." He needed our reassurance. I doubted that my tired bedraggled appearance helped.

His face, completely drained of color, was almost grey. Sweat beaded up profusely as he told us what had (or had not) taken place at the other hospital. I double, triple checked my examination to be sure I had not missed anything. But I just had to take one look at the bloody gaping hole in his chest to realize how close he had come to having both his chest and life blown away. It was inches at most—that's all there was between life and death—from becoming yet another homicide statistic.

"No one seemed to know what they were doing," he said, describing events at the 'other hospital'. He was clearly still very agitated and impatient for more to be done now that he was here. "They all kept standing around, asking each other questions about what to do. No one seemed to know anything," he said, as he looked directly at me with piercing interrogating eyes. Was he thinking that we weren't any better?

"They finally shipped me here," he continued, stuttering slightly.

"Don't worry sir. You are in the right place, and we know precisely what to do," I fibbed, as I tried to reinforce the confidence exuded by our nurses.

His anxiousness certainly did not diminish as I shared more details with him as to the extent of his injury. Following a third check, I sent him over to get a more detailed set of X-rays. I knew that might take a while, so before I let him disappear into the bowels of radiology, we sat him up for a portable chest X-ray to at least make sure that he did not have an occult pneumothorax.

He didn't. But it showed piles of 'scrap metal' everywhere. There was birdshot scattered beyond his armpit, up in his chest and neck. Finally, he returned with a more complete set of X-rays that were almost identical to the films that had accompanied him. His left armpit was still chock full of lead. However, the new films now showed a few pieces of metal that were some distance away from the main grouping, more specifically a couple that appeared to be superimposed on his cardiac silhouette on both views. The only explanation for this was that these fragments must have somehow made their way into the heart itself. As is always true and especially in medicine, more facts led to more questions and then to more problems that needed to be solved. How did they get there? Would they cause any harm? What should we do about it? Should we leave it alone or go after it? Was there more damage hiding that might bust loose and cause us to regret our actions?

We decided to hold off on telling him all this just yet. He was agitated enough as it was, and we needed more information before we could come up with a game plan. There was also the real possibility that he might have a serious vascular injury. We certainly needed to know this before proceeding further.

The main grouping of 'shot' appeared to be in the area of the axillary vessels, an index-finger-sized artery that supplied blood to the upper extremity and returned it to the heart by means of the even larger, but thinner walled, vein. Our next step was to get an arteriogram, a contrast study that would further delineate the blood vessels, allowing us to detect any significant vessel injury and certainly any that might require surgical intervention. It would give us a 'road map' of the area. However, obtaining the study was never easy, and in the middle of the night could be near to impossible, even in a major, level one trauma center such as ours. That night we were fortunate, and things ran uncharacteristically smoothly and within an hour our patient was up in the arteriogram suite being studied.

Today we would get the answer very rapidly by the use of a CT angiography. With this, we can see if, where, and to what extent the blood vessels are involved and even visualize them in three dimensions.

Dan, who had just finished a third OR case, wandered by and took a look at the wound of woman with the straddle fracture. He stared into the wound for a few moments and then broke the awkward silence.

"Nick, why don't you go ahead and sew up that laceration here?"

"OK," I replied, pretty much automatically. I knew you never said 'No' to your chief. It was just not done, and anyway, I still had not had a chance to get a really good look at the extent of it. When I finally did, I was completely taken aback, stunned really. This was no little laceration. It was huge. I could not believe that he really wanted me to fix it here. I did not feel at all comfortable with the idea. I really thought that it needed to go to the operating room to be fixed.

But then who was I to argue with my chief? He had clearly seen many of these before. I needed to trust his decision (and therein lay the issue and my problem). On the other hand, if I was the one sewing it up, it should be my call as it would be my neck on the line if a problem arose. I know, it should be my chief's problem, right? But that's just not the way things worked. If I did something based on his decision, it was still my responsibility. That was the way that we were taught. Never to do things blindly. Always be accountable for your actions. So I, and only I, would need to be accountable for why I decided to try and repair it under less-than-optimal conditions. I thought it over. I knew that we could better evaluate her wound, debride it, irrigate it, and close it with better lighting and help under the more ideal conditions of the operating room. The whole side of her leg was sliced open, right down to bare bone. In addition, I could see a large U-shaped piece of muscle and skin just flopping around in it. I knew I needed to go and talk to Dan about it but also knew that was not going to be fun. I found him over by the OR front desk, reading a book (hopefully about surgery!).

"Hey, Dan," I said, slightly subdued, but still trying to respectfully get his attention. He briefly looked up from his book and gave me a brief but clearly translatable 'Why the hell are you bothering me?' look.

I waited for a few seconds but with no reply forthcoming, continued. "That gal in the module with the thigh laceration?"

His expression remained unchanged. I was waiting for some reaction. There was none.

"I took a closer look at the wound, and I think she might need to come to the OR to get fixed. It's really huge," I continued explaining, my voice trailing off, almost pleading. "I think we should do it over here."

"Just fix it there. It'll be fine," he said. This time he looked up, swallowed hard, then looked back at his book, hoping that I would just go away. "Just take your time," he concluded, flatly, as if reading verbatim from the pages open in front of him.

"No. It's really huge, Dan. It's gonna need to be explored." I paused for a moment. "I think."

I think? Damn it. I knew. Grow some 'cajones' why don't you? I chastised myself.

"I can't even see what is going on at the bottom," I replied, or perhaps pleaded (just a little), trying hard not to sound confrontational. I was really worried that something might let loose in there.

"You sure?" He looked up again, still purposefully not making eye contact. "Sure you can't just do it there?" he replied, still really not interested in being bothered with another case.

Finally I could sense him starting to cave a bit but felt that I was still meeting too much resistance, so it was time for plan B, I thought.

"I know Dr. Ledgerwood would be really mad if something went wrong because we fixed it over there. You know how she likes these to be done in the operating room." Now I was gently digging my heels in. "But of course, it's your call."

He was very frightened of Dr. Ledgerwood (let's face it, we all were), so I knew that time I had hit a homer. He stiffened up, slowly clenching his hands, his knuckles becoming whiter, then rapidly raising both his eyes from his book, took a deep breath in and exhaled slowly.

"OK. I guess that's probably a good idea," he conceded. "Go ahead and get her ready."

I knew that I wanted to end up going to the OR with our shotgun case, so I let Jeff go in to repair this laceration. After they were all done, Jeff reaffirmed my decision not to do it in the module, as it had indeed gone all the way down to the bone where there were some pretty large vessels that they had to ligate, and a large amount of 'junk' that to be washed out. Jeff sarcastically described what a 'wonderful' time he had, so I was extra grateful that I had not scrubbed it. Dan was left-handed, and so doing things right-handed always seemed a little strange to him. (That could account for a lot.) Jeff explained that in the OR, Dan would constantly correct every single thing that he did, to the point that he even made Jeff put in sutures at an awkward angle because it looked better to him that way.

Meanwhile, still lost within the bowels of the hospital where the mysterious arteriogram suite was located, they were finishing up the study on our shotgun victim and very much to our surprise, it was completely negative. However, when we reviewed the films there was nevertheless still something a little peculiar, as there were now three pieces of metal overlying the cardiac shadow, whereas before there had been only two. Now, where did the extra piece come from and how did it get there? On the video one of the pieces appeared to be mobile, moving with every cardiac contraction. It most likely was moving around in the right ventricle itself. The most likely explanation, at least the one that we came up with, was that this piece of shot had penetrated the subclavian vein and had subsequently been whisked away with the returning blood back to the heart. This was also most likely how the first two fragments found their way there. So now what should we do about it? Trying to get the fragments out would involve extensive intervention, and it did not seem to be worth the risk. If we left them, they might just stay in the heart and lodge in the muscle or they might embolize out into a small branch of the pulmonary artery. Neither of these possibilities were likely to be problematic, and either one was still better than the risk of intervention. After we had discussed it at length amongst ourselves and the radiologist, we presented the case to Dr. Ledgerwood, who immediately told us to leave them alone but to get the patient ready to debride his wound. In the end, the study showed that there was no major arterial injury, so we completed his work-up before heading off to the OR. When I talked to him again, he was far more relaxed as he sat up with just a couple of 4x4s over the wound. He looked dramatically improved with some color having finally returned to his olive skin. His previously tight facial muscles were relaxed, as he now believed us when we reassured him that he would be fine.

At around 2:00 am, we were able to take him to surgery. I wheeled him back into the assigned room, then shaved and prepped him. I not only scrubbed the area around the injury but also the entire chest as well. There was really no telling what we might find and have to fix once we got going. Even with this seemingly superficial injury, there was still the possibility that we might have to go into his chest to repair something or just to get control of his blood vessels in case something big were to let loose. It was imperative to prep 'high and wide' (yet another axiom of trauma surgery). We needed to be prepared, both physically and mentally, for anything that we might encounter.

With Dan hovering over my left shoulder, I began cutting away the dead tissue from within and around the wound. I cut away the dead tissue from the chest wall muscles (pectoral), heading out towards the armpit (axilla). There in the depths of the wound (really just a bloody great hole), the main axillary vessels could clearly be seen. The blast had done the majority of the dissecting work for me but had still left the wound a junkyard; littered with fragments of his shirt, dead flesh, and bloody birdshot.

I had barely started trimming when Dan nervously chimed in.

"Nick. Careful. Don't cut so much," he pleaded. "Be more gentle," he continued, trying his hardest to slow me down, rein me in, as I cut my way through the thick jungle of macerated and necrotic tissue.

"Not so deep! Careful! You're going too deep! Stay superficial." His voice broke slightly as he pleaded, almost frantically. He appeared very scared that I was going to cut into something, and all hell would bust loose.

Not wanting to aggravate him further, I slowed down and pretended to concentrate hard on cutting away at the edges of the wound. There, too, I did not have much luck as even my minimal attempts were thwarted.

"That's good skin. Leave it and get some of this dead stuff," he prodded at a small piece of dead tissue with the tips of his pick-ups.

"Good skin," I thought to myself. I've seen better looking tissue on cadavers. The skin around the wound was riddled with holes and was as good as dead, likely containing more lead than skin. I recalled another surgical axiom: remove all non-viable tissue. But at this moment it was contradicted by another axiom: Chief knows best.

We were not making any headway—just picking slowly and ineffectually at that.

Meanwhile, unbeknownst to us, Dr. Ledgerwood had snuck in and was intently observing our distinct lack of progress. We were so focused on the wound that neither of us saw her. Without saying a word, she left the room, scrubbed, and returned.

"Come on Maxwell, cut!" she said. "This is an operation. Isn't it?"

I must have jumped a mile, or at least my heart felt like it did, and I felt like I'd lost continence. The adrenaline was certainly flowing now. "Yes," came my feeble and surprised reply. As always, she managed to instill the fear of God into me.

"Well, cut then. Get rid of all that messed up skin," she said, "It's not doing him any good now," she continued, outlining a circle with her finger wide around the perimeter of the macerated, pockmarked skin.

Without further prompting, I took the scalpel and excised a doughnut of macerated shot-pocked skin from around the wound. I thought Dan was going to have the big one as he slowly cowered behind me, watching me excise the skin that he had given me strict instructions to save just minutes earlier.

"Now, that's more like it," she said, almost complementary.

I could see Dan quivering, pretending that he was in full agreement.

"Now, let's get some of this other junk out of here," she said, prodding on the dark shredded contents of the wound that was alive muscle a few hours earlier. As I cut out a large hunk of tissue, a squirt of arterial blood shot up from the wound, narrowly missing her right eye.

"Well, at least there is good blood supply there," she said with a low, slow, chuckle, that helped defuse the tension slightly as she clamped the offending vessel with a hemostat.

The remainder of the operation was straightforward, but after Dr. Ledgerwood left, we really didn't do any more. Dan was still very apprehensive about cutting away too much and immediately returned to his previous overly-conservative plan.

"Let's get done and get out of here," he said. "I've had enough of this."

Despite everything, the patient did very well and left the hospital a few days later, still with a lot of birdshot deep in his shoulder, which would be his lifelong companion and souvenir. He would still need to change the dressing on his left chest a few times a day. When the wound showed signs of healing, he would return for a skin graft.

No doubt, he would forever trigger airport security detectors. It was a minor inconvenience and far better than the alternative. Many of our gunshot patients went on with life with a hunk (or more) of lead in them. It was just something they got used to and took in stride.

When it comes to lead, leaving it alone is almost always preferable to going after it (another axiom?).

Postscript

THREE YEARS later—I stood in the very familiar resuscitation room, looking into the eyes of my 'interns'. I could see their apprehension, almost feel the frightening insecurities that went hand in hand with being a first-year resident. I looked at them and saw myself, just a few years, but then also a lifetime, ago.

We waited for the arrival of a code: a gunshot wound. I no longer had the same sense of foreboding, yet exhilarating, heart-pounding excitement. It was business as usual, another patient to be taken care of, and perhaps another surgery. Now that part was still exciting. There were (are) few things more satisfying than taking a severely injured patient to the operating room and fixing them. I wondered how many gunshots and stabbings I had seen over the last few years? Certainly hundreds. They were all similar, yet individually all so very different.

I looked intently at my juniors, as they milled around waiting for the code to arrive. They appeared so confident. Was this really how they felt? Unlikely. It was much more likely they were just keeping their insecurities in, deeply hidden, just as I had done when I was in their shoes and putting on a show so we could not see their real anguish and worry. They also had learnt the mantra: *Never let them see you sweat.*

I knew how they really felt. I had been there, and not that long ago either. Hell, some days, I was still there. I had felt their pain, their nagging insecurity. But I certainly was not going to let on that I knew how they felt. They needed to gain their own confidence.

Surgical training came as a bit of a shock for all of us. I really had no idea what I had signed up for, and I'm guessing that went for the majority of first year residents. I thought that the process of learning to be a surgeon would involve long hours in the operating room (which of course it did, but that came much later), learning how to operate. I soon learnt that I knew nothing even about the process. Alarmingly, most future physicians knew little and had minimal knowledge of what 'real' practice entailed when choosing their future specialty or even their decision to go into medical school.

Operating skills although important was a surprisingly small part of what was necessary to become a good surgeon. It was neither the most important nor the most difficult.

Surgical decision-making is the most important skill that we needed to master, but in order to do that, we first needed to learn and control our ego. Sadly (for their patients), some surgeons never manage it. We are taught to make a decision and stick to it, occasionally trying to save face when clearly we are wrong. But then we must remember that it's not our face that we should be trying to save.

Learning to be humble, although not part of the surgeon's repertoire, is essential. It is imperative to have awareness of what you know and even more so of what you don't. This goes double for what we can and cannot do. Continuing with unrelenting, arrogant, stubbornness can lead to dangerous and potentially lethal consequences We needed to learn that there are times when it is right not to do something, and in fact at times critical that we don't. This underlines the most important attribute of being a surgeon: Knowing when not to operate.

The great majority of poor outcomes originate with the poor decision to proceed to the operating room in the first place rather than from an error during the procedure itself. However, once you have made that first error, the chances are high that you will make a second.

We must be much more than just 'cutters'. We need to know how and when to cut and most importantly when not to. Our every step, every move must be carefully planned, choreographed in our minds. We need a plan for every scenario we might encounter and limit surprises.

We must be confident, yet not cocky; efficient, yet not too fast; organized, but never rigid. Cockiness kills. Yet on the flip side, we cannot be paralyzed by fear and insecurity.

It was my first day back at 'receiving', now as a chief resident, and I had just finished staffing my intern on draining a thick, smelly abscess on a drug addict's scarred and pock-marked leg. I was barely out of my surgical gown when my pager went off. I listened, then looked at it, but the number drew a blank. It had been over 18 months since I had last rotated here, and the small portion of my brain that had been partitioned for the storage of this hospital's phone numbers had long since been replaced with others. However, my ears perked up, and I listened more intently the second time as the string of numbers were preceded by 'oo'. There was trouble somewhere. 'oo' always meant an emergency. I racked my brain trying to think from where the call might be originating. I made my way to the nearest phone, about 50 yards down the corridor. It must be from Tony, my second year in the module, I surmised, and the number must be that of the 'bat-phone', on the resuscitation room wall. But then why had he not just paged me with a string of ones, which was our universal signal for a surgical code? My hunch was right, and I could hardly hear a word over the deafening commotion, typical of a resuscitation in full swing. He spoke up.

"Nick, there's a woman here, who was brought in as a medical code with practically no blood pressure," He began at an almost incomprehensible pace, but after taking an audible deep breath, slowed. "Blood's pouring out of her NG. They have no idea where it's coming from."

Great, another medical code disaster, I thought. I can't wait. Those stinking GI bleeds were always special, I thought facetiously.

"I'll be right there," I replied. I hung up and briskly made my way the short distance to the resuscitation room, a route on the worn, tired linoleum that I could have made blindfolded. I no longer had the sense of dread and worry of a few years ago. I was there to help my juniors and take care of the patient. I knew how to do that now.

When I walked into the room, it was pandemonium, a boiling cauldron of hands going every which way. I could hardly imagine that our surgical codes were ever that messy, but of course, they were. Tony began to tell me the history as I looked through the seething mass of hands attempting to locate the object of so much attention. Finally I caught sight of her. She was so pale, a ghastly, ghostly, deathly white; her color only interrupted by intermittent splotches of blood. An NG tube came out of one nostril sucking copious amounts of blood. Between her teeth was an opaque plastic endotracheal tube through which she was being ventilated by hand (bagged). She already had lines in place, with at least one subclavian and two peripherals that I could see through which saline and blood were being pushed. Her chest, meanwhile, remained under attack by a couple of nurses and some students who were taking turns performing CPR. In my head I was trying to piece it all together. Where was all this bleeding coming from? Had a stomach ulcer bust loose? Or worse, was she a drinker? Could this bleeding be coming from a ruptured, engorged esophageal varix?

I looked at her and racked my brain but still could not come up with a diagnosis that made any sense. Nevertheless, whatever was going on was life-threatening and was not going to stop itself. The only hope, if this woman had any, was to immediately get her to the operating room. I had Tony call ahead and we brought her right over to the OR. They knew to set up to go into the chest and abdomen.

The bleeding could be coming from anywhere, the esophagus, the stomach, the lungs. We needed more information, but we didn't have the time. She was bleeding to death. Where should I start. The chest or belly? We were missing something. But she could not help us. She was dying, bleeding to death right in front of us.

The EMS team could not shed any light, but I was informed her mother was here, and I found her pacing in the meditation room. I certainly did not have any encouraging news for her, explaining that I thought it was very unlikely that her daughter would survive whatever was going on. Our short exchange was helpful but did not make me feel any better about her chances.

The patient was 40 and had gone with her mother to the annual auto show that was taking place at Cobo Arena. Just outside the entrance, she had collapsed and was found by the EMS crew, lying in a pool of blood, with no blood pressure and a fading heart rhythm.

Her mother explained that her daughter had recently experienced a few episodes of vomiting blood, but her doctors were unable to find the cause. She had a thoracotomy 17 years earlier for the repair of a coarctation of the aorta (a congenital narrowing of the artery in the chest), and more recently she had been re-operated, on for an aneurysm in the same area. Could her current predicament be related? At first I thought not, as the blood was only coming out of her NG tube, and so it appeared to be of GI origin; but we were always taught never to pick two diagnoses if just one fit the bill. The more I thought about it, the chances were that this was all related.

On the way over to surgery, she began having torrential bleeding from her endotracheal tube. This was much more than just a GI bleed! Unlike the dark blood of the NG tube, this was a bright crimson red and just kept coming, requiring almost constant suctioning.

With a blood pressure barely 50 and a chest X-ray that did not help, we pushed her into the surgical suite. Some pushed the cart, some pushed fluids while others pushed on her chest, standing on the cart to perform cardiac compressions.

Despite pouring in blood and fluids, it was coming out just as fast.

We were having difficulty keeping up. I decided that it would be best to attack the chest first as this appeared to be the most likely area causing her life-threatening bleeding. While performing a cursory scrub, the nurses rapidly squared off her iodine doused chest and abdomen with blue sterile towels. We never got her blood pressure above 50. Had her previous repair bust loose? That was always a possibility, despite the chest X-ray looking fine. Then there was still the not insignificant matter of the bright red blood pouring out of her endotracheal tube. So I went for the left side of her chest, the side with the long scar.

I made a long steady confident incision. It was amazing what a difference three years had made. I followed the old scar. Once I was in, the chest was full of bright red blood. I wondered why it had not shown on her chest film. Slipping in the rib spreader, I cranked it open as wide as I could. Cupping my right hand, I began scooping out huge dollops of dark bloody clot. I immediately knew that this was going to be even harder than I thought, for even with all of the clot out of the way, I still could not see where the blood was coming from. The more we sucked, the more it kept filling back. It appeared to be bleeding from everywhere. I knew I had the right body cavity, but still where was the source? What was it? The lung itself was a 'goner', a destroyed bloody soaked sponge of tissue. Everywhere the lung was stuck—stuck to the chest wall, stuck from the scarring of all her previous surgeries, making it infinitely harder to identify anything let alone figure out where the bleeding source was. I knew it must be somehow related to her previous aortic surgery. I needed help. I had the circulator call over to Harper Hospital (which was right next door to us and easily reached by a connecting underground tunnel) to get a hold of the thoracic surgery resident on call, to see if he could come over and give me a hand.

I was a fifth-year chief and would shortly be out in practice, so I should be able to deal with traumatic chest injuries. But was this really trauma? I didn't think so. Any help was welcome, even though I knew there was probably nothing that anyone else would be able to do except reinforce that which we already suspected.

It took only about five minutes before Rob, the on-call cardio-thoracic resident, rushed into the room, still a little short of breath. I knew Rob well, as he was a year ahead of me and had now entered his first year of his cardiac surgery residency following graduation. He was a competent, caring, and knowledgeable individual and someone whom I had always trusted. After immediately scrubbing in to help, he had few words of encouragement especially after I had shared with him the history I had obtained. He reinforced to us that which we all feared but expected. This was most likely a ruptured aorta at the site of her previous aneurysm repair and was uniformly fatal.

Even with the likely poor outcome, we continued with our struggle, hoping that we might find a more easily correctable problem. We were loathe to give up. Despite everything, it was futile. We just could not keep up with her massive blood loss, and very soon her powerful young heart began to fail. Not wanting to let her succumb, we began open cardiac massage. Feeling her now feeble contractions in our hands, it was about ten minutes before it was over, and we still had not been able to make it to the aorta. There was nothing more we could do. Her heart, now just an empty flaccid bag of smooth muscle, had contracted for the last time. Even if we could magically get the bleeding stopped, there was no way she could survive such an insult let alone the possibility of any type of repair. Once she was pronounced, we spent a little time looking around in what had rapidly become a bloodless field. This type of exploration was always difficult, leaving us all feeling empty. In reality it was an on-table thoracic autopsy. Soon the air was filled with that unmistakable and unpleasant odor that seems to occur about ten minutes after death. Finally, we dissected out the aorta and located the cause of her demise. At the site of the previous aortic repair, where the Dacron graft had been sutured to the aorta, there was a huge hole, easily large enough to admit the tip of my index finger.

Infection had likely caused the disruption. This rare complication could have occurred at any time, but it would have ended with the same catastrophic results.

As we walked away, I was overcome with a strange sense of deja-vu. I stopped, looked back, and stared at her lifeless chest, gaping wide under the harsh cold operating room lights. My heart skipped a beat as I could not help but be reminded of my recurring nightmare.

APPENDICES

Surgical Golden Rules

* Never let 'them' (or anyone else) see you sweat.

* When in doubt contact your senior resident, at any time, day or night.

* The senior resident is always right.

* Slower is safer and often quicker.

* Always cut away dead stuff.

* The time to act is when you first think about it. If you wait until it becomes obvious, it is frequently too late.

* Skin incisions heal from side to side, not up and down, so make a bigger cut if you need to.

* Approximate, don't strangulate.

* Poor outcomes are most frequently the result of poor decisions.

* Exposure is always the key to 'safe and sound' surgery.

* Don't fuck with the pancreas.

* Always prep a much larger area than you think you might need. High and wide.

* Never look away from a bleeder (presuming you are wearing glasses or eye protection).

* Leaving a projectile (bullet or fragments) in place is usually safer than going after it (them).

* Survivability was inversely proportional to the number of tubes entering and exiting a patient.

* Never assume knowledge. It is far safer to assume the lack of it.

Surgical Glossary

ADD Attention Deficit Disorder.

analgesic Pain killer.

anastomosis Connection between two adjacent tubular structures, usually portions of the gastro-intestinal (GI) tract or blood vessels

aneurysm A swelling of the wall of an artery, which may enlarge and rupture.

amps Ampules—standard pre-packaged doses in syringes or glass 'ampules'.

apnea Lack of respirations (breathing).

ascending reticular activating system (ARAS) A neural network in the brain stem, responsible for controlling wakefulness.

auscultation Listening using a stethoscope.

BAC Blood alcohol concentration.

bed pan A steel or plastic receptacle used as a toilet by bedridden patients.

bilaterally Both sides (right and left).

boarded An expression used for scheduling patients, when the patient's information was put onto the OR 'board', and we were given a time for the surgery.

bovie Electrocautery: named after William Bovie, a biophysicist who invented the electrocautery device, which was then popularized by Harvey Cushing in 1926 for brain surgery.

butt pus Abscess in the peri-anal area.

cardiac tamponade A dangerous situation where the heart cannot relax between cycles due to external pressure.

c-arm A type of portable 'live motion' X-ray machine.

Cc Cc, cubic centimeter or ml, milliliter are identical and interchangeable measurements of volume.

c-collar Cervical collar, often foam, used to protect the neck from further injury. Also called Philly collar.

central line An IV catheter placed into a central vein.

coagulation factors Components of blood that enable blood to clot.

coagulopathic A decreased ability to coagulate.

code A cardiac or respiratory arrest.

consult A request for another physician's opinion, frequently in another specialty.

cornea The transparent layer at the front of the eye.

CPR Coronary-pulmonary resuscitation.

crepitus A crackling sound usually in the subcutaneous tissue, due to air or gas. Sounds like Rice Krispies.

cricothyrotomy A cut in the cricothyroid membrane, just below the 'Adam's apple', to allow access to the airway (trachea) in an emergency.

crossmatch A sequence of tests performed to make sure that donor blood is compatible with the recipient.

cut A street term used when a street drug is diluted by adding some similar appearing substance.

cutdown A cut in the skin to expose a vein and enable access.

debride/debridement The removal of devitalized or foreign material from a wound.

decorticate Abnormal positioning (posturing) of arms and legs, signaling severe brain damage.

defibrillation Application of a controlled electrical shock to attempt to stop cardiac fibrillation.

D50 An intravenous solution containing 50 grams of dextrose (sugar) in every 100 millileters.

DFO Acronym for 'Done Fell Out'.

dispo (disposition) Plan for the patient.

epinephrine (epi) Known in Europe and Canada by the more familiar name adrenaline. A powerful cardiac stimulant.

ether screen A 'screen' made from elevating the top of the surgical drapes hooked to IV poles, separating the head of the patient (anesthesia area) from the surgical field. A term left over from the days when ether was administered.

fascia The fibrous sheath that encompasses muscles and some organs.

fasciotomy An operation where fascia is cut to release the built up pressure, usually following trauma.

fibrillation An uncoordinated quivering of (cardiac) muscle.

flail chest A section of the rib cage no longer attached to the rest of the chest wall.

foley catheter Balloon tipped catheter used to drain the urinary bladder

GCS score (Glasgow Coma Scale) A numerical neurological objective scale to record the level of consciousness.

guarding The contraction of the abdominal wall to protect (guard) the inflamed intra abdominal structures. May be voluntary or involuntary.

hematuria Blood in the urine.

hemostat A surgical tool—a clamp used to control bleeding.

hypoglycemic Low blood sugar.

hypovolemic Low blood volume.

ICP Intracranial pressure.

innervate To supply an organ or part with nerves.

intern First year in training after medical school. First year of residency.

iris The colored membrane behind the cornea of the eye, which adjusts allowing varying amounts of light through.

ischemia Inadequate blood supply.

IVP (Intravenous pyelogram) A contrast X-ray study to evaluate the urinary system.

jaws of life A hydraulic spreading and cutting tool that is used by emergency rescue squads to help with the extrication of trapped victims. They have been around in various iterations since the early 1970s.

laparoscopy Surgery using the insertion of a fiber-optic-lit camera to look inside the abdomen.

laparotomy (exploratory) Lap, lapped, ex-lap. An incision made in the abdomen through which it is then explored.

lap sponges Face cloth sized absorbent cotton cloths used in operating rooms.

log-roll A method used to move a patient so as to keep the spine straight, 'in column'

LR 'Lactated ringers'. 'Ringers'. An intravenous fluid concoction favored in trauma.

M & M (morbidly and mortality conference). A weekly 'teaching' conference where the surgical residents discussed complications in front of the entire system-wide surgical staff.

Mannitol An osmotic diuretic, used to help remove extra water from swollen brain tissue.

mediastinum The area of the chest above the heart and between the lungs containing the great vessels (the main blood vessels entering and leaving the heart), lymphatics, and thymus gland.

meninges The three membranes that enclose the brain and spinal cord.

mesentery The attachments of intra-abdominal organs within which are its blood supply.

module one The specific potion of our emergency room dedicated to surgical and trauma patients.

module one breath A colloquial term used to describe the breath of highly intoxicated individuals.

morgue The location in a hospital where bodies are examined and stored temporarily after death.

myocardium Heart muscle.

MVA Motor vehicle accident.

Narcan A narcotic antagonist that works by blocking the narcotic receptors in the brain and so prevents them from working. Used in drug overdoses.

necrotic Dead.

needle driver The surgical instrument used to hold suture needles while suturing.

NGT (nasogastric tube) A plastic tube placed through the nose and down into the stomach where it is used to evacuate both fluid and air.

OCU (observation care unit) Known, tongue in cheek, as the occasional care unit.

operative report A typed narrative of the why, how, and what took place during surgery.

palpate Examination (of a portion of the body) by touch.

paradoxical respiration A portion of the chest goes in rather than out with inspiration and the opposite with expiration.

paraplegic Interruption of nerves supplying the lower extremity, most often from spinal injury.

peritoneal lavage Washing of the abdominal cavity, looking for blood or contamination.

peritoneum The one cell thick, shiny, smooth innermost lining of the abdominal cavity.

peritonitis Inflammation of the peritoneum, most commonly as the result of blood or some other irritant (bowel contents) in the abdomen.

pick-ups Tweezers used to pick up tissue.

platelets A small cellular blood component involved in the first stage of blood clotting.

Pleur-evac A brand of chest drainage system.

pneumo (pneumothorax) Collapse of a lung.

postictal Following a seizure.

pupil The hole at the center of the iris that allows light to pass through.

recovery room The room next to the operating room where patients wake up after anesthesia.

retina The inside portion of the back of the eye that converts light into nerve signals.

rigors Extremes of shivering with alternating spikes in temperature.

rigor mortis The 'third' stage of death, which is characterized by stiffening of the muscles.

ringers See **LR.**

Sabiston Our textbook of surgery—our 2000-paged small-print surgical bible!

scrubs Clothes worn by surgical staff in the operating room.

sinus A cavity, usually within bone, commonly of the face and communicating with the nasal cavities.

spinal shock Autonomic dysfunction following spinal cord injury.

stethoscope An instrument used to listen to the internal sounds of the body.

straddle fracture Pelvic fractures involving both superior and inferior pubic rami. Can have significant associated genitourinary injuries.

stridor A vibrating, difficulty-with-breathing sound caused by respiratory tract obstruction, internal or external.

suture The actual material, thread that is used for the stitches.

resident Physician in training after medical school.

tap (abdominal) See **peritoneal lavage.**

ureter The long, thin (pencil-sized), muscular tube that drains urine from the kidney to the bladder.

urinal A plastic hand-held container used for males to urinate in.

vertical mattress A suture technique used to close skin.

Vicryl A brand of absorbable suture.

ACKNOWLEDGMENTS

THE WRITING of this book has been a very long journey, taking about eight years, once I had rediscovered the pages of disorganised scribble (notes) that I made during many half awake days and nights in the Emergency room. Trying to make sense of them was another project in of itself. Even during the timeframe of writing I have seen medicine and surgery change more than I could have imagined (but that's for another time).

Firstly I would like to thank Dr. Izzie Weisglass, who was my senior resident during my third year medical school surgery rotation at the Montreal General Hospital, and unlike my experiences to that point, he made me understand that surgery could be both enjoyable (some might even say fun!) and rewarding. Up until then I had never known anyone who said that they had enjoyed their surgical rotation.

I then must give great credit to Dr. Michael Busuito who impressed me so much, with his infectious enthusiasm during my residency interview, that I decided (and was very thankful I did so) to rank Detroit high on my 'match list'. I consider myself even more fortunate that the department chairman, Dr. Alex Walt (1923–1996), chose to accept me into the program.

However the most thanks and credit must go to my many, sometimes but not always, patient mentors during my five years of training. I particularly need to name Dr. David Bouwman, Dr. Robert Wilson, Dr. Anna Ledgerwood and Dr. Charles Lucas, whose guidance (and significant ass kicking) allowed me to succeed. The latter two (L&L), I can still feel, are watching over my shoulder on difficult cases to this very day. Their dedication to education was nothing short of inspirational (even though at the time, we called it torture!).

There were also a few physicians who, sadly, I did not get the opportunity to work with very often, but still whose short exposure to their skill and advice I still heed to this day. Dr. Choichi Sugawa, our surgical endoscopist was one such person, whose almost miraculous skill wielding endoscopes, I still marvel at.

I was also fortunate to learn so much (mostly good) from my many more senior residents (who will remain anonymous) with whom I had the opportunity to work so closely with every day.

Most importantly I want to thank my family: my parents who always gently nudged me in the correct direction; my wife, Christa, who not only had the misfortune of having to scrub many difficult cases for me, but who I also tortured in return with the reading and rereading of my manuscript and whose suggestions were invaluable.

I must also give recognition to Jim and Erin from the M&M Café, Monticello, who kept the coffee flowing while I spent far too long working and reworking the manuscript.

But this list would not complete without thanking the industry and patience of both my editor, Karen Barrett-Wilt, and my book designer, Sara DeHaan.

ABOUT THE AUTHOR

GRADUATING FROM high school in Cambridge, England, Dr. Maxwell went on to spend a 'gap year' working for the British government and the United Nations in New York City. Returning to continue his education he completed a bachelors in human genetics at McGill University in Montreal where he also went on to receive his medical degree. Deciding to pursue surgery he began his surgical journey at the many and varied hospitals of The Detroit Medical Center.

After interviewing all over the country he settled on a hospital in southern Wisconsin where he continues to practice general, vascular and minimally invasive surgery. When not caring for his patients he is an avid sailor and enjoys both racing and cruising. He is married with two daughters and two step-sons.